1865

1865

America Makes War and Peace in Lincoln's Final Year

Edited by Harold Holzer and Sara Vaughn Gabbard

Southern Illinois University Press
Carbondale

18 17 16 15   4 3 2 1

Publication of this book has been made possible through a generous
donation from Friends of the Lincoln Collection of Indiana. For more
information about Friends of the Lincoln Collection of Indiana, write to
P.O. Box 11083, Fort Wayne, IN 46855, or visit www.lincolncollection.org.

**The directors of Friends of the Lincoln Collection of Indiana
thank Ian and Mimi Rolland for their sponsorship of this book.**

Cover illustration: Painting, *Lincoln's Drive through Richmond*, 1866,
by Dennis Malone Carter. Cropped, ICHi-52424, Chicago History
Museum.

Library of Congress Cataloging-in-Publication Data
1865 : America makes war and peace in Lincoln's final year / edited by
Harold Holzer and Sara Vaughn Gabbard.
    pages cm
Includes bibliographical references and index.
    ISBN 978-0-8093-3401-8 (cloth : alk. paper)
    ISBN 0-8093-3401-1 (cloth : alk. paper)
    ISBN 978-0-8093-3402-5 (ebook)
    ISBN 0-8093-3402-X (ebook)
1. United States—History—Civil War, 1861–1865. 2. Lincoln,
Abraham, 1809–1865—Influence. 3. United States—Politics and
government—1861–1865. I. Holzer, Harold. II. Gabbard, Sara Vaughn.
III. Title: America makes war and peace in Lincoln's final year.
E470.A1195 2015
973.8—dc23   2014030944

Printed on recycled paper. ♻
The paper used in this publication meets the minimum requirements
of American National Standard for Information Sciences—Permanence
of Paper for Printed Library Materials, ANSI Z39.48-1992. ∞

Contents

Contents

Appendixes

1865

Introduction

Harold Holzer

$\mathcal{T}$oward the end of his tragically curtailed life, Abraham Lincoln belatedly acknowledged a handsome gift that had arrived six months earlier from William Lloyd Garrison, the outspoken abolitionist editor who for years had ardently, sometimes disobligingly, pushed the seemingly reluctant president toward emancipation.

The gift was a large freedom painting by artist William Tolman Carlton titled *Watch Meeting—Dec. 31st 1862—Waiting for the Hour*, which Garrison described as portraying "a group of negro men, women and children waiting with heartfelt emotion and thrilling delight for the midnight hour of December 31, 1862, to pass, and the introduction of that new year which was to make them forever free." Added the once hostile Garrison, making no effort to disguise his newfound admiration, "Many photographic copies were made of it, and it was by my advice that it was presented to you and the most fitting person in the world to receive it."[1]

It is hard to understand why Lincoln neglected to acknowledge such a gratifying presentation. Was he perhaps still reluctant to identify with the "extremists" who had advocated the immediate abolition of slavery long before it was politically correct? Was he still resentful that Garrison had uttered such highly critical things about him for so long? Or did he simply feel more comfortable with artist Francis B. Carpenter's recently completed emancipation painting, then on temporary display at the White House, which depicted not the African American beneficiaries of his initiative, but its white proponents, Lincoln and his cabinet?

Perhaps Lincoln felt less than grateful for the gift for all these reasons, yet Garrison had visited the White House a few months earlier, in the summer of 1864, and the meeting of the two great but often squabbling freedom advocates had proved cordial in the extreme. According to New York antislavery editor Theodore Tilton, who accompanied his Boston colleague to the meeting, "the President's face wore an expression of satisfaction rather than elation. His reception of Mr. Garrison was an equal honor to host and guest." And Lincoln undoubtedly wanted the old abolitionist to know that he had indeed firmly joined the ranks of the once radical cause. For when one of the visiting newspapermen mentioned to Lincoln that he was delighted that New York senator Edwin D. Morgan had recently proposed a Republican Party platform plank advocating a constitutional amendment abolishing slavery, Lincoln "instantly" took credit for the initiative. "It was I," he corrected Garrison and Tilton, "who suggested to Mr. Morgan that he should put that idea into his opening speech [to the national convention]."[2] It was not long after this summertime visit to Washington that Garrison dispatched the celebratory emancipation painting to the White House.

By 1865, Garrison had become sufficiently convinced of Lincoln's sincere commitment to extending freedom that he joined in the chorus of praise for the man he had so long doubted. "Having full faith in your integrity of purpose, and inflexible determination to stand by every word and syllable enunciated by you in your emancipation proclamation, come what may," Garrison effused in his January 21, 1865, letter, "I have frequently had occasion, both in my editorial capacity and as a lecturer, to defend you against the many sweeping accusations that have been brought against you, sometimes even on the anti-slavery platform." Now all he wanted in return was an acknowledgment "stating that the painting aforesaid was duly received by you."[3]

More than two weeks later, on February 7, Lincoln finally dispatched his long-awaited thank-you note, apologizing for "the seeming neglect occasioned by my constant engagements" and explaining, "When I received the spirited and admirable painting 'Waiting for the Hour' I directed my Secretary not to acknowledge its arrival at once, preferring to make my personal acknowledgment . . . and waiting for some leisure hour, I have committed the discourtesy of not replying at all."[4] Garrison graciously welcomed Lincoln's delayed but heartfelt letter, even though it had been written by John Hay, one of his private secretaries, and merely signed by the still preoccupied chief executive.

By then, the incontrovertible fact that Lincoln had come to accept—and, moreover, strongly advocate—equality under the law had become obvious not only to philosopher advocates like Garrison, but to Union commanders in the field as well. This included those ostensibly fighting for the same goal by leading regiments of "colored" troops, but in at least one case practicing the kind of prejudice more common among slave masters. In response, the president made clear he would countenance no retreat from the new national commitment to freedom and, moreover, was ready to hint at an embrace of the next step in the national transition: racial equality.

In fact, the same day he replied to Garrison, Lincoln also took up the case of Lieutenant Colonel John Glenn of the 120th Colored Infantry, stationed in Henderson, Kentucky. Glenn had been accused, in Lincoln's unforgiving words, of "forcing negroes into the Military service, and even torturing them—riding them on rails and the like—to extort their consent. I hope this may be a mistake." Admonished the president, "The like must not be done by you, or any one under you." And then Lincoln justified his instructions with Sermon on the Mount simplicity: "You must not force negroes any more than white men."[5] This small, mysterious incident in Kentucky had elicited from the president a large but seldom acknowledged commitment to equal treatment for all men regardless of race.

Lincoln had come a long way by 1865, and though he lived to see only three and a half months of this climactic year, he used his brief time remarkably well and with resounding impact on American history, as this book attempts to demonstrate. For one thing, most momentously of all, as historian Michael Vorenberg discusses in chapter 1, Lincoln expended unprecedented energy and influence to shepherd House passage of the resolution sending the Thirteenth Amendment to the states for ratification. And then he signaled his pride and joy in the result by adding his bold signature to the congressional document. This in turn provoked the Senate to pass another, far less exalted, resolution petulantly declaring that "such approval was unnecessary." By then, Lincoln hardly minded such quibbling. He had clearly wanted his name on the historic freedom document he had so ardently supported, which, as he put it, finally put the fatal "harpoon in the monster" of American slavery. And he got his wish.[6]

During these same eventful months, Lincoln also oversaw—and when he could, personally observed—the Union army's final efforts to extinguish the rebellion. In chapter 2, military historians John F. Marszalek and Michael B. Ballard portray General Ulysses S. Grant's crucial last thrusts against Robert E. Lee in Virginia in "partnership" with the commander in chief, under his exceptional management of the overall war effort—particularly during the costly battles leading up to the final Union triumph. Lincoln's steely nerve and unwavering commitment to black freedom were never on more dazzling display than at Hampton Roads, Virginia, where in

February, as historian Richard Striner recounts in chapter 3, the president faced down Confederate emissaries who tantalizingly proposed immediate armistice if Lincoln would order the Emancipation Proclamation reversed. But its author would not bend: peace would not come without freedom.

A month later, Lincoln made clear his view that the blame for what might be called the nation's "birth defect"—American slavery, as consecrated by the U.S. Constitution—deserved to be shared by South and North alike. In perhaps the greatest inaugural address ever delivered, he invoked Old Testament fire and brimstone to declare that the suffering caused by the Civil War might well have been the punishment of a just God for our tolerating such a sin. And then Lincoln asked the mortal citizens of the warring sections to treat each other, when peace finally came, "with malice toward none" and "charity for all." In chapter 4, Ronald C. White, Jr., the leading expert on the Second Inaugural Address, offers a new appraisal of the extraordinary oration that Lincoln viewed as his rhetorical zenith, predicting that it would "wear as well as" any he had ever made.[7] After Richmond fell and the Confederate government evacuated its capital, Lincoln paid an unprecedented visit to the city—a tour brilliantly reconceived in chapter 5 by the leading authority on the dramatic trip, Richard Wightman Fox.

But the 1865 event that truly made Lincoln immortal—and, in its wake, tested America's legal system and its ability to survive a violent presidential transition—was his April 14 assassination. In chapter 6, Edward Steers, Jr., one of the nation's most respected experts on the tragedy, revisits and reinterprets his years of research into the drama and its leading actors. Then in chapter 7, former Rhode Island chief justice and longtime Lincoln scholar Frank J. Williams carefully and definitively explores the question of whether or not American military—or, alternatively, civilian—justice should have been applied to the prosecution of the Lincoln assassination conspirators.

No historical exploration of the momentous year of 1865 would be complete without an understanding of the African American experience in the final year of the war, which became the initial year of peace and reconstruction. Did a cessation of hostilities bring with it a cessation of stubborn white resistance to black liberty and civil rights? As Howard University historian Edna Greene Medford explains in chapter 8, frustratingly, the struggle for "a new birth of freedom" far outlived the martyred leader who first spoke those inspiring words at Gettysburg. Finally, in chapter 9, I offer an illustrated exploration of post-assassination American visual memory, as seen in the paintings, prints, sculptures, and photographs recorded during Lincoln's last months alive, as well as those produced in the frenzy of public interest that followed his death.

Appendices guide the reader further through the eventful final year of both Lincoln's life and the Civil War, offering a detailed look at the president's activities and writings from January 1 to April 15, 1865; a list of events that occurred during the entire year, both in the United States and throughout the world; selections from the introspective and challenging speech that Frederick Douglass gave on September 29, 1865, at the dedication of the Douglass Institute in Baltimore; and a sad letter that the bereaved Mary Lincoln wrote to artist Francis Bicknell Carpenter in November 1865, seven months after the assassination. We believe this material provides both context and texture to augment these writings on the emotional final months of Lincoln's life and the memories his passing inspired.

Of course, it is impossible to know precisely where Lincoln might have steered the country had he lived. But we have an important clue from his final days. On April 11, 1865, the president delivered a long policy address from the windows of the Executive Mansion in Washington. In an otherwise dry oration, Lincoln momentously suggested that the "elective franchise" at last be "given to the colored man"—that is, "conferred on the very intelligent, and on those who serve our cause as soldiers."[8] The sentiment, which seems tentative and proscribed to modern ears, sounded radical enough to John Wilkes Booth, who heard the remarks from the White House lawn and vowed that because it merely hinted at a future of racial equality, it would be the last speech Lincoln ever made. And Booth made certain it was.

Two months earlier, William Lloyd Garrison had sent one final, enthusiastic letter to the president, acknowledging Lincoln's recent acknowledgment of the emancipation painting. "Happily, you are blessed with an elastic and a cheerful spirit," Garrison gushed, adding the prayer, "may you be inspiringly sustained to the end!"[9]

Tragically, the end came not long thereafter. But as the long neglected Garrison correspondence suggests, during the president's final months alive, even one of the most uncompromising freedom advocates of the nineteenth century had come to believe that Abraham Lincoln had "done a mighty work for the millions who have so long pined in bondage in our land—nay, for the freedom of all mankind."[10]

Notes

1. William Lloyd Garrison to Abraham Lincoln, January 21, 1865, Abraham Lincoln Papers, Library of Congress. Mary Lincoln took the painting with her when she left the White House, but it has since returned to the White House Collection. See William Kloss, *Art in the White House: A Nation's Pride* (Washington, DC: White House Historical Association, 1992), 152.

2. Francis B. Carpenter, *Six Months at the White House: The Story of a Picture* (New York: Hurd and Houghton, 1866), 167–68.

3. Garrison to Lincoln, January 21, 1865.

4. Lincoln to Garrison, February 7, 1865, in *The Collected Works of Abraham Lincoln*, ed. Roy P. Basler, 8 vols. (New Brunswick, NJ: Rutgers University Press, 1953–55), 8:265–66.

5. Lincoln to "Lt. Col. Glenn," February 7, 1865, *Collected Works*, 8:266.

6. Remarks by Senator Lyman Trumbull, *Congressional Globe*, 38th Cong., 2nd sess., February 7, 1865, 629–30; "Harpoon" comment, John Taliaferro, *All the Great Prizes: The Life of John Hay, from Lincoln to Roosevelt* (New York: Simon and Schuster, 2013), 97.

7. Lincoln to Thurlow Weed, March 15, 1865, *Collected Works*, 8:356.

8. *Collected Works*, 8:403.

9. Garrison to Lincoln, February 13, 1865, Lincoln Papers.

10. Ibid.

1

The Thirteenth Amendment

Michael Vorenberg

*Thirteenth Amendment to the Constitution
of the United States of America*

Section 1. Neither slavery nor involuntary servitude, except as a punishment for crime whereof the party shall have been duly convicted, shall exist within the United States, or any place subject to their jurisdiction.

Section 2. Congress shall have power to enforce this article by appropriate legislation.

The year 1865 was defined by the constitutional abolition of slavery. It began and ended with the Thirteenth Amendment. When the second session of the Thirty-Eighth Congress reconvened a few days after New Year's Day, the most pressing matter the lawmakers faced was adoption of the amendment. When the first session of the Thirty-Ninth Congress convened eleven months later, at the beginning of December, the amendment needed the approval of only a few more states for ratification, and the most pressing matter for the new Congress was how to enforce the measure with new legislation. Between the beginning and end of the year, "*the* Constitutional amendment," as it was generally called—it was not known by its number until well after 1865—became a topic of discussion throughout the country. During that time, its ratification became more and more certain, yet its meaning and impact grew ever more elusive.

As 1865 dawned, the likelihood that slavery would be abolished by constitutional amendment was much in doubt. Given that his party's platform included a plank endorsing the amendment, President Abraham Lincoln had good reason in his December message to Congress to declare his party's electoral success in the fall of 1864 a popular mandate for the amendment. He called on the House of Representatives to pass the measure during the coming weeks. The Senate had adopted it back in April 1864. Lincoln's decision to push for the amendment now was risky. The chances of getting it through the House would be much better in March 1865, when he could call a special session of a new Congress dominated by newly elected Republicans.

Republican leaders in Congress at first shared his optimism. Yet the partisan rancor was fierce in those first weeks in the House, and by the holiday recess the amendment's adoption was in jeopardy. A Washington newspaper correspondent reported that Republicans were no longer "so sanguine of its success in the House."[1] On Christmas Day, Congressman James Ashley of Ohio sent a desperate note to Republican congressmen who had returned home for the holidays. Soon after New Year's Day, the House would vote on the amendment, Ashley explained, yet it looked to be a few votes short of the two-thirds majority it needed for adoption. The Ohio congressman asked fellow Republicans to persuade Democratic representatives from their delegation to support the measure. "Is there not one sinner among the opposition from your State who is on praying ground?" he asked.[2]

Article V of the Constitution describes the procedure for amending the Constitution:

> The Congress, whenever two thirds of both Houses shall deem it necessary, shall propose Amendments to this Constitution, or, on the Application of Legislatures of two thirds of the several States, shall call a Convention for proposing Amendments, which, in either Case, shall be valid to all Intents and Purposes, as Part of this Constitution, when ratified by the Legislatures of three fourths of the several States, or by Conventions in three fourths thereof, as the one or the other Mode of Ratification may be proposed by Congress; Provided that no Amendment which may be made prior to the Year One thousand eight hundred and eight shall in any Manner affect the first and fourth Clauses in the Ninth Section of the first Article; and that no State, without its Consent, shall be deprived of its equal Suffrage in the Senate.

As 1865 opened, however, the sin of slavery still seemed a stain not soon to vanish. Ashley knew that he did not have the numbers. He postponed the vote to the end of January. Secretary of State William Henry Seward at this point sent word to Albany for lobbyists who could help secure votes for the amendment.

Meanwhile, Francis P. Blair, Sr., was jeopardizing the amendment by trying to negotiate a peace, unofficially, with Jefferson Davis in Richmond. Blair, who had once been a member of President Andrew Jackson's inner circle, the Kitchen Cabinet, was now something of an elder statesman among the more conservative supporters of Lincoln. He had pestered the president to allow him to go to Richmond until Lincoln finally relented. Lincoln knew that Davis would agree to no peace unless it came with Confederate independence. And that is probably why he let Blair go. A public report from Blair that only the permanent division of the Union would satisfy Davis might cut the legs out from under the argument made by Lincoln's opponents that Davis was anxious for peace and only Lincoln's insistence on emancipation stood in the way. But the plan could just as easily backfire. If news leaked of a peace talk, even an unofficial one, passage of the amendment would have to wait even longer. The prospect of peace would give further negotiation priority over the amendment or any other antislavery measure that might antagonize the South.

Also, emancipation seemed to be progressing just as well without an antislavery amendment as with one. The Union state of Maryland had abolished slavery in October 1864; Missouri followed in January 1865. In that same month, the seceded state of Tennessee, now under rule of a provisional Union government, also abolished slavery. At least two other seceded states now under Union rule, Arkansas and Louisiana, seemed likely to end slavery by state action within a few months. Why, then, abolish slavery by a national constitutional amendment?

The reasons were in part political but primarily legal. The sooner the national government made a definitive move against slavery, the sooner the institution could be omitted as a topic of discussion in any peace negotiation. And Lincoln would no longer be plagued, as he had been for the past six months, by the false charge that it was his insistence alone on emancipation that prolonged the war. Also, if Democrats and border-state Unionists could be brought on board the pro-amendment wagon, the Republican Party, now fashioning itself the National Union Party, could legitimately claim a broader constituency. Most important, the amendment put abolition on the soundest possible constitutional footing. No court could claim that any of the wartime emancipation measures, including the Emancipation Proclamation, were unconstitutional. No government of a state readmitted to the Union on the basis of its new antislavery constitution could then fiddle with that constitution to allow slavery to persist or to reenslave freed people.

The amendment's backers agreed on the importance of adopting the amendment to end slavery, but they were divided on whether the measure would then become the foundation for future laws that would strike yet more blows for legal equality among different races. On one side were Radical Republicans like Senator Charles Sumner of Massachusetts, who saw the amendment as but one piece of a slate of measures needed to obliterate the color line. The same session of Congress that would give the final vote on the amendment would also approve Sumner's bill ending racial discrimination on Washington, DC, streetcars. On the other side were conservatives like Montgomery Blair, Francis Sr.'s son. The younger Blair, once Lincoln's postmaster general, wrote to a kingpin of the Democratic Party that the amendment represented the end, not the beginning, of partisan division over racial issues. With the slavery issue disposed of, Blair explained, the Radicals, with their egalitarian position, would be a minority faction isolated politically. These "malignants of the confiscating disfranchising party," Blair said, would have only one issue to stand for, "the Negro equality question," and on that issue they would fall.[3]

Blair had a point: many whites in the Union who supported universal emancipation were far from enthusiastic about the prospect of whites and blacks living as equals, even though as many as 180,000 African American men were now taking on equal risks and burdens by serving in Union armies and navies. Evidence of persistent racism landed on Lincoln's doorstep at the start of the new year. On January 2, 1865, the White House hosted its annual New Year's levee for the public (the event would have occurred on January 1, but that was a Sunday). As at previous New Year's levees, African Americans came to the event and lined up at the rear of the receiving line. But when the doors opened, a surge of black visitors displaced waiting whites. "Put 'em out," shouted some of the whites. Local police tried to hold back some of the African Americans, and Ward Lamon, the marshal of the district, was seen ejecting some from the line entirely. Mrs. Lincoln, who had come to receive the guests, saw the melee and retired to the interior. Only after whites had been admitted, offered their good wishes to the president and First Lady, and departed were the few African Americans who remained allowed to enter. Some were ordinary men and women; others were Union soldiers; still others were church leaders, who, in the words of one observer, tried to "gain a victory over the devil every time they succeed in obtruding themselves in white society upon pretended terms of equality."[4]

In the final debate on what would become the Thirteenth Amendment, opponents of the measure hoped that they could use racial prejudice to defeat it. The trick was getting Republicans to admit that they hoped

African Americans would become equal citizens, not just free people. Steven Spielberg's 2012 film *Lincoln* depicted the gambit well, though the congressman who led the race-baiting was "Sunset" Cox of Ohio, not Fernando Wood of New York. Cox asked Thaddeus Stevens of Pennsylvania, the best-known Radical in the House, if he would renounce his "doctrine of negro equality." "I never held to that doctrine of negro equality," Stevens replied. Cox saw the chance to catch Stevens in a lie. He asked, "Then I understand the gentleman . . . not to hold that all men are created equal?" "Yes, sir," Stevens answered, "but not equality in all things—simply before the laws, nothing else."[5]

"Equality before the laws" was a phrase that congressmen understood well. It meant that laws and their enforcers should not explicitly discriminate among types of people. It did not mean that governments should go beyond this minimal procedural equality and act proactively to bring different groups of people to the same political, economic, and social status. In his heart, though, Stevens, like many of his fellow Republicans, believed that proactive legislation was in order. That was why, at the very time he was advocating for the amendment, he was pushing for laws that would confiscate the property of former rebels and distribute it to freed people. Yet, as the film *Lincoln* showed, Stevens was savvy enough not to reveal the full extent of his egalitarianism during the amendment debate.

Lincoln also offered an accurate depiction of the way the peace issue threatened to stall the amendment even further. Blair's mission to Richmond was only partly a failure. He failed to secure any sort of promise of peace from Jefferson Davis, just as Lincoln knew he would. But he did persuade Davis to send envoys to Washington, not on the condition that the Confederacy prepare for surrender—Davis never would have gone along with such a scheme—but rather on the pretext that the Union and Confederacy, acting as two distinct nations, might discuss a joint venture against Mexico. Such a scheme would get nowhere with Lincoln, who refused to acknowledge the Confederacy as a nation and had nothing to talk about with Southern envoys unless they came bearing a promise that Southern whites were ready to lay down arms and rejoin the Union. Davis knew Lincoln's position, but he nevertheless sent the three men, one of whom was Alexander Stephens, his vice president, hoping that at the very least their mission would stir up antiwar feelings in the North and perhaps even lead to a cease-fire.

By January 31, the day scheduled for the final vote on the amendment in the House, rumors that the three envoys were on their way north had spread through the Union, and opponents of the amendment demanded that the vote be postponed. The measure was sure to antagonize the negotiators, these congressmen argued, so it had to be tabled until after the peace talks. Lincoln intervened at this moment with a disingenuous note saying that he knew of no peace commissioners on their way to Washington. In fact, he did know of these men. He had ordered them detained at City Point, Virginia. That was how he could write with confidence that they were not on their way to the capital.[6]

By the time Lincoln met with the Southern peace men, the amendment abolishing slavery had been adopted by Congress. The vote took place on January 31. In one of the most tense, dramatic moments in the history of Congress, the tallying of votes held everyone in suspense, congressmen and a packed gallery of spectators alike. The measure barely had the two-thirds majority needed. Only the suspicious absence of some lame-duck Democratic congressmen, at least a few of whom were later rewarded with Republican patronage, allowed the measure to be adopted.

When the final numbers were announced, 119 for the amendment and 56 against, the crowd erupted. "Such rejoicing I never before witnessed . . . (white people I mean)," Charles Douglass wrote to his father Frederick.[7] Frederick Douglass's fellow abolitionist, Congressman George Julian, remembered years later that when the vote was announced, "it seemed to me I had been born into a new life, and that the world was overflowing with beauty and joy."[8] Lincoln was equally moved. Although he regarded the Emancipation Proclamation as the measure he most wanted and expected to be remembered for, he believed, as he told a group of celebrants after the amendment's passage, that the "proclamation falls far short of what the amendment will be when fully consummated." It was "a King's cure for all the evils."[9]

Aside from curing the possible evils of the enslaved never becoming free and freed people again becoming slaves, the amendment put an end to the Confederates' trick of fomenting pro-peace, anti-Lincoln sentiment in the North by pretending that only Lincoln's demand for emancipation, not their insistence on independence, kept the war alive. Now that the amendment was headed to the states for ratification, it was out of Lincoln's hands, and emancipation was no longer something to be bargained at the peace table. That was precisely the point the president made at the meeting at Hampton Roads on February 3, when he and Seward sat down with the three Southern men who, three days before, Lincoln had told Congress were not coming to Washington. The pretext for the meeting that Francis Blair had concocted, a joint invasion of Mexico by the North and South, quickly crumbled, as Lincoln made it clear that there were no plans to make until the seceded states were back in the Union. As for slavery, Secretary Seward told the envoys something they probably did not yet know, that the amendment had been passed by Congress. The slavery issue was out of the president's hands.

Yet, as Lincoln and Seward explained, Southern states did not have to sit idly by while ratification ran its inevitable course toward the final adoption of the amendment. To Alexander Stephens at Hampton Roads, he suggested returning to Georgia and persuading the legislature there to ratify the amendment. That would smooth the path to Georgia's readmission to the Union. The implications of Lincoln's statement were significant and perhaps surprised even the Southerners. Southern states were to be counted for the purposes of determining how many states were needed for ratification, and they would have the power to vote on ratification. These were positions that Congress had yet to endorse. Indeed, right after Congress adopted the resolution sending the amendment to the states, Charles Sumner had proposed a bill, quickly rejected by his colleagues, that would have left the formerly seceded states out of ratification on the basis that those states were no longer in the Union.[10]

Lincoln's stance on ratification, by contrast, was consistent with the understanding that the states had never actually left the Union. Lincoln was putting the practice of reconstruction before theory, and using the amendment to play his gambit. He wanted hasty reconstruction, and he knew that members of his party in Congress were ready to prevent readmission of Southern states until they exacted a broad program of punishment of former rebels and civil and political rights for African Americans. Yet, Lincoln calculated, if former Confederate states voted for the amendment, would Congress really dismiss those votes? And if those votes counted toward ratification, how then could Congress deny those states readmission to the Union? Lincoln asked that question directly in the speech that turned out to be his last, on April 11, 1865. By then the newly formed pro-Union government of Louisiana had ratified the amendment. How could Congress now deny that it was part of the Union? Lincoln asked. "If we reject Louisiana," he said, "we also reject one vote in favor of the proposed amendment." In the same speech, he stressed the importance of including all the formerly seceded states in ratification. Keeping those states out of the process would make ratification "questionable," he argued, "while a ratification by three fourths of all the States [i.e., the Southern states as well as Northern] would be unquestioned and unquestionable."[11]

Lincoln's statement about Louisiana and the other states of the Confederacy suggested that he was paying close attention to the progress of ratification. If one counted the seceded states as still being in the Union for the purposes of ratification, which obviously Lincoln and Seward did, then there were thirty-six states, and twenty-seven needed to vote for the amendment for ratification. While Lincoln was still alive, Seward, whose Department of State had responsibility for tracking ratification, counted Louisiana's ratification, and he did the same for the former Confederate states of Virginia and Tennessee. He also counted the ratification of West Virginia, a state created with the urging of the Lincoln administration and hastily admitted to the Union in early 1863. Lincoln tacitly approved all these questionable ratifications.

He tried to go even further. By offering compensation to states where slaves had been emancipated, he hoped to induce a defection of states that would leave the Confederacy, ratify the amendment, or both. He hinted to the governor of the Union state of Maryland, Augustus Bradford, that compensation would come to the border state if it ratified the amendment. The legislature voted for ratification almost immediately, but former slave owners never did receive compensation. To the peace commissioners at Hampton Roads, Lincoln promised that he would try to secure $400 million of federal funds to compensate slave owners of the former states of the Confederacy. When he returned to Washington, he suggested this plan to his cabinet, which quickly rejected it. Compensated emancipation— something that Lincoln had been pressing for since the start of the war and a program that Congress had incorporated into its act emancipating slaves in the District of Columbia—was no longer palatable to a Union population that had suffered the loss of hundreds of thousands of lives and hundreds of millions of dollars.[12]

While Lincoln and Congress discussed and monitored the progress of ratification in the slave states, Northern legislatures began to hold their ratification debates, some of which were far more contentious than Northerners would choose to remember. For later generations of Northerners, 1865 was yet one more year when the North showed its moral superiority. In 1861, it had done so by going to war against the "Slave Power," though in fact most Northerners were explicit in claiming that the war was about reunion only, not emancipation. In 1863, it had done so by supporting Lincoln's Emancipation Proclamation, though in fact some Northerners were ambivalent about the measure and others demanded that Lincoln rescind it. In 1865, lore has it, the North followed up on the proclamation by pushing the Thirteenth Amendment speedily toward adoption. In fact, Democrats and border-state Unionists blocked or at least stalled ratification in a number of Northern states.

Kentucky and Delaware, the only border states that had failed to abolish slavery, rejected ratification outright. Opponents in both states voiced concerns that the measure would lead inevitably to black suffrage. In Kentucky, opponents voiced an additional concern: that the amendment would be used by the federal government to overturn its law prohibiting the use of African American testimony against white defendants. Well after the amendment was adopted, Kentucky conservatives held on to that law tenaciously—and successfully.

In Northern states that had strong Democratic parties, the opposition to the amendment in the legislatures was able to stall its ratification for months. The focus of the opponents' attack was the amendment's second clause, which empowered Congress to enforce the prohibition of slavery with "appropriate legislation." That clause, the opposition warned, would be used by the federal government to overturn state legislation in the North as well as the South and perhaps even to seize control of all state governments. The rhetoric had no basis in reality—even the most radical congressmen had no designs on remaking Northern state governments— but it nonetheless revealed that states' rights ideology was as powerful in the North as in the South. An Ohio state legislator responded to the amendment's passage through Congress with a proposal that lawmakers wear a "badge of mourning" for thirty days, out of sorrow for a measure that was "the first step towards a centralized despotism."[13]

New England, which would boast of its abolitionist tendencies in the decades to come, was hardly unified in its support of the amendment. Rhode Island, Massachusetts, and Maine ratified the measure quickly. But Democrats in Connecticut, who had successfully blocked proposals for black suffrage throughout the war, kept the legislature from rendering a positive vote on the amendment for five months, arguing that it would allow the federal government to overturn the state's prohibition against black voting.[14]

Ultimately, what turned the tide in favor of the amendment in politically divided Northern states was Lincoln—not his arguments in favor of the measure, not his behind-the-scenes dealings, but rather his death. The shocking assassination of the president made opponents of the amendment vulnerable to the charge that they were defiling the memory of the slain emancipator. As Lincoln's funeral train approached Albany, New York, a Democratic editor in the city advised Manton Marble, the powerful editor of the *New York World*, the most widely circulated Democratic newspaper in the country, "from this point let us refuse to allow the Dem. party to ever *seem* in a disloyal position or as the defenders of Slavery."[15] The next day, the Democrats in the legislature yielded the fight. As Lincoln's body lay in state in New York's capitol, the state could claim that it had ratified the measure that had become so important to him in the last months of his life.

When Andrew Johnson took up the presidency, the ratification of the amendment was by no means assured. Votes in favor of ratification were still needed from at least eight states. Johnson followed the course of his predecessor. He encouraged newly formed Unionist legislatures in the formerly seceded states to ratify the amendment, and he and Seward, still the secretary of state, accepted those ratifications as legitimate. What Johnson did *not* do was require former Confederate states to ratify the amendment as a precondition to their readmission to the Union. Yet much modern history and lore has Johnson issuing such a prerequisite. The history of Reconstruction written in the century after that period was distorted by tales of federal despotism against the South. The Reconstruction amendments appear as measures adopted outside the guidelines of proper constitutional procedure, with the president demanding that Southern states ratify the Thirteenth Amendment and Congress going further by requiring states to ratify all the amendments.

It is true that the Republican-dominated Congress of the post-1866 years did require states seeking readmission to ratify the amendments, and perhaps Congress lacked the authority to do so.[16] But in 1865, neither Congress nor President Johnson imposed a requirement that formerly seceded states had to ratify the Thirteenth Amendment in order to have their representatives and senators readmitted to Congress. What Johnson in fact told the governors was that he expected their states to abolish slavery by *state* constitution, and he encouraged but did not require them to ratify the Thirteenth Amendment. In other words, Johnson took the same approach that Lincoln had in regard to the Southern states and ratification. He wanted the amendment ratified as quickly as possible, and he knew that if the formerly seceded states took part in the process, this would be more likely to assure their full restoration into the Union.

So eager for hasty ratification were Johnson and Seward that they were sometimes negligent about proper procedure, but only at first. In many states, as soon as word was received from Washington, DC, telegraph operators that Congress had passed the amendment on January 31, officials moved to have their state ratify the measure immediately so that it could have the honor of being listed first, or at least among the first, in the ratification record. The result was that some states, like Illinois, voted on ratification before they should have—that is, before receiving an official transmission from the secretary of state that the amendment was submitted to the state for ratification. Illinois took another vote after it received the official transmission from Seward. But in the meantime, Rhode Island had ratified the measure. So which state was the first to ratify, Illinois or Rhode Island?

The answer depends on how one regards technicalities. During this early period of ratification, technicalities did not trouble the Lincoln or Johnson administration. Seward counted a state as having ratified the amendment as soon as he learned of the results of the vote from any source and did not wait for or even demand an official transmission of the record of the vote from the state governor or legislature. Indeed, even the question of whether state *legislatures* had to ratify the amendment seemed at first not to matter to the president and secretary of state; they seemed satisfied with ratification by state *conventions*, even though the resolution for the amendment passed by Congress required ratification by legislatures.

There was precedent for the Executive Department to be inattentive to such procedure. In March 1861, the Thirty-Sixth Congress had passed the measure sometimes called the "first Thirteenth Amendment," which prohibited forever federal interference with slavery where it already existed. The resolution for the amendment required ratification by legislatures, and indeed two state legislatures (Maryland and Ohio) did ratify the measure, yet Illinois in 1862 ratified the measure in its state convention, and that ratification became part of the official record.[17] So it was understandable that the technicality of whether the antislavery Thirteenth Amendment required ratification by state legislature or convention was lost on members of both the Lincoln and Johnson administrations. It had been more than sixty years since the Constitution had been successfully amended, and knowledge about procedure was hazy.

Eventually, though, Seward and Johnson realized the confusion that they had helped cause, and they standardized ratification procedure. After hearing from Senator Jacob Collamer of Vermont in October that ratification had to be done by legislatures, President Johnson, who had assumed that ratification by a state was done as soon as either the legislature or a convention voted in the affirmative (a procedure that would have made progress on ratification even faster, as most of the Southern states during the summer and fall of 1865 had conventions that were rewriting state constitutions), Johnson adhered to procedure.[18] He and Seward informed Southern state governors that ratification had to be done by legislature. Meanwhile, Seward recognized that some of the ratifications in the North had never been officially transmitted to the State Department, and he sent word to all state governors that ratification was not official until a message announcing the legislature's vote had been properly transmitted to his office. He also took the occasion to urge those states that had not yet ratified the measure to do so as quickly as possible.[19]

The substance of the amendment, much more than poorly followed procedure, was likely to be the measure's undoing. Specifically, the enforcement clause in the amendment's second article was a sticking point for formerly seceded states. As governor after governor in the South explained to Johnson, white lawmakers in their states worried that Congress would use the measure to overturn state laws denying civil or political rights to African Americans. A Mississippi delegate to the state convention declared that the second clause "gives to Congress broad, and almost, I may say, unlimited power."[20] The Southern whites' greatest fear was that the enforcement clause would lead quickly to federally enforced black suffrage throughout the South. As Benjamin Perry, the governor of South Carolina, explained, white legislators in the state feared "that the second section [of the amendment] may be construed to give congress power of local legislation over the Negroes and white men, too, after the abolishment of slavery."[21]

To pacify Southern white fears, Seward wrote a remarkable letter to Governor Perry, which was reprinted in newspapers across the North and South. Any objection about the second clause leading to black suffrage was "querulous and unreasonable," Seward explained, as the clause was "really restraining in its effect, instead of enlarging the powers of Congress."[22] In other words, the point of the word "appropriate" was that Congress could not use the amendment for anything that went beyond the prohibition of slavery; plenty of free people, most notably white women, did not enjoy political equality, so there was no reason for Southern whites to fear that "appropriate" could somehow entail suffrage rights. Benjamin Butler, a former Union general and Massachusetts politician, spoke for many Radicals when he denounced Seward's "sophistry" in suggesting that "'appropriate' is a restrained word."[23]

It is not clear whether Seward's efforts at calming the racist fears had any effect. Within a month of issuing the message, he received official word that South Carolina, North Carolina, Alabama, and Georgia had ratified the amendment. Indeed, Georgia's vote sealed the amendment's adoption, as it was the twenty-seventh state to ratify. Yet two of those states added qualifiers to their ratification that suggested Seward's assurances had had little effect. South Carolina attached to its ratification a declaration "that any attempt by Congress towards legislating upon the political status of former slaves, or their civil relations, would be contrary to the Constitution of the United States, as it now is, or as it would be altered by the proposed amendment."[24] Alabama attached a similar rider stating that "this amendment to the constitution of the United States is adopted by the Legislature of Alabama with the understanding that it does not confer upon Congress the power to Legislate upon the political status of Freedmen in this State."[25] Seward accepted both of these ratifications as legitimate. He counted South Carolina and Alabama on the "yes" side when he issued an official statement on December 18, 1865, declaring that the amendment had been adopted.

These qualifying resolutions from Southern legislatures, far more than informal efforts by national lawmakers to secure the amendment's ratification, put the amendment's legitimacy in doubt. At no time did a member of Congress or the executive suggest that a state legislature could impose limits on the amendment. The one exception may have come at the Hampton Roads conference in early February. Alexander Stephens reported well after the meeting that Lincoln suggested that Stephens's state of Georgia might ratify the amendment ", so as to take effect—say in five years."[26] Yet it is almost certain that Stephens fabricated this statement. He had political reasons for doing so when he wrote his memoirs—mainly, to support the myth that Lincoln had always prized state over national power—and when Georgia voted to ratify the amendment, it put no qualifier about the timing of emancipation or anything else in its resolution.[27] A constitutional scholar might in fact opine that because South Carolina and Alabama did not ratify the amendment unconditionally, their ratifications were illegitimate and the amendment was not officially adopted—or at least not adopted by December 18, when Seward issued his message.

Even someone who believes that a state may attach conditions to a ratification must concede that South Carolina's condition was violated, for within six months of Seward's December 18 message, Congress had adopted two measures, the Civil Rights Act of 1866 and the new Freedmen's Bureau Act, which both affected the "civil relations" of former slaves and had been authorized explicitly by the Thirteenth Amendment's second clause, according to congressional Republicans. When Congress adopted these enforcement measures, did South Carolina's ratification become void? That question and others related to ratification had become moot by the end of 1865. Congress simply chose to accept the amendment as adopted, and it was already pushing for new constitutional amendments that more explicitly granted civil and political rights to African Americans. It would adopt the first of those amendments, the Fourteenth Amendment, in the spring of 1866 and send it to the states for ratification.[28]

Regardless of what we might say now about the procedural legitimacy of the Thirteenth Amendment, there is no questions that Americans by the end of 1865—lawmakers, Northern whites, Southern whites, Republicans, Democrats, abolitionists, and most important, the former slaves most directly affected by the measure—accepted the amendment as a legitimate law, if not a monumental one.

Indeed, the amendment might be said to be the defining measure of 1865. The debate on the measure opened the year, and Seward's declaration of its adoption closed the year. "No event of this period, or any other period, is so remarkable or so grand," an editorial in the *Cincinnati Gazette* declared on December 21.[29] The timing of Seward's declaration had an added poignancy. On the day that the secretary of state issued his message, Senator Thomas Corwin died. The Ohio senator had been the sponsor of the "first Thirteenth Amendment" of 1861, promising noninterference with slavery in the South. As 1865 came to an end, Corwin, a symbol of the Northern compromise with slaveholders that had bedeviled the nation for so long, was gone. So, too, was slavery.

Notes

1. Letter by "the Washington Correspondent" of the *Rochester Democrat and American*, December 28, 1864, 2.

2. J. M. Ashley to "Dear Sir," December 25, 1864, Edward McPherson Papers, Library of Congress, Washington, DC.

3. Montgomery Blair to Samuel L. M. Barlow, December 12, 1864, Barlow Papers, Henry E. Huntington Library, San Marino, CA.

4. *Cincinnati Daily Enquirer*, January 13, 1865, 1.

5. *Congressional Globe*, 38th Cong., 2nd sess., January 5, 1865, 125.

6. Edward C. Kirkland, *The Peacemakers of 1864* (New York: Macmillan, 1927), 226–37; S. S. Cox to Manton M. Marble, February 1, 1865, Manton M. Marble Papers, Library of Congress; *The Collected Works of Abraham Lincoln*, ed. Roy P. Basler, 8 vols. (New Brunswick, NJ: Rutgers University Press, 1953–55), 8:248.

7. Charles R. Douglass to Frederick Douglass, February 9, 1865, Frederick Douglass Papers, Library of Congress.

8. George W. Julian, *Political Recollections, 1840–1872* (Chicago: Jansen, McClurg and Company, 1884), 251.

9. *Collected Works*, 8:254. See Michael Vorenberg, "The Thirteenth Amendment Enacted," in *Lincoln and Freedom: Slavery, Emancipation, and the Thirteenth Amendment*, ed. Harold Holzer and Sara Vaughn Gabbard (Carbondale, IL: Southern Illinois University Press, 2007), 180–94.

10. Michael Vorenberg, *Final Freedom* (New York: Cambridge University Press, 2001), 225–26.

11. *Collected Works*, 8:399–405.

12. Vorenberg, *Final Freedom*, 224.

13. *Cincinnati Enquirer*, February 3, 1865, 2.

14. For the record of states voting on ratification, though the record is not entirely accurate, see *Documentary History of the Constitution of the United States of America, 1786–1870* (Washington, DC: Department of State, 1894), 2:520–637.

15. C. Comstock to Manton Marble, April 21, 1865, Manton M. Marble Papers, Library of Congress.

16. See, for example, E. H. Randle, "The Three Last Amendments to the Constitution of the United States," *American Law Review* 44 (1910): 561–71. On the issue of proper amendment procedure and the Reconstruction amendments, see Bruce Ackerman, *We the People*, vol. 2, *Transformations* (Cambridge, MA: Harvard University Press, 2000), 101–6.

17. *Documentary History of the Constitution*, 2:518–19.

18. Collamer to Johnson, October 5, 1865, in Paul H. Bergeron, ed., *The Papers of Andrew Johnson* (Knoxville: University of Tennessee Press, 1991), 9:189–90. See also Johnson to William Marvin, November 20, 1865, ibid., 9:412, in which Johnson indicates to the governor of Florida that while he is pleased that Florida's convention has voted for ratification, its legislature still must render the deciding vote.

19. Vorenberg, *Final Freedom*, 232–33.

20. Howard Devon Hamilton, "The Legislative and Judicial History of the Thirteenth Amendment" (PhD diss., University of Illinois, 1950), 29.

21. Benjamin F. Perry to Andrew Johnson, November 1, 1865, in Bergeron, *Papers of Andrew Johnson*, 9:324.

22. Senate, Messages from the President of the United States, 39th Cong., 1st sess., 1966, Ex. Doc. 26, 254, 198.

23. Butler to Thaddeus Stevens, November 20, 1865, Thaddeus Stevens Papers, Library of Congress.

24. *Documentary History of the Constitution*, 2:606.

25. Ibid., 2:610. Florida adopted the exact same resolution, though its ratification came after Georgia's and thus was not needed for the amendment's adoption. See ibid., 2:625.

26. Alexander H. Stephens, *A Constitutional View of the Late War between the States* (Philadelphia: National Publishing Company, 1870), 611–14.

27. Vorenberg, *Final Freedom*, 223–24.

28. Ibid., 233–39.

29. *Cincinnati Gazette*, December 21, 1865, 2.

2

Grant and Lincoln: Partnership for Victory

John F. Marszalek and Michael B. Ballard

*A*s the year 1865 opened, two men stood poised to seal victory in the Civil War for the Union. Their stories had many of the same roots, but their personalities and styles differed. The fate of war brought them together, and together they joined forces to bring the bloodiest contest ever fought on American soil to an end. They not only saved the Union but also destroyed slavery, the institution that had divided the nation for so long. Of these two victors, one was a novice executive and uneducated military man, the other a seasoned, down-on-his-luck veteran of the Mexican War who hoped and expected to play a greater role in the upcoming Civil War. No one could have predicted in 1861 that their ultimate merger would change history.

Ulysses S. Grant had much further to go than President Abraham Lincoln. Thinking that his West Point training should give him access to more than the company command that his hometown offered, Grant was disappointed when Illinois did not make him a regimental commander. He traveled to the state capitol to try to remedy the situation, only to be snubbed by Governor Richard Yates. Then the governor unexpectedly told Grant that Yates needed his help in the Illinois adjutant general's office. Grant wound up pushing papers, not commanding troops. He had to wait until June 15, 1861, before Yates gave him command of the ragamuffin Twenty-First Illinois Volunteer Regiment. This unit needed discipline. Grant successfully provided it, and his Civil War military career was launched.[1]

President Abraham Lincoln knew nothing about this unimpressive-looking army officer who was a West Point graduate. As the new president of the United States in 1861, he was too busy trying to make sense out of what was happening in the entire nation. The United States looked to him to solve the secession problem, and this meant raising troops, supplying them, finding the right leaders for them, and going on the offensive against the newly organized Confederate States of America. It was not an easy task, and Lincoln had major difficulties all along the way. His biggest problem was the selection of officers—not regimental commanders like Grant, but overall commanders to lead the expanded army of the prewar years. The Northern public demanded a quick victory from its president, and he wanted to provide it.

At first Lincoln looked to Winfield Scott, the hero of the War of 1812 and the Mexican-American War, and the commanding general of the army for forty-seven years. Scott, a Virginian, was highly revered in the nation, so when he declared his loyalty to the Union and did not join the Confederate war effort, federals, especially Lincoln, rejoiced, and Confederates were disappointed. Lincoln had available the best soldier the nation possessed. Surely Scott would lead the nation to victory, just as he had defeated Santa Anna in Mexico City. Or so Lincoln and the nation hoped.

This hope proved to be illusory. Scott was infirm and set in his ways, unable to provide the leadership the nation needed. Lincoln then turned to a younger man, a charismatic leader who, by all appearances, was just the person for the job. George B. McClellan became commanding general while also leading the Army of the Potomac, the military force that would have to implement victory in the Virginia, or eastern, theater. Lincoln worried that this was too much to ask of any one man, but McClellan responded, "I can do it all."[2]

It turned out that McClellan could not do it all, and he could not even do very much of it. He exhibited an unwillingness to move his army against the Confederates, demonstrating not the confidence of his earlier statement to Lincoln, but hesitation and worry. Lincoln was terribly disappointed in McClellan and all but took over the role of commanding general himself. McClellan did no better leading just the Army of the Potomac than he had done when serving as commanding general. He forced Lincoln to look elsewhere, and the president initiated a series of unsatisfactory changes for that army's command: Ambrose Burnside, Joseph Hooker, and George Gordon Meade.

Under inept leadership by commanding generals, Federal forces seemed to stumble upon themselves—or, more accurately, stumble before the Army of Northern Virginia under Robert E. Lee. Burnside foolishly made a frontal attack up Mayre's Hill at Fredericksburg and suffered a horrendous repulse. At Chancellorsville, Joe Hooker had the right battle plan but lacked the nerve to execute it. Robert E. Lee split his forces in front of the Federals and won an important victory. George B. McClellan did fight Lee to a stalemate at Antietam and forced him to withdraw, but he made no effort to pursue the retreating Confederates. George Meade inflicted a bloody defeat on Lee at Gettysburg, but he considered his own army too battered to risk another fight against Lee, who surely would strongly contest any Union pursuit. When all was said and done, nothing ever seemed to change fundamentally. The Federals and the Confederates continued to face each other in a standoff between Washington and Richmond.[3]

Conversely, Lincoln noted the military victories in the western theater, the region between the Appalachian Mountains and the Mississippi River. This is where General Henry W. Halleck's successes persuaded Lincoln to bring him to Washington to become commanding general. Unfortunately, Halleck did not replicate his western theater successes in the East. In truth, his earlier progress was less the result of any aggressiveness on his part and more the result of the aggressiveness of his subordinate commanders there, especially Ulysses S. Grant.[4]

As Lincoln grew ever more frustrated about the lack of movement in the East, the little-known Grant became the epitome of aggressive action in the West. He took his regiment into battle at Belmont, Missouri, in November 1861, and though he was forced to retreat, his war experiences to that point convinced him that his enemy feared him even more than he feared his enemy. He talked Henry W. Halleck, who at the time commanded the region, into offensive action against Fort Henry on the Tennessee River and Fort Donelson on the Cumberland River. His February 1862 victories at both places crumpled the northernmost defensive line of Confederate general Albert Sidney Johnston, established from the Cumberland Gap in the East to the Mississippi River in the West. At Shiloh in April 1862, Grant's Army of the Tennessee took a pummeling on the first day of the battle, but then Grant, with the help of reinforcements, drove the Confederates back to Corinth on the second day. He was not always correct in his estimation of the enemy, but he kept pushing forward.

In July 1863, Grant conducted what many scholars consider to be among the greatest campaigns in military history. He captured Vicksburg, Mississippi, and its defending army and opened the entire Mississippi River to Federal control. In the fall, when the Confederate Army under General Braxton Bragg defeated Federal general William S. Rosecrans at Chickamauga Creek near Chattanooga, Grant ultimately came to the rescue and drove the Confederates out of Chattanooga.[5]

Lincoln was in Washington, far away from the western theater, so his attention tended to remain focused on Virginia. But he could not fail to see what Grant was doing in the West. Grant was conquering Confederate resistance. He forged ahead, leaving the Confederates little time to rest. Grant and Lincoln seemed to be on the same page. The war must cease being a gentlemanly conflict, where civilians watched from the sidelines and Southern society had been protected. The enemy must be defeated, even if collateral damage to property caused civilians to suffer. Hard war had become necessary.

When Lincoln issued his Preliminary Emancipation Proclamation in September 1862, he demonstrated this fact. Slavery would no longer be protected. On January 1, 1863, he signed the final proclamation, freeing slaves in those areas of the nation still in opposition to federal jurisdiction and accepting black men into the Union army. While Grant was defeating the Confederate Army before him, Lincoln was grappling with the issue of slavery and deciding that its destruction was essential to the Union war effort.[6]

Lincoln also realized that, once again, he had to appoint a new commanding general. He needed someone willing to push the Federal armies to defeat and destroy the Confederates before them. Henry W. Halleck was still in charge, but he refused to lead, telling his field commanders that they might do whatever they thought best. Lincoln wanted more. He wanted his commanding general to initiate direct action, and he wanted it immediately and persistently.

At this same time, many in Congress, led by Grant's political supporter Elihu Washburne, were also losing patience with Halleck. Congressmen wanted to see the war forced to a victorious conclusion, and they too looked to the West—to Ulysses S. Grant. They moved to pass a law establishing the rank of lieutenant general, and they made it clear, if it was not already obvious, that Grant was the intended beneficiary. To make sure that someone else, particularly Halleck, would not receive this rank, the House passed an amendment specifically naming Grant as the person who should get this promotion. The Senate refused to go along with this amendment, however, citing it as a violation of the president's constitutional right to make appointments. Lincoln made it clear that he intended to give Grant the slot, and legislative resistance dissipated. On February 26, 1864, the lieutenant general bill made it through the House and the Senate. Now all that was required was Lincoln's signature.[7]

The president liked what he saw in Grant, but he was worried that the general might have political ambitions. After all, this was a presidential election year, and more than a few politicians wanted to replace Lincoln on the Republican ticket. Moreover, the uncertain direction of the war made Lincoln's reelection uncertain. Grant would make a good candidate, identified as he was with military victories. First it was whispered, and then forthright conversations began: replace Lincoln with Grant.

In fact, Grant had no political ambitions. He wrote letters to politically influential individuals disavowing any interest in the presidency. After a lapse of twenty years, he heard from his old boyhood friend Daniel Ammen, now a commodore in the navy, telling him to avoid politics like the plague and continue fighting to win the war. Grant gratefully responded, "My only desire will be, as it has always been. To whip out the rebellion in the shortest way possible and to retain as high a position in the Army afterwards as the Administration then in power may think me suitable for."[8]

As one of the most astute politicians ever to occupy the White House, Lincoln wanted to make sure. He investigated further on his own and became convinced that Grant indeed had no political ambitions. On February 29, Lincoln sent Grant's name to the U.S. Senate to become the new lieutenant general, a rank that only George Washington had previously held. On March 6, Halleck wrote to Grant to tell him that Lincoln had signed his commission as lieutenant general, and it was waiting for him in the War Department when he arrived in Washington. Halleck added his congratulations.[9]

Grant arrived in Washington four days later. He and his son Fred walked up to the registration desk of Willard's Hotel, only to be told as he signed the register "U.S. Grant and son, Galena, Illinois" that the only available room was a small, obscure one on the top floor. But when the clerk saw the signature, he quickly changed that reservation to a better room. When Grant and his son walked into the hotel's crowded dining room, the diners immediately recognized the unimpressive-looking general and cheered vociferously.

Grant next went to the White House to see Lincoln, walking into the middle of a reception in his honor, and he was placed on a sofa so that the celebrants could see him. Cheers rang out, Lincoln shook the general's hand, and the crowd surged forward. The general had to be rescued. Lincoln said that he would give Grant his commission the following day. He handed Grant a copy of his own prepared comments for that day and asked Grant to be ready to respond. Hating to speak in public, Grant clumsily read a few words the next day in response to Lincoln's kind words of praise. Yet Lincoln had to have liked what he heard. After thanking the president for this honor, Grant said, "I feel the full weight of the responsibilities now devolving on me and know that if they are met it will be due to those armies, and above all to the favor of that Providence which leads both Nations and men."[10]

This ceremony signaled an important change in the military direction of the Civil War and in American military history too. Lincoln made Grant his new commanding general and appointed Henry W. Halleck to a new position: chief of staff. Grant would be commanding general, but he would be present with General George Meade and his Army of the Potomac, while Halleck and Secretary of War Edwin M. Stanton would be headquartered in Washington. Grant would tell Meade how the Army of the Potomac should operate against Robert E. Lee, while Halleck and Stanton would provide both logistical and political support. In the West, William T. Sherman became overall commander.[11]

On May 4, 1864, Grant implemented the kind of warfare Lincoln had long been calling for. Since early in the war, Lincoln had been trying to convince his generals that the old Jominian ideas of mass and maneuver only helped the undermanned enemy. Instead of allowing the Confederates to shift troops and thus negate the numerical Federal advantage, Lincoln wanted his generals to attack simultaneously on all fronts. Capture of geographic locations was not as important as destruction of the enemy armies. Lincoln had long been pushing this policy on his previous generals, but to no avail. Lincoln understood that if the Federal armies applied widespread, coordinated pressure, they would win this war and preserve the Union.

Grant agreed. His plan for the eastern theater was to put the Army of the Potomac into action while other Union armies also went on the offensive up the James River peninsula and throughout the Shenandoah Valley. At the same time, Sherman's western army—actually three armies organized into one, the Army of the Tennessee, Army of the Cumberland, and Army of the Ohio—would march against Confederate general Joseph E. Johnston's army in what came to be called the Atlanta Campaign.

Farther west, Grant had wanted Nathaniel P. Banks to move against Mobile, but he went along with Lincoln's desire to have Banks begin the Red River Campaign into northwest Louisiana. If successful, this would bring Federal pressure on Confederate Texas and, it was hoped, convince Napoleon III that his desire to control Mexico through support of Emperor Maximilian would not be tolerated. Maximilian, an Austrian invited into Mexico by Mexican monarchists, became a puppet of the French, but he proved to be unpopular. Banks's campaign failed, but Napoleon III now sensed that the U.S. government would send aid to anti-Maximilian forces; the French abandoned Mexico.

Lincoln had long been concerned about the French presence in Mexico because of its proximity to California, other contiguous U.S. territories (the future states of Arizona and New Mexico), and especially Texas, which, like other Confederate states, the president considered as still being in the Union. Lincoln told Grant after the fall of Vicksburg that it would be better to keep an eye on Napoleon III than to attack Mobile. So Grant had come to understand that there was more to the war than defeating the Confederacy. Lincoln could not take his eyes off potential European threats, and Grant grew to appreciate Lincoln's determination to look beyond Confederate defeat. That fourth day of May in Virginia, the Civil War, under the unforeseen combination of Lincoln and Grant's leadership, signaled the beginning of a Federal offensive that Grant was determined to keep pushing until the enemy's ability to resist melted away.

As Grant made his plans, the president sent him a message of support. "I wish to express, in this way, my entire satisfaction with what you have done up to this time, so far as I understand it." Lincoln added, "I wish not to obtrude any constraints upon you." Grant greatly appreciated these words, responding, "The confidence you express for the future . . . in my Military experience is acknowledged with pride. It will be my earnest endeavor that you, and the country, shall not be disappointed." This exchange was the hallmark of the Lincoln-Grant relationship: mutual trust and a determination to win the war.[12]

Even with Lincoln's support, Grant had many obstacles to overcome. He knew he had to learn about the abilities of his new team of generals as well as the nature of the huge Army of the Potomac he would be traveling with. George Meade had qualities Grant appreciated, but he also noted that other generals resented Meade's harsh temperament. He decided to use this aspect of Meade's reputation to his advantage. Grant stayed away from the front lines, leaving Meade to overlook operations and to discipline those not doing their jobs. In the West, Grant had known his generals well, and he trusted most of them, but that advantage did not exist in Virginia at the beginning of the 1864 campaign.[13]

Grant also quickly realized that both commanders and soldiers in his army felt cowed by Robert E. Lee. During the Wilderness Campaign, a near hysterical Federal officer warned Grant about Lee's prowess. Grant responded firmly, "Oh I am heartily tired of hearing about what Lee is going to do. Some of you seem to think he is suddenly going to turn a double somersault, and land in our rear and on both of our flanks at the same time. Go back to your command, and try to think what we are going to do ourselves, instead of what Lee is going to do." Eliminating such thoughts was essential to the success of the campaign. Grant told Meade, "Lee's Army will be your objective point. Wherever Lee goes there you will go also." As the campaign evolved, Grant learned that wherever he went, Lee would go also. The contest proved to be between Lee's tactical genius and Grant's tenacity and patience. With double the number of Lee's army, some 119,000 to Lee's 64,000, Grant had more time and flexibility to carry out his plans and to react to Lee's movements. But Grant also had the pressure of coordinating a multifront war across the country.[14]

Grant pondered what route to take to assault Lee. He ultimately decided to go after him from the east side of the Army of Northern Virginia, thus making it easier to keep in contact with supply boats following the Union army down the Atlantic seaboard. The fight began at the Wilderness, southwest of Fredericksburg. The bloody two-day battle, May 5–6, 1864, tested the mettle of both armies. The dense terrain and gun smoke frequently kept soldiers from seeing more than a few feet ahead of them. In a tactical sense, Lee won the battle, and in times past, the Army of the Potomac would have retreated. Not Grant. He determined to continue moving south, trying to outflank Lee. If that did not work, he would still keep pressuring him. Lee had no intention of allowing Grant to get behind his army, because this would open the way to Richmond. Grant's top priority was Lee, but Lee's was protecting the Confederate capital.

While the fighting raged, Abraham Lincoln and Secretary of War Stanton anxiously waited for news from the front. Was Grant going to be successful, or would he be just another in the long list of military failures in the East? Lincoln asked Assistant Secretary of War Charles Dana, who had gotten to know Grant well during the Vicksburg Campaign, to leave Washington and visit Grant. Dana arrived after the fight in the Wilderness had ended, finding that Grant and Meade had individual headquarters, close but separate. The procedure they followed was to have Grant send orders to Meade, who then sent them on to corps commanders in the field. Dana saw no preparations being made to retreat. Grant had already sent a message to Lincoln via a reporter, assuring the president that retreat was not an option. Grant wrote to Halleck several days later, "[I] propose to fight it out on this line if it takes me all summer." These were reassurances that Lincoln was excited to hear, particularly after the years of inaction and complaints.[15]

As he fought his way south, Grant made time to send updates to Halleck, knowing that Halleck would pass those messages of importance to Stanton and Lincoln. From time to time, Grant did communicate directly with Lincoln, but many of these notes were mundane exchanges about personnel. No serious correspondence passed between the two until late in the summer of 1864.[16]

The next great battle came at Spotsylvania Court House, and it was one of the bloodiest of the war. Grant suffered over 18,000 casualties, bringing his total number of killed, wounded, and missing, counting the Wilderness, to more than 35,000. Rumblings about these staggering losses began to be heard in the North, but Lincoln determined to stand by Grant. He knew that Grant had to suffer losses to defeat the stubborn, well-led Southern army.[17]

In the coming battles at the North Anna River and Cold Harbor, Grant incurred another 15,000 losses. Lost in the smoke of almost continual fighting, however, was the fact that Lee, although suffering fewer casualties in the battles, was losing men in greater proportion, and he could not replace them. In fact, Grant, while losing many men, was bleeding Lee. Grant had lost some 55,000 from his initial force of 119,000, compared with Lee's losses of 33,000 out of 64,000. Grant's losses represented 45 percent of his manpower, while Lee's represented nearly 50 percent. And Grant could call up replacements, giving his army stability of numbers, whereas Lee could not bring in nearly enough men to replace his losses. Lee's overall casualties continued to shrink the size of his army.[18]

Still, this was a different Grant than the general who had won the Vicksburg Campaign. After two failed attacks at Vicksburg against formidable defensive works, Grant had settled for a siege. Lee's defensive positions in Virginia were often much more formidable than those in Mississippi, yet Grant kept trying to crash through them. The problem was that his commanders simply could not coordinate attacks as Grant wanted, and he grew increasingly frustrated as the campaign progressed. Yet he determined that he must do whatever it took to defeat Lee, and if that meant continual assaults, so be it. Grant had earlier sent General Philip Sheridan with most of the army's cavalry south to raid the area around Richmond, but he should have kept him closer and thus would have known more about Lee's activities.

The Union campaign from the Wilderness through Cold Harbor led to charges that Grant was a butcher who coldly sacrificed his men. Yet a close study of the campaign reveals that Grant did not wait until after his repulse at Cold Harbor to use maneuver as a tactic. He regularly combined maneuver with force, and had Meade and the corps commanders been more aggressive, more skilled, and more of a team, Grant would have been more successful. Grant had to play the hand dealt him; he could not build a solid command corps from scratch in the time allotted him. Grant also believed, especially in the wake of Cold Harbor, that morale in Lee's army was dissipating. Lee's irreplaceable losses kept mounting, and many Confederate soldiers realized they could not last much longer against such pressure. Grant, however, underestimated their devotion to Lee; they seemed willing to fight as long as the old man told them to fight.[19]

After Cold Harbor, Grant managed one of the great feats of the war. He crossed the James River with his entire army. Grant knew the defenses around Richmond were strong and extensive, and he had no inclination to try to overwhelm them. By bypassing Richmond, Grant could establish a supply and manpower depot to support a movement against Petersburg, cutting Lee's railroad supply line from the south. Grant set up headquarters at City Point, Virginia, and though he was disappointed that the initial assault against Petersburg had failed, he determined to take the city.

Grant set up a supply base and hospital at City Point (modern day Hopewell, Virginia), which became, after the general made his decision to besiege Petersburg, one of the busiest ports in the country. Overlooking the confluence of the James and Appomattox Rivers, City Point was an ideal place for Grant's headquarters. Soon he established personal contact with Lincoln; the president was eager to see him now that the campaign had become stabilized into a siege operation at Petersburg. Finally, the two architects of the war were able to spend time together.

Lincoln visited City Point on June 21, 1864, to check on naval operations up the James River toward Richmond. The president and the general rode together along the rear of the army, no doubt discussing more men for the war and how they might be used. Lincoln left before the end of the day. Prior to Lincoln's visit, Grant had telegraphed the president calling for additional troops, suggesting that another 300,000 men should be brought into the army. Such an increase in Union numbers probably would have allowed Grant to drive back the Confederates from their fronts in Richmond and Petersburg "without attacking fortifications." Grant believed that Lee could not get any reinforcements, and reports of rebel desertions were common. Lincoln responded that a call had already been sent out the previous day for 500,000 men.[20]

On July 26, Grant received a message from Secretary of War Stanton to the effect that Lincoln wanted to meet him at Fortress Monroe off the Virginia coast. Grant responded that he could see Lincoln Friday of that week, though the time was later changed to Sunday, July 31. Confederate general Jubal Early was threatening Washington, and rumors had it that an attempt would be made to free Confederate prisoners at Point Lookout, Maryland, on a tip of land southeast of Washington. Grant sent cavalry commander Phil Sheridan to beat down these Confederate threats. Lincoln was not sure that would be enough unless Grant came and personally supervised operations. Grant promised to rush to Washington on August 4. The Early threat evaporated.[21]

Grant hurried back to City Point to find that a disaster had occurred during his absence. His engineers had dug a tunnel under Confederate works, similar to a Grant operation near the end of the Vicksburg siege, and filled it with gunpowder. After the explosive was detonated, the Union attack turned into a disaster. The crater formed by the gunpowder's explosion turned out to be a death trap for the charging Federal soldiers. Confederate troops hurried to the rim around the crater and fired relentlessly into the masses of Federal troops. Grant lost 2,450 killed and 2,000 wounded. He was disgusted. "It was the saddest affair I have witnessed in this war," he said. "Such opportunity for carrying fortifications I have never seen and do not expect again to have." Grant was so upset that he sent forward a request for Lincoln to set up a court of inquiry into the failed attack. A court was established and led to the resignation of one officer, the transfer of another, and permanent leave for corps commander Ambrose Burnside.[22]

The fighting around Petersburg dragged on for months. Both sides made sorties that accomplished nothing of note and led to the taking of many prisoners, a result Lee could ill afford. Desertions in the Confederate army continued as time dragged by. Grant kept lengthening his line, forcing Lee to do the same, until the Confederate defenses had thinned considerably. Petersburg was not a classic siege; Lee had the freedom to pull back at any time. Yet he was trapped by circumstances. To pull back would allow Grant to cut a vital supply line and likely force the capitulation of Richmond. Lee had to stay where he was, and his army became more and more depleted by increases in desertions, casualties, and men taken prisoner.

Both Lincoln and Grant were relieved when Sherman captured Savannah, Georgia, in time to help the president overcome war-weariness in the North. Lincoln had won reelection prior to Sherman's taking of Savannah, but Sherman's and Grant's progress had done much to solidify the president's political fortunes. In private letters, Grant wrote, "The overwhelming majority received by M. Lincoln, and the quiet with which the election went off, will prove a terrible damper to the rebels. It will be worth more than a victory in the field both in its effect on the rebels and in its influence abroad." To Grant, Lincoln's reelection would force the Confederates to take drastic measures to survive. It was also a defeat for the Copperheads (pro-peace Democrats). Earlier, to Grant's disgust, Copperheads had accused Lincoln of interfering with the army. Elihu Washburne had written evidence to the contrary and asked Grant's permission to use the letters to defend Lincoln. Grant quickly responded, "I have no objection to the President using any thing I have ever written to him as he sees fit," adding with a touch of humor, "I think however for him to attempt to answer all the charges the opposition will bring against him will be like setting a maiden to work to prove her chastity."[23]

Though the end was in sight, Grant had to deal with the annoyance of what he perceived was General George Thomas's reluctance to defeat a

Confederate army at Nashville. Lincoln, meanwhile, threw himself into the battle over the passage of the Thirteenth Amendment to the U.S. Constitution, which would abolish slavery.

Grant saw Thomas win his battle in December 1864, and Lincoln won his political victory at the end of January 1865. The climactic final year of the war began with an unusual event that thrust Lincoln and Grant into a difficult situation. Pressured to search for peace possibilities, Lincoln allowed Francis P. Blair to visit Jefferson Davis unofficially. Blair met twice with Davis in mid-January, but exchanges of messages proved there could only be a stalemate. Lincoln insisted on reunion, while Davis demanded that the Confederacy remain a separate entity. All this led to the Hampton Roads peace conference at Fortress Monroe off the Virginia coast, a further fruitless effort to bring peace. Davis felt he must make an effort, and since Lincoln had agreed to Blair's visits to Richmond, perhaps both presidents could deflate criticism for doing nothing, though both knew their positions were incompatible.

On January 31, 1865, Grant notified Lincoln that he had received a request from Southern officials who wanted to pass through the general's lines to have a conference with the president to discuss how the war might be ended. Blair worked behind the scenes to set up the meeting. Three Confederates received permission from Jefferson Davis to contact Grant: Alexander Stephens, vice president of the Confederacy; J. A. Campbell, assistant secretary of war; and R. M. T. Hunter, a Virginia senator. Grant told Lincoln that directions had been sent to the three men with the intent of allowing them to come to his headquarters. From that point, he would wait for Lincoln's instructions. Lincoln responded that written instructions were being sent by a messenger, Major Thomas T. Eckert, assistant superintendent of the U.S. Military Telegraph Office.[24]

Stanton wrote an additional note telling Grant to set up an interview with the three Confederates. If Eckert should later request that a meeting with Lincoln be scheduled, Grant should allow the rebel commissioners into Fortress Monroe and provide protection and "comfortable quarters." Meanwhile, Stanton directed Grant, "Let none of this have any effect upon your military movements or plans."[25]

On February 1, Grant sent a brief message to Lincoln assuring the president that there would be a truce, but that his troops remained alert and ready to carry on as if nothing were happening anywhere else. The three Confederates told Grant they wanted to go to Washington to speak to Lincoln, but Grant had no authority to authorize such a visit. When Eckert arrived, he told Grant that the general should not be present for any of the talks, explaining, "You are the commanding general of the army.

If you make a failure or say anything that would be subject to criticism it would be very bad. If I make a mistake I am nothing but a common business man and it will go for naught. I am going to take the responsibility, and I advise you not to go to the conference." Grant responded that it would be ill-mannered for him not to welcome the Confederates. Eckert noted that Grant seemed upset that he was being kept in the dark about Lincoln's proposals.

When Grant entered the room during Eckert's second round of talks, one of the Confederates (possibly Hunter) told him the talks with Eckert seemed stalled. The Confederates wanted to go to Washington, as Lincoln had allegedly promised. Before Grant could say anything, Eckert interjected, "General Grant, you are not permitted to say anything officially at this time." Eckert then elaborated, "If you will read the instructions under which I am acting you will see that I am right." Grant stayed for a few minutes, listened to the conversations, and then left.

Grant never seemed to forgive Eckert for his behavior. The commanding general of any army could not be expected to be happy about being cut off by a major. Eckert regretted the bad feelings he had created, but he insisted that his actions had been based on his orders from Lincoln.[26]

At 10:30 that same evening of February 1, Grant sent a message to Stanton:

> I will state confidentially but not officially to become a matter of record, that I am convinced, upon conversation with Messrs Stevens, & Hunter that their intentions are good and their desire sincere to restore peace and Union. I have not felt myself at liberty to express even views of my own or to account for my reticency. This has placed me in an alquerd [awkward] position which I could have avided by not seeing them in the first instance. I fear now their going back without any expression from any one in authority will have a bad influance. At the same time I recognize the difficulties in the way of receiving these informal commissioners at this time and do not know what to recommend. I am sorry however that Mr. Lincoln can not have an interview with the two named in this dispatch if not all three within our lines.[27]

Lincoln accepted Grant's reasoning. He decided to meet with the Confederates at Fortress Monroe because, on the heels of winning his battle for the constitutional amendment abolishing slavery, he had no intention of inviting the rebel officials to Washington. On February 2, he notified Grant of his decision, and Grant notified Secretary of State William Seward that the Confederate commissioners had agreed to the meeting place.

The conference accomplished nothing. Predictably, Lincoln demanded that the Union must be reunited, and Davis stood by his position, via his commissioners, that the Confederacy must be recognized. Grant arranged for the passage of the three representatives back through his lines, and Lincoln asked him on February 8 if he could use some of Grant's words contained in his earlier message to Stanton in his report to Congress. Lincoln thought that Grant's point about a "bad influence" if the rebel agents left without having met with anyone in authority was a good one to share with House members. Grant had no objection. His frustration provided Lincoln with political cover, and the two men once again, though in an unusual manner this time, reinforced one another.[28]

As Lee's army neared collapse on the Petersburg line, Grant decided he wanted to see Lincoln. "Can you not visit City Point for a day or two?" he wrote. "I would like very much to see you and I think the rest would do you good." Lincoln responded that he had already thought of making the trip and expected to bring his wife, Mary, and "a few others."[29]

Lincoln arrived on March 24 with Mary, son Tad, and "several ladies." The next day, Lee made one last desperate assault on Grant's line at a fortification named Fort Stedman. Grant and Lincoln, who were on the boat that had brought the presidential party upriver, soon learned that the Confederates had been beaten back with heavy losses. After the fighting had settled down, Grant invited Lincoln to ride with him closer to the front. Lincoln happily accepted and spent time with Union troops, who vigorously cheered him. That evening, Lincoln sat at a campfire and reviewed the war, the hardships, foreign issues, pressure on his administration, patriotism in the North, and the pride he had in Federal troops. Grant asked Lincoln if the president had ever had any doubts about the outcome of the war. Lincoln answered firmly that he had not. Lincoln seemed to thoroughly enjoy himself, telling stories, petting homeless kittens, reviewing the troops, and riding with Grant and Phil Sheridan. Julia Grant and Mary Lincoln went along, but Mrs. Lincoln did not seem to enjoy the muddy roads. The two women did not like each other, but this rift had no impact on their husbands' friendship.[30]

As the end of the war grew imminent, an odd occurrence led Lincoln to make sure that Grant knew who was boss. Confederate general James Longstreet and E. O. C. Ord, one of Grant's generals, talked about peace during an exchange of prisoners in late February. Afterward, Longstreet shared the conversation with Lee, who wrote Grant regarding a possible meeting between the two commanders to talk about ways to end the war. Grant wanted to see his old friend Longstreet, but he was wise enough to contact Stanton before initiating a meeting. Stanton responded with a strongly worded message from Lincoln: "The president directs me to say to you that he wishes you to have no conference with Gen. Lee unless it be for the capitulation of Lee's army, or on solely minor and purely military matters. He instructs me to say that you are not to decide, discuss, or confer upon any political questions: such questions the President holds in his own hands; and will submit them to no military conferences or conventions— mean time you are to press to the utmost, your military advantages."

Grant responded defensively to Lincoln's words of caution. Clearly he knew he could not negotiate on behalf of Lincoln. To Stanton, Grant wrote that he had sent a message to Lee to that effect. "I can assure you," Grant continued, "that no act of the enemy will prevent me pr[e]ssing all advantages gained to the utmost of my ability. Neither will I under any circumstances exceed my authority or in any way embarrass the Govt. It was because I had no right to meet Gen. Lee on the subject proposed by him that I refered [*sic*] the matter for instructions."[31]

This incident gave Lincoln an opportunity to clear the air. With the end of the war looming, the president could not afford to have officers acting on his behalf or as self-styled diplomats. He had to be sure that Grant clearly understood his place regarding negotiations, which the general certainly did.

By March 28, Lee's military options had nearly run out. The morning of April 2, Jefferson Davis and his government evacuated Richmond. Meanwhile, that same day, Lincoln met with Grant, Sherman, and Admiral David D. Porter at City Point. Grant brought Lincoln up to date on the military situation, noting that "the crisis of the war was at hand." Grant expected to block any attempt Lee might make to go south, and the only immediate concern was keeping Lee from successfully escaping west from the Petersburg lines. Sherman said he could come up through North Carolina, pressing Joe Johnston to the point that he could occupy Lee and Johnston until Grant could close in for the kill. Lincoln wanted to know if the war could be ended without another battle, but neither Grant nor Sherman had control over what the Confederates might do. The president commented that once the shooting stopped, he inclined toward "a generous policy." He said he would not care if Confederate political leaders escaped, as their absence might make it easier to cope with the war's aftermath.[32]

The end came quickly after the meeting. On April 4, 1865, Lincoln was in the evacuated Confederate capital at Richmond, and on April 9, Grant accepted Lee's surrender at Appomattox Court House. Grant gave Lee generous terms, as he understood them from the meeting with Lincoln. On April 13, the Grants were in Washington and invited to tour the capital, cloaked in celebration at the news of Lee's surrender. The next morning,

Lincoln and his cabinet met with Grant at the White House. Lincoln invited the general and his wife, Julia, to attend a play at Ford's Theatre that evening. Grant declined, saying that he and Mrs. Grant had already made plans to travel to Burlington, New Jersey, to see their children. At Ford's that evening, Abraham Lincoln was assassinated as Grant rode on a train traveling north.[33] As soon as he received the news, Grant returned to Washington.

Though Lincoln lived to rejoice in Lee's surrender, he would never know of Johnston's capitulation to Sherman on April 26. Death could not take from him a few days of celebration and the pleasure of knowing that his major purpose as president had been achieved. Grant had to go on alone to do what he could to see that the fruits of victory were not squandered. He would be limited to overseeing the military aftermath, and he did so without the firm hand he had so counted on in the White House. When Grant became president in 1869, after the disastrous presidency of Andrew Johnson, his task was to complete the work of the Civil War. He tried valiantly and had some notable successes. Yet he was unable to complete the work of including African Americans fully in American society as Lincoln had planned. Still, Grant knew that he and Lincoln had done something worthwhile: their combined tenacity had saved a nation and ended slavery. This was a great achievement for these two individuals from Illinois, a little-known soldier and an untried president.

Notes

1. James M. McPherson, *Tried by War: Abraham Lincoln as Commander in Chief* (New York: Penguin Press, 2008) is the Lincoln Prize–winning book on the military history of the Civil War. The most thorough study of Ulysses S. Grant's military role in the Civil War is Brooks D. Simpson, *Ulysses S. Grant: Triumph over Adversity, 1822–1865* (New York: Houghton Mifflin, 2000), especially pages 78–96.

2. Timothy D. Johnson, *Winfield Scott: The Quest for Military Glory* (Lawrence: University Press of Kansas, 1998); Stephen W. Sears, *George B. McClellan: The Young Napoleon* (New York: Ticknor and Fields, 1988); November 1, 1861, *Inside Lincoln's White House: The Complete Civil War Diary of John Hay*, ed. Michael Burlingame and John R. Turner Ettlinger (Carbondale: Southern Illinois University Press, 1997), 30.

3. William Marvel, *Burnside* (Chapel Hill: University of North Carolina Press, 1991); Walter H. Herbert, *Fighting Joe Hooker* (Indianapolis: Bobbs Merrill, 1944); Freeman Cleaves, *Meade of Gettysburg* (Norman: University of Oklahoma Press, 1991).

4. John F. Marszalek, *Commanding General of All Lincoln's Armies: A Life of Henry W. Halleck* (Cambridge, MA: Belknap Press of Harvard University Press, 2004).

5. Michael B. Ballard, *Vicksburg: The Campaign That Opened the Mississippi* (Chapel Hill: University of North Carolina Press, 2003).

6. Harold Holzer, Edna Greene Medford, and Frank J. Williams, *The Emancipation Proclamation: Three Views* (Baton Rouge: Louisiana State University Press, 2006).

7. Simpson, *Ulysses S. Grant*, 257; Elihu B. Washburne to Ulysses S. Grant, February 26, 1864, *The Papers of Ulysses S. Grant*, ed. John Y. Simon et al., 32 vols. (Carbondale: Southern Illinois University Press, 1967–2012), 10:188n (hereafter cited as *PUSG*).

8. Daniel Ammen to Ulysses S. Grant, February 5, 1864, *PUSG*, 10:133.

9. Abraham Lincoln to U.S. Senate, February 29, 1864, *PUSG*, 10:188n; Henry W. Halleck to Ulysses S. Grant, March 6, 1864, *PUSG*, 10:189n.

10. Simpson, *Ulysses S. Grant*, 258–61; Ulysses S. Grant, "Speech," March 9, 1864, *PUSG*, 10:195.

11. "Order Assigning Ulysses S. Grant to Command of the Armies of the United States," March 10, 1864, and "General Orders No. 98," March 12, 1864, in *The Collected Works of Abraham Lincoln*, ed. Roy P. Basler, 8 vols. (New Brunswick, NJ: Rutgers University Press, 1953–55), 7:236, 239–40.

12. Abraham Lincoln to Ulysses S. Grant, April 30, 1864, *Collected Works*, 7:324; Ulysses S. Grant to Abraham Lincoln, May 1, 1864, *PUSG*, 10:380.

13. The most thorough military analysis of the Overland Campaign is Gordon C. Rhea's multivolume study, published by Louisiana State University Press (Baton Rouge), including *The Battle of the Wilderness, May 5–6, 1864* (1994); *The Battles for Spotsylvania Court House and the Road to Yellow Tavern, May 7–12, 1864* (1997); *To the North Anna River: Grant and Lee, May 13–25, 1864* (2000); and *Cold Harbor: Grant and Lee, May 26–June 3, 1864* (2002). A fifth and final volume is forthcoming. Unless otherwise noted, our discussion of the campaign from the Wilderness to Cold Harbor is based on Rhea's volumes.

14. Gordon C. Rhea, *In the Footsteps of Grant and Lee: The Wilderness through Cold Harbor* (Baton Rouge: Louisiana State University Press, 2007), 36; Ulysses S. Grant to George G. Meade, April 9, 1864, *PUSG*, 10:274.

15. Charles A. Dana, *Recollections of the Civil War* (New York: D. Appleton, 1902), 187–90; Ronald C. White, Jr., *A. Lincoln: A Biography* (New York: Random House, 2009); Ulysses S. Grant to Henry H. Halleck, May 11, 1864, *PUSG*, 10:422.

16. Grant's communications with Meade, Halleck, and Lincoln during this campaign are found in *PUSG*, 10–14.

17. White, *A. Lincoln*, 632.

18. Gordon Rhea's statistical evaluations are quoted in Edward H. Bonekemper III, *A Victor, Not a Butcher: Ulysses S. Grant's Overlooked Military Genius* (Chicago: Regnary, 2004), 196.

19. James M. McPherson points out that Lee had the advantage of fighting on the defensive. See McPherson, "The Unheroic Hero," *New York Review of Books* 46 (October 4, 1996): 16–19.

20. Ulysses S. Grant to Benjamin Butler, June 21, 1864, Ulysses S. Grant to George Meade, June 21, 1864, Ulysses S. Grant to Abraham Lincoln, July 19, 1864, *PUSG*, 11:97–98, 103–104n, 280.

21. Ulysses S. Grant to Edwin M. Stanton (EMS), July 26, 1864, Edwin M. Stanton to Ulysses S. Grant, July 26, 27, 1864, Abraham Lincoln to Ulysses S. Grant, July 28, 29, 1864, Ulysses S. Grant to Abraham Lincoln, July 28, 30, 1864, Abraham Lincoln to Ulysses S. Grant, August 3, 1864, Ulysses S. Grant to Abraham Lincoln, August 4, 1864, *PUSG*, 11:315–16, 360.

22. Ulysses S. Grant to Henry W. Halleck, August 1, 1864, *PUSG*, 11:361, 164n; regarding Burnside, see *PUSG*, 11:414–15n.

23. Edwin M. Stanton to Ulysses S. Grant, August 19, 1864, Elihu B. Washburne to Ulysses S. Grant, September 20, 1864, Ulysses S. Grant to Elihu B. Washburne, September 21, 1864, *PUSG*, 12:25n, 185. See ibid., 12:416, regarding Grant's private correspondence.

24. Brian Steel Wills, *George H. Thomas: As True as Steel* (Lawrence: University Press of Kansas, 2012); Harold Holzer and Sara Vaughn Gabbard, eds., *Lincoln and Freedom: Slavery, Emancipation and the Thirteenth Amendment* (Carbondale: Southern Illinois University Press, 2007); White, *A. Lincoln*, 656–57; Michael B. Ballard, *Long Shadow: Jefferson Davis and the Final Days of the Confederacy* (Jackson: University Press of Mississippi, 1986), 18; Ulysses S. Grant to Abraham Lincoln, August 31, 1864, Abraham Lincoln to Ulysses S. Grant, January 31, 1865, *PUSG*, 13:332–34n. On Eckert, see *PUSG*, 13: 347n.

25. Edwin M. Stanton to Ulysses S. Grant, January 30 [13], 1865, and Ulysses S. Grant to Stephens, Campbell, and Hunter, January 31, 1865, *PUSG*, 13:334n, 224–35.

26. Ulysses S. Grant to Abraham Lincoln, February 1, 1865, *PUSG*, 13:344–45; David Homer Bates, *Recollections of the United States Military Telegraph Corps during the Civil War* (New York: Century, 1907), 336–37.

27. Ulysses S. Grant to Edwin M. Stanton, February 1, 1865, *PUSG*, 13:345–46 (misspellings in original).

28. Abraham Lincoln to Ulysses S. Grant, February 2, 1865, Ulysses S. Grant to William Henry Seward, February 2, 1865, Ulysses S. Grant to Abraham Lincoln, February 8, 1865, *PUSG*, 13:346–47n.

29. Ulysses S. Grant to Abraham Lincoln, March 20, 1865, Abraham Lincoln to Ulysses S. Grant, March 20, 1865, *PUSG*, 14:213n.

30. Horace Porter, *Campaigning with Grant* (New York: Century, 1897), 403–16.

31. White, *A. Lincoln*, 658; Ulysses S. Grant to Edwin M. Stanton, March 3, 1865, Edwin M. Stanton to Ulysses S. Grant, March 3, 1865 (two messages), Ulysses S. Grant to Edwin M. Stanton, March 3, 1865, *PUSG*, 14:90–91n, 100.

32. Porter, *Campaigning with Grant*, 423–24.

33. Ibid., 497; White, *A. Lincoln*, 672–73.

3

Lincoln and the Hampton Roads Conference
Richard Striner

$\mathcal{A}$ colorful episode—in some respects inconsequential but in other ways important and suggestive—took place in early 1865 when Abraham Lincoln met with a delegation of Confederate commissioners.[1]

This had not been Lincoln's idea. Early in December 1864, in the aftermath of some events that effectively doomed the Confederacy—the battlefield victories of William T. Sherman, Philip H. Sheridan, and George H. Thomas and the massive electoral victories of Lincoln and Republicans generally—Francis Preston Blair, Sr., a veteran Democratic Unionist, came up with a scheme that he believed would shorten the war: Confederate and Union forces, he believed, should join together and invade Mexico. The pretext for this intervention would be to counteract a previous intervention by the French, which had been supported by the British and Spanish. Napoleon III had attempted to collect some Mexican debts by landing troops, creating a monarchy in Mexico, and foisting an Austrian archduke, Maximilian Ferdinand, on the Mexican people as their ruler.

Blair met with Lincoln on December 28 and, without telling the president the details of his scheme, requested a pass to visit Richmond and confer with Confederate leaders. Lincoln gave him the pass and Blair went to Richmond, courtesy of the U.S. Navy, which supplied a ship from the Potomac flotilla to carry Blair to Aiken's Landing on the James River. Blair had written ahead to Jefferson Davis, so a steamer was ready to carry Blair to Richmond when he arrived.

Lincoln's reasons for giving Blair the pass are unclear. There is no doubt that Lincoln regarded the prospect of talking to Confederates, except for discussions of the terms for their surrender, as distasteful. The last thing he wanted or intended was to confer legitimacy on the rebellion in any way. In his annual message to Congress earlier that month, Lincoln had declared that "no attempt at negotiation with the insurgent leader [Jefferson Davis] could result in any good." Lincoln argued that Davis "would accept nothing short of severance of the Union—precisely what we will not and cannot give. His declarations to this effect are explicit and oft-repeated."[2]

On the other hand, Lincoln sometimes gave permission for talks with Confederates when politicians put pressure on him to give "peace talks" a try. On such occasions, Lincoln permitted them to talk to the rebels in the hope that they would discover for themselves how naïve their expectations were. It was for this reason that Lincoln sent *New York Tribune* editor Horace Greeley in the previous summer to confer with some Confederate agents on the Canadian side of Niagara Falls.

In addition, it is also possible that Lincoln regarded Blair's mission as an opportunity to gain firsthand information on attitudes in Richmond. Perhaps this was part of the reason why Lincoln also approved a simultaneous but lesser-known visit to Richmond by James W. Singleton, a Democrat from Illinois. Singleton had offered to inform the rebel leaders that their estimation of Northern war-weariness was greatly exaggerated. With Lincoln's approval, Singleton set off for Richmond on January 9, 1865.

Lincoln found himself in a position of supreme strength at the time. He had another four years in the White House. The Republicans would control the new Congress by huge supermajorities. General Sherman had captured the city of Savannah and would soon be turning north to join forces with Grant at Petersburg and deliver the coup de grâce that would destroy Lee's army. And when that happened, Lincoln allegedly told some White House visitors, at least according to a reminiscence recorded years later, "the Southern Confederacy can kiss my ass."[3]

Blair got to Richmond safely on January 12 and conferred with Jefferson Davis, who rejected the idea of a joint U.S.-Confederate invasion of Mexico but expressed willingness to discuss the restoration of amicable relations between the North and South. He gave Blair a written statement in which he proclaimed, "I . . . am willing now, as heretofore, to enter into negotiations for the restoration of peace; and am ready to send a commission whenever I have reason to suppose it will be received, or to receive a commission, if the United States government will choose to send one . . . with a view to secure peace to the two countries."[4] When Blair conveyed this message to Lincoln on January 18, the president—careful to express himself in language that would pass muster with very different audiences—wrote a note addressed to Blair, to be delivered to Jefferson Davis. In the note, Lincoln stated, "I have constantly been, am now, and shall continue, ready to receive any agent whom he, or any other influential person now resisting the national authority, may informally send to me, with the view of securing peace to the people of our one common country."[5]

Blair met with Davis again on January 21. The two men discussed the possibility of an armistice to be arranged by Generals Ulysses S. Grant and Robert E. Lee. But when Davis consulted with Alexander H. Stephens on January 27, the Confederate vice president recommended the appointment of a peace commission to meet with Lincoln himself. Davis agreed and appointed three commissioners—Stephens, Senator Robert M. T. Hunter, and Assistant Secretary of War John A. Campbell—to confer with Lincoln. He instructed them "to proceed to Washington City for an informal conference . . . upon the issues involved in the existing war, and for the purpose of securing peace to the two countries."[6]

As news of these developments reached Washington, Radical Republicans became disgruntled and even alarmed. Zachariah Chandler wrote, "Blair is an old fool for going to Richmond upon a peace mission and the Administration is little better for permitting him to go upon any pretense whatever."[7] Navy Secretary Gideon Welles reflected in his diary, "The President, with much shrewdness and much good sense, has often strange and incomprehensible whims. . . . It would hardly surprise me were he to undertake to arrange terms of peace without consulting anyone."[8]

On January 31, the news that Confederate peace commissioners had been appointed threatened to derail the urgent Republican efforts to secure House passage of the Thirteenth Amendment to the Constitution, which would outlaw slavery. Congressman James Ashley, the floor manager for the measure, wrote Lincoln a note asking him to take some countermeasures: "The report is in circulation in the House that peace Commissioners are on their way or are in the city, and is being used against us. If it is true, I fear we shall lose the bill. Please authorize me to contradict it, if not true."[9] The president crafted the following message for release to the public: "So far as I know, there are no peace commissioners in the city, or likely to be in it."[10]

Ashley later reflected that the Thirteenth Amendment would have been defeated if he had not secured Lincoln's message. A number of Democrats, he recalled, "could easily have been prevailed upon to vote against it, on the ground that the passage of such a proposition . . . would have been offensive to the Commissioners."[11]

As to the likelihood of rebel peace commissioners arriving in Washington, Davis's emissaries had explicitly requested permission to visit the city, per the Confederate president's instructions, when they arrived at Grant's lines in Petersburg on January 30. Lincoln agreed on principle to give them safe passage so long as they were prepared to enter into discussions "with a view of securing peace to the people of our one common country."[12] But to ascertain whether the Confederates were willing to parley along lines consistent with the "one common country" principle, Lincoln sent Major Thomas Eckert, head of the telegraph service in the War Department, to interview the rebel commissioners and report back to him.

In the meantime, however, the commissioners had sent a letter to General Grant requesting a conference with Lincoln "in pursuance of the course indicated by him in his letter to Mr. F. P. Blair of January 18th. 1865."[13] In other words, the Confederate commissioners discarded Davis's language in regard to the "two countries." Grant cabled Lincoln about the commissioners' letter and permitted the delegation to enter his lines at City Point. As the commissioners crossed the lines, loud cheers broke out from troops on both sides.

Lincoln took the preliminary precaution of sending Secretary of State William H. Seward to confer with the Confederates at Hampton Roads before committing himself to providing the rebels safe conduct for a visit to Washington. Lincoln gave Seward explicit written instructions. He told the secretary of state to make clear to the rebels that "three things are indispensable": "the national authority" must be acknowledged "throughout all the states"; there was to be no "receding, by the Executive of the United States on the Slavery question"; and there would be "no cessation of hostilities short of an end of the war, and the disbanding of all forces hostile to the government." Lincoln then instructed Seward that "all propositions of theirs not inconsistent with the above, will be considered and passed upon in a spirit of sincere liberality." Seward was to "hear all they may choose to say, and report it to" Lincoln. But the president admonished Seward that he should "not assume to definitely consummate anything."[14] The next day, Lincoln wrote to General Grant, "Nothing which is transpiring" should "change, hinder, or delay your Military movements."[15]

Meanwhile, Major Eckert, Lincoln's first emissary, arrived on February 1. After talking with the rebel commissioners, Eckert was not convinced that the "two countries" proposition had been discarded altogether, so he sent a cable informing Lincoln that he had not received the assurances that the president had demanded. Moreover, on February 1, Lincoln conferred with James Singleton, who had just returned from Richmond. Singleton's reports about his conversations were also conveyed to William Cornell Jewett, who forwarded them to the *New York Tribune*, where they were published.[16]

Singleton reported that the Confederates would "not consent to Reconstruction upon any other basis than the clearest recognition of the rights of the States respectively to determine each for itself all questions of local and domestic government, Slavery included." On the other hand, Singleton alleged, the rebel leaders might promise the abandonment of slavery if Confederate independence were granted; they "will not permit Slavery to stand in the way of Independence—to that, it would be promptly surrendered, but to nothing else—unless it should be a fair compensation coupled with other liberal terms of Reconstruction secured by Constitutional Amendments."[17]

Lincoln briefly considered recalling Seward and allowing the pressure of events—military events—to soften rebel attitudes further. But on February 1, Grant, who disagreed with Eckert's conclusions, cabled Secretary of War Edwin M. Stanton, advising him to urge the president to meet with the rebel commissioners. "I am convinced, upon conversation with Messrs. Stevens [*sic*] and Hunter," wrote Grant, "that their intentions are good and their desire sincere to restore peace and union." Grant told Stanton that to send the commissioners back "without any expression from any one in authority will have a bad influence."[18]

And so it was that Lincoln made the decision to join Seward at Fortress Monroe, at the tip of the peninsula between Virginia's York and James Rivers, and meet the Confederates himself. The president left Washington and traveled by train to Annapolis, Maryland, where he boarded the steamer *Thomas Colyer* for the trip to Fortress Monroe. The conference with the rebel commissioners took place on February 3 aboard the steamer *River Queen*, which lay at anchor in Hampton Roads (one of the various arcane denotations of the word *road*, a nautical usage referring to a point where rivers empty into a larger body of water, in this case the Chesapeake Bay). Seward joined Lincoln for the meeting with the three Confederate commissioners.

Upon Lincoln's departure, Republican discontent increased. Welles wrote that "without exception," cabinet members were unhappy in regard to the fact that the "Chief Magistrate should have gone on such a mission."[19] The *New York Tribune* reported that "radical war men made no concealment of their anger and their apprehensions."[20]

The participants agreed that no notes would be taken during the meeting. Much of our knowledge of what happened is dependent on the accounts of two of the three Confederate commissioners: Alexander Stephens and John Campbell. Stephens gave an account in 1865 to the editor of the *Augusta (Georgia) Chronicle and Sentinel*. Years later, he reminisced about the meeting to Evan P. Howell, who shared the recollections with Henry Watterson, editor of the *Louisville Courier-Journal*. Stephens also included a lengthy account in his book *A Constitutional View of the Late War between the States*. John Campbell wrote a "Memorandum of the Conversation at the Conference in Hampton Roads."[21]

Lincoln affected a friendly demeanor as the conference began, especially with Stephens, who had served with him in Congress almost twenty years earlier. Stephens came aboard the steamer wearing a heavy topcoat, and Lincoln joked affably, "Now, gentlemen, you see what a large amount of 'shuck' Mr. Stephens has—just wait a minute and you will be surprised to find what a small 'nubbin' he is."[22]

Stephens opened the discussion by asking, "Is there no way of putting an end to the present trouble?" Lincoln replied right away: "The restoration of the Union is a *sine qua non* with me, and hence my instructions that no conference was to be held except upon that basis." Stephens attempted to ignore this edict and discuss Blair's proposal for an armistice followed by a U.S.-Confederate invasion of Mexico. Lincoln responded, "I suppose you refer to something that Mr. Blair has said," adding that Blair "had no authority to speak for me." He then dismissed the idea of an armistice as well as the proposal for the joint invasion. As to the former, it would constitute a "*quasi* recognition of the States then in arms against the National Government, as a separate power," a proposition he would never consider.[23]

As to the latter, "there could be no war without the consent of Congress, and no treaty without the consent of the Senate of the United States." Since any joint operation would have to be based on formal understandings between two sovereign powers, the same arguments precluding an armistice would rule out the possibility of a joint operation: Lincoln would never negotiate a treaty with the Confederate states because to do so "would be a recognition of those States," which "could not be done under any circumstances." Besides, he observed, there was a danger that a "quarrel would break out in the midst of the joint operations" and that "one party might unite with the common enemy to destroy the other."[24]

Campbell tried to turn the discussion to the possible terms of Reconstruction, but Seward—no doubt to Lincoln's irritation—suggested that Stephens be given more time to develop his proposals. Perhaps Seward was inclined to indulge the idea of a joint invasion, since he had once suggested a comparable notion—to pick a quarrel with a European nation as a way to reunite the North and South—during the secession crisis of early 1861. But Lincoln had no more interest in this idea at the end of the war than he had had at the beginning.

Robert Hunter objected that "the recognition of Mr. Davis's power to make a treaty" was "the first and indispensable step to peace." He cited seventeenth-century English history, referring to "the correspondence of King Charles the First, and his Parliament, as a reliable precedent, of a constitutional ruler, treating with rebels." Lincoln made short work of this gambit with the wry observation that "Charles lost his head."[25]

After this, the conference got down to practicalities. Lincoln told the commissioners that as soon as their troops stopped fighting, he would use his presidential power to expedite the resumption of "practical relations" between the so-called Confederate states and the rest of the Union. Moreover, the rebels could rely on him to use his executive powers with the "utmost liberality." But Lincoln insisted he "never would change or modify the terms" of the Emancipation Proclamation "in the slightest particular." Then Lincoln and Seward discussed the more consequential emancipating power of the newly passed (though yet to be ratified) Thirteenth Amendment to the Constitution. Seward produced a copy of the amendment and suggested that if the Confederate states abandoned the rebellion right away, they might be able to prevent its ratification.

Stephens later asserted that Lincoln made the following suggestion: he told Stephens to go back to his home state of Georgia, "get the Governor of the State to call the Legislature together, and get them to recall all the State troops from the war; elect Senators and Representatives to Congress, and ratify the Constitutional Amendment prospectively, so as to take effect—say in five years." Lincoln said that "such a ratification would be valid in my opinion," according to Stephens.

But after dangling this carrot, Lincoln brandished the stick: he warned the commissioners of the "increasing bitterness of feeling in Congress." "The time might come," he continued, when rebels would no longer be considered "an erring people, invited back to the Union as citizens." The Confederates should face the realities, cut their losses, and take advantage of Lincoln's "liberal" attitude while it lasted.[26]

Lincoln shifted back and forth between conciliation and firmness on the slavery issue. According to one account, when Stephens blurted out that "negroes will not work, unless forced to it, and . . . we shall all starve together," Lincoln retorted that Southern white people should indeed "go to work like honest people or starve."[27] But then he reverted to a more philosophical and visionary approach to the slavery issue. Ever since his "Peoria speech" of October 16, 1854, Lincoln had proclaimed that the white people of the North, as well as the South, had been blameworthy for slavery. Just a month after the Hampton Roads conference, the president would make this point with biblical resonance in the course of his Second Inaugural Address. Feeling as he did, he had for years been in favor of assisting Southern whites in the work of emancipation through financial help. So Lincoln urged the commissioners to take action on emancipation well before the ratification of the Thirteenth Amendment would make the issue moot. According to Stephens's account:

> He went on to say that he would be willing to be taxed to remunerate the Southern people for their slaves. He believed the people of the North were as responsible for slavery as the people of the South, and if the war should then cease, with the voluntary abolition of slavery by the States, he should be in favor, individually, of the Government paying a fair indemnity for the loss to their owners. He said he believed this feeling had an extensive existence at the North. He knew some who were in favor of an appropriation as high as Four Hundred Millions of Dollars for this purpose.[28]

Chafing under the weakness of the Confederate bargaining position, Stephens complained that the South was being forced to surrender unconditionally. Seward begged to differ, reminding the commissioners of the relative leniency of the terms that were being offered. Seward argued that "yielding to the execution of the laws under the constitution of the United States, with all its guarantees and securities for personal and political rights," could not "be properly considered as unconditional submission to conquerors, or as having anything humiliating in it."[29]

The meeting broke up without substantive results except for an agreement to reopen the issue of prisoner exchanges.

On the Confederate side, the Hampton Roads conference did nothing to shorten the war. Jefferson Davis responded to Lincoln's proposals with surly contempt. He swore to "teach the insolent enemy who has treated our proposition with contumely in that conference in which he so plumed himself with arrogance."[30] One of the Confederate commissioners, John Campbell, regretted that Davis had reacted as he did.[31]

Lincoln was guardedly pleased when he returned to the White House. "I have not brought back peace in a lump from the conference," he told Singleton, "but I am glad I went down."[32] Lincoln was particularly keen on his own proposal to pay $400 million to the slave states. On February 5, he drafted a congressional resolution that expanded the scope of the payment to cover both surrender and ratification of the Thirteenth Amendment. This was a supreme demonstration of Lincoln's audacity: he would actually pay the Confederates to surrender. Even more extraordinary was that he would pay the states to ratify a constitutional amendment. There is nothing in the Constitution forbidding such a course of action, but who among the Founders would have thought it conceivable, let alone proper, to entertain such a thought? Here in part is the text of what Lincoln presented to the cabinet on February 6:

> The President of the United States is hereby empowered, at his discretion, to pay four hundred millions of dollars to the States of Alabama, Arkansas, Delaware, Florida, Georgia, Kentucky, Louisiana, Maryland, Mississippi, Missouri, North Carolina, South Carolina, Tennessee, Texas, Virginia, and West-Virginia . . . on the conditions following, to wit: . . . [that] all resistance to the national authority shall be abandoned and cease, on or before the first day of April next; and upon such abandonment and ceasing of resistance, one half of said sum to be paid . . . and the remaining half to be paid only upon the amendment of the national constitution recently proposed by congress, becoming valid law, on or before the first day of July next, by the action thereon of the requisite number of states.[33]

Lincoln told his cabinet that the plan was defensible for its economic merits alone. "How long has this war lasted, and how long do you suppose it will last?" he asked his department chiefs and advisers. "We cannot hope that it will end in less than a hundred days. We are now spending three millions a day, and that will equal the full amount I propose to pay, to saying nothing of the lives lost and property destroyed. I look upon it as a measure of strict and simple economy."[34] No doubt he also viewed the proposal as a way to help the slave states recover from the devastation of the war. Gideon Welles recalled that Lincoln "frequently expressed his opinion that the condition of affairs in the rebel states was deplorable, and did not conceal his apprehension that, unless immediately attended to, they would, in consequence of their disturbed civil, social, and industrial relations, be worse after the rebellion was suppressed."[35] But the cabinet rejected the proposal.

As fragmentary news of the Hampton Roads conference reached Washington, the Radical Republicans who had taken a dim view of the conference believed that the results had validated their viewpoint. Zachariah Chandler wrote, "The peace fizzle has ended as I supposed it would in national disgrace." He proclaimed that it had been "ridiculous for the President to go 200 miles to meet the representatives of these accursed Rebels and then come back with a flea in his ear."[36]

Amid rumors that Lincoln had humiliated himself at the conference, congressional leaders requested a report from the president, and Lincoln submitted one to the House of Representatives. He included copies of the pertinent correspondence, such as his instructions to Seward. Lincoln stated:

On our part, the whole substance of the instructions to the Secretary of State . . . was stated and insisted upon, and nothing was said inconsistently therewith; while, by the other party it was not said that, in any event, or on any condition, they *ever* would consent to re-union, and yet they equally omitted to declare that they *never* would so consent. They seemed to desire a postponement of that question, and the adoption of some other course first, which, as some of them seemed to argue, might, or might not, lead to re-union, but which course, we thought, would amount to an indefinite postponement. The conference ended without result.[37]

Journalist Noah Brooks wrote of the reaction when Lincoln's report was read aloud to the House. At first the clerk read amid "absolute silence," but soon, Brooks reported, "the appearance of grave intentness passed away, and members smilingly exchanged glances as they began to appreciate Lincoln's sagacious plan for unmasking the craftiness . . . of the rebel leaders." At least, this was the intention that many Republicans chose to impute to Lincoln's actions. When the reading was finished, "an instant and irrepressible storm of applause" began.[38]

The report seemed to mollify Lincoln's Republican critics. Congressman Thaddeus Stevens, for instance, wrote that "the President thought it was best to make the effort, and he had done it in such a masterly style, upon such a firm basis and principle," that people "who thought his mission there was unwise will accord to him sagacity and patriotism, and applaud his action."[39] The *New York Times*, which had opposed the Blair mission, rejoiced that no harm had come from the conference, "due to the practical good sense of President Lincoln."[40] The *New York Herald* proclaimed Lincoln "one of the shrewdest diplomats of the day" and a "giant among pygmies." The *Herald* also claimed that Lincoln's actions proved beyond doubt that they could "have no peace with the so-called Confederate States short of the expulsion of Jeff. Davis from Richmond and the defeat and dispersion of Lee's army." Even so, Lincoln's conciliatory gestures would "widen the distractions, dissensions, demoralizations and confusion exiting throughout the rebellious States."[41]

Though the Hampton Roads conference led to no major short-term results, it illustrates the deftness and virtuosity with which Lincoln handled most issues right down to the final weeks of his life. The broad expressions of praise for his conduct in the course of the negotiations, with even the virulent Democratic Copperhead Fernando Wood of New York having some good things to say, were one among innumerable examples of what the nation was to lose just a few months later, when Lincoln was murdered in the second month of what would have been his second four-year presidential term.

Notes

1. For general coverage of the event, see William C. Harris, "The Hampton Roads Conference: A Final Test of Lincoln's Presidential Leadership," *Journal of the Abraham Lincoln Association* 21 (2000): 30–61; Ludwell H. Johnson, "Lincoln's Solution to the Problem of Peace Terms, 1864–1865," *Journal of Southern History* 34 (1968): 576–86; Charles W. Sanders, Jr., "Jefferson Davis and the Hampton Roads Peace Conference: 'To Secure Peace to the Two Countries,'" *Journal of Southern History* 63 (1997): 803–26. The meeting acquired new and widespread fame after being dramatized in the 2012 Steven Spielberg film *Lincoln*.

2. Abraham Lincoln, "Annual Message to Congress," December 6, 1864, in *The Collected Works of Abraham Lincoln*, ed. Roy P. Basler, 8 vols. (New Brunswick, NJ: Rutgers University Press, 1953–55), 8:151.

3. Carl Sandburg's notes on an interview with Joseph Fifer, [1923], Sandburg-Barrett Collection, Newberry Library, Chicago, cited in Michael Burlingame, *Abraham Lincoln: A Life*, 2 vols. (Baltimore: Johns Hopkins University Press, 2008), 2:990, n. 118.

4. Jefferson Davis to Francis Preston Blair, Sr., January 12, 1865, *Collected Works*, 8:275.

5. Abraham Lincoln to Francis Preston Blair, Sr., January 18, 1865, ibid., 8:220–21.

6. Jefferson Davis, *The Rise and Fall of the Confederate Government*, 2 vols. (New York: Thomas Yoseloff, 1958), 2:617.

7. Zachariah Chandler to his wife, January 25, 1865, Chandler Papers, cited in Burlingame, *Lincoln*, 2:990, n. 120.

8. Gideon Welles, *Diary of Gideon Welles: Secretary of the Navy under Lincoln and Johnson*, with an introduction by John T. Morse, Jr., 3 vols. (Boston: Houghton Mifflin Co., 1911), 2:231, 235.

9. James Ashley to Lincoln, January 31, 1865, *Collected Works*, 8:248.

10. Lincoln to Ashley, January 31, 1865, ibid.

11. Ashley to William Herndon, November 23, 1866, group 4, reel 8, Herndon-Weik Collection, Manuscript Division, Library of Congress.

12. Burlingame, *Lincoln*, 2:753.

13. Alexander Stephens, John A. Campbell, and Robert M. T. Hunter to Ulysses S. Grant, January 30, 1865, in U.S. War Department, *The War of the Rebellion: A Compilation of the Official Records of the Union and Confederate Armies*, 128 vols. (Washington, DC: Government Printing Office, 1880–1901), ser. 1, vol. 46, pt. 2, 297.

14. Lincoln to William Seward, January 31, 1865, *Collected Works*, 8:250–51.

15. Lincoln to Ulysses S. Grant, February 1, 1865, ibid., 8:252.

16. Burlingame, *Lincoln*, 2:755.

17. *New York Tribune*, February 2, 4, 6, 1865, cited in Burlingame, *Lincoln*, 2:991n135.

18. Grant to Stanton, February 1, 1865, *Collected Works*, 8:282.

19. Morse, *Diary of Gideon Welles*, 2:235.

20. *New York Tribune*, February 3, 1865.

21. Burlingame, *Lincoln*, 2:991n137–40; Alexander H. Stephens, *A Constitutional View of the Late War between the States: Its Causes, Character, Conduct and Results, Presented in a Series of Colloquies at Liberty Hall*, 2 vols. (Philadelphia: National Publishing Company, 1868–70); John A. Campbell, "Memorandum of the Conversation at the Conference in Hampton Roads," in *Reminiscences and Documents Relating to the Civil War during the Year 1865* (Baltimore: John Murphy and Co., 1887), 11–17.

22. Reminiscence of Alexander Stephens to Evan P. Howell in 1882, cited in Burlingame, *Lincoln*, 2:991n137.

23. Stephens, *Constitutional View*, 2:599–601, 608.

24. Campbell, *Reminiscences and Documents*, 12–13.

25. Quotes in this and the next two paragraphs from Stephens, *Constitutional View*, 2:611–14.

26. *Augusta (GA) Chronicle and Sentinel*, June 7, 1865.

27. *Springfield (MA) Republican*, February 25, 1865, cited in Burlingame, *Lincoln*, 2:991n146. See also Stephens, *Constitutional View*, 2:615.

28. Stephens, *Constitutional View*, 2:617.

29. Ibid., 616–17.

30. William J. Cooper, *Jefferson Davis: American* (New York: Alfred A. Knopf, 2000), 513.

31. John A. Campbell to Benjamin R. Curtis, July 20, 1865, cited in *Century Magazine* 38 (October 1889): 952.

32. James Singleton, interviewed in the *Chicago Times*, December 26, 1885, cited in Burlingame, *Lincoln*, 2:991n152.

33. Lincoln, "To the Senate and House of Representatives," February 5, 1865, *Collected Works*, 8:260.

34. John Palmer Usher interviewed by John G. Nicolay, October 11, 1877, cited in Burlingame, *Lincoln*, 2:991n155.

35. Gideon Welles, "Lincoln and Johnson: Their Plan of Reconstruction and the Resumption of National Authority," *Galaxy* 13 (April 1872): 522.

36. Zechariah Chandler to his wife, February 10, 1865, cited in Burlingame, *Lincoln*, 2:991n153.

37. Lincoln, "Message to the House of Representatives," February 10, 1865, *Collected Works*, 8:274–85.

38. Noah Brooks, *Washington in Lincoln's Time* (New York: Rinehart, 1958), 206–7.

39. *Congressional Globe*, 38th Cong., 2nd sess., February 10, 1865, 733.

40. *New York Times*, February 7, 1865.

41. *New York Herald*, February 8, 1865.

4

Abraham Lincoln's Sermon on the Mount:
The Second Inaugural

Ronald C. White, Jr.

*T*he movie *Lincoln* brought Abraham Lincoln once again front and center to audiences—not simply in the United States but around the world. Some moviegoers quibbled about the ending, believing the film should have concluded when Lincoln left the White House for the last time to attend a play at Ford's Theatre. Instead, it ended by circling back a month earlier to March 4, 1865, when Lincoln delivered his Second Inaugural Address.

But Lincoln's film counterpart delivered only part of the address. As Daniel Day-Lewis intoned, "Yet, if God wills that it continue . . . ," we were carried forward to the majestic final paragraph, which begins "With malice toward none, with charity for all." These last 143 words are marvelous, but they do not convey the full meaning of the address. With no criticism of the moviemakers, Lincoln's Second Inaugural Address deserves not a zoom but a wide-angle lens if we are to appreciate its full import for understanding the conclusion of the Civil War.

Vindication marched with victory in the early spring of 1865. The Confederacy found itself splintered, if not shattered. After four years as a war president, Lincoln could look ahead to four years as a peace president. Gamblers in the streets were betting that the sixteenth president would be inaugurated for a third term and serve all the way until March 1873. Friends and supporters, believing the president had been unfairly criticized during much of his first term, declared that recent events vindicated his leadership. The

Washington Daily Morning Chronicle's lead story for the morning of March 4 declared, "The reinauguration suggests the proud reflection that every prediction as to himself, made by the friends of the Union at the beginning of his Administration, has been confirmed." This second inauguration, his supporters argued, ought to be a time for Lincoln to crow a bit.[1]

March 4, 1865, dawned with incessant rain. The streets oozed with soft mud, described by locals as "black plaster." The noted Washington photographer Alexander Gardner prepared to record the event for posterity. The correspondent for the *London Times* was particularly struck by the presence of so many African Americans.[2] Lincoln recognized Frederick Douglass, the African American abolitionist leader, reformer, and newspaper editor, in the crowd. Up behind the right buttress, thirty-five feet from the president, stood the actor John Wilkes Booth. Filled with hatred, Booth had been planning to abduct Lincoln, but now that the South's military fortunes had taken a turn for the worse, he resolved that stronger measures would be necessary.

When Lincoln was introduced, the expectant crowd exploded. At fifty-six, he looked older than his years. As the president rose, he held in his left hand his Second Inaugural Address, printed in two columns. Lincoln prepared to speak.[3] He then began his address in a subdued tone. In the highly charged atmosphere of wartime Washington, with sharpshooters posted on buildings and soldiers everywhere, it was as if he wanted to lower anticipations. Lincoln did so in the first paragraph with the words *less*, *little*, and *no*. He began with impersonal language, sounding more like an observer than the main actor. Lincoln directed the focus away from himself by speaking in the passive voice. After the first paragraph, he used no more personal pronouns.

In the second paragraph, we first hear Lincoln's strategy for his address. He was asking the question no one else was asking: how could the South be brought back into the Union when the war finally ended? He understood that if the South was meant to bear the blame and shame alone, it would never be able to reenter the Union.

His first rhetorical move promoted a renewed unity by employing inclusive language. Over and over again in the second paragraph, he used the inclusive adjectives *all* and *both*:

All dreaded it—all sought to avert it.

Both parties deprecated war.

Lincoln imputed the best possible motives to the enemy. He knew the crowd would cheer if he demonized the South. That is what we usually do in times of war. During World War I, we forbade the teaching of German in our public schools. In World War II, we moved the Japanese away from the West Coast into internment camps. Lincoln, by his use of inclusive language, emphasized that the people of the South did not want this war any more than did the people of the North.

But then how are we to understand the rest of Lincoln's penultimate sentence of the second paragraph? He went on to say:

> *but one of them would* make *war rather than let the nation survive; and the other would* accept *war rather than let it perish.*

Was Lincoln not blaming the South for the war?

Yes, but . . . When we listen to politicians, it is important to listen to what they do not say. Just imagine if Lincoln had said, "but those rebels, those traitors." His audience would have erupted in cheers—and jeers. I believe he consciously used the generic phrase "but one of them" to tamp down the emotions of his audience.

One word dominates the second paragraph. In the ninety-nine words of this paragraph, Lincoln used the word *war* seven times and the pronoun *it* twice in reference to war. He knew that war permeated the conversations of everyone in attendance.

In most cases in this paragraph, Lincoln made *war* or its pronoun equivalent the direct object, both grammatically and historically, of the actions of the soldiers, the generals, and himself as commander in chief. In other cases, it was the object of a preposition. Until he arrived at the final sentence:

> *And the war came.*

Four words. Four syllables. War was no longer an object in the last sentence of the paragraph; now it had become the subject. Lincoln understood what we still do not understand. The North began the war convinced that with more manpower and greater industrial might than its opponent, it would win the war within a matter of months. The United States began the war in Iraq believing that with more manpower and greater industrial might, we would win the war in a matter of months. Lincoln, after four long years of war, understood that neither he nor his generals were in charge of the war, but that any war takes on a life of its own. War became the subject.

How did he voice this sentence? We have photographs of him delivering his address, but no audio. I can imagine Edward Everett, the greatest orator of the day, who spoke at Gettysburg, speaking it with great force and volume. But I think Lincoln would have said it softly, mournfully, slowly:

And the war came.

In the third and longest paragraph, Lincoln recapitulated the cause and meaning of the war. A 2011 Pew Research Center survey on current attitudes toward the Civil War revealed that only 38 percent of Americans believe slavery was the cause of the Civil War.[4] Lincoln, however, after describing slavery as *a peculiar and powerful interest*, went on to say:

> *All knew that this interest was, somehow, the cause of the war.*

When Lincoln introduced the Bible and God into the Second Inaugural, he entered new territory in presidential inaugural addresses:

> *Both read the same Bible, and pray to the same God; and each invokes His aid against the other.*

Before Lincoln, in the previous eighteen inaugural addresses, the Bible was quoted only one time—by John Quincy Adams. Each address had referred to God or the Deity, but only in the last paragraph in the sense of "we need God's help too." But Lincoln, in the second shortest inaugural address ever offered, just 701 words, named God fourteen times, quoted the Bible four times, and invoked prayer three times. The point here is not to add up the references but to probe their meanings in Lincoln's speech. The introduction of God and the Bible signals Lincoln's determination to think theologically as well as politically.

From the moment Abraham Lincoln invoked the presence of God so prominently in his Second Inaugural Address, questions have been raised about Lincoln's religion. How could a person who never joined a church employ such language about God?

Some have argued that Lincoln tailored his words to fit the beliefs of his audience. A shrewd politician, Lincoln understood the "marketplace." Religious language, coming on the heels of the Second Great Awakening, present in the revivals among both Union and Confederate soldiers, suffused much of the public speech and private conversations of Americans during the Civil War. Lincoln, so the argument goes, knew he was speaking to a largely Protestant audience and simply co-opted their language.

Others have claimed that Lincoln excluded beliefs or language that would have put off his audience. Thus he did not draw upon enlightenment ideas about God, often expressed in the language of Deism or fatalism. David H. Donald, in his Lincoln biography, argues that the author of the Second Inaugural wanted to use other words. "He might have put his argument in terms of the doctrine of necessity, in which he had long believed, but that was not a dogma accepted by most Americans."[5]

Neither of these suggestions offers a sufficient explanation for Lincoln's religious language. Nor does it take into account the development of Lincoln's faith during the tumultuous years of the Civil War.

After recognizing the use of the Bible and prayer by the soldiers on both sides, Lincoln probed the appropriate use of the Bible. Throughout his life, Lincoln was keenly aware of the misuse as well as the use of religion. Through his wartime experience of hosting delegations of ministers and politicians, most of whom were quite confident that God was on the side of the Union, Lincoln entered into the dilemma of how to read, interpret, and apply the Bible. He observed directly opposite readings of the Bible. On one side stood those who believed the Bible sanctioned slavery. On the other side were those who understood the Bible as encouraging the abolition of slavery.[6]

Lincoln offered here not only affirmation but also interrogation. The last part of the sentence, *and each invokes His aid against the other*, is not framed grammatically as a question, but it is clear that Lincoln was now beginning a section where he would ask questions both about human actions and God's actions. He was suggesting that the Bible and prayer could be used as weapons to curry God's favor for one side or the other. Lincoln inveighed against a tribal God who would take the side of a section or party.

Lincoln had experienced this kind of religion in an interview three months to the day before the Second Inaugural. On December 4, 1864, two Tennessee women called on him to seek the release of husbands being held as Confederate prisoners of war. One woman pleaded that her husband was a religious man.

Lincoln objected. "In my opinion, the religion that sets men to rebel and fight against their government, because, as they think, that government does not sufficiently help *some* men to eat their bread on the sweat of *other* men's faces, is not the sort of religion upon which people can get to heaven!"[7] In his answer, he quoted from memory Genesis 3:19, which he now applied to slavery. For Lincoln, the sanction of slavery from the Bible was the ultimate pretension. Less than three months later, this interview surely was in Lincoln's memory as he delivered his Second Inaugural and worked with the first of four passages from the Bible.

But as if in midsentence, Lincoln caught himself and determined to balance judgment from the Old Testament with mercy from the New Testament, invoking Matthew 7:1:

> *but let us judge not that we be not judged.*

These words came from the Sermon on the Mount, in which Jesus advocated an ethic of humility and compassion. Lincoln, whose religious beliefs have sometimes been portrayed as coming from the Old Testament, here employed Jesus's words from the New Testament. Lincoln contrasted a legal understanding of human relationships with a practice of mercy and forgiveness. It was this section that secured the appellation "Lincoln's Sermon on the Mount" after his delivery of the Second Inaugural Address.

This second biblical quotation is central. How we would like to hear Lincoln's tone as he quoted these words of Jesus. A speaker could employ such words as a fencer would make a return thrust following a parry. Understood as a retaliatory sally, the intent of Lincoln's words is undermined. These words retain their integrity when used, as Lincoln did here, in humility and confession.

The arc of his remark was toward the North. Northern politicians, press, and people had been harsh in their judgment of the South. Lincoln struggled with abolitionists because of their moral pretentiousness. His dispute with the Radical Republicans of his own party was because of their determination to punish the South. His contention with some of the churches was with their self-righteousness.

Lincoln, throughout his address, balanced pretension with possibility. The pretension of the misuse of religion would now become a transition to the possibility of God's activity in the Civil War. At the architectural and rhetorical center of his Second Inaugural Address, Lincoln offered his major theological affirmation:

The Almighty has His own purposes.

After discussing different actors, Lincoln concentrated on God as the primary actor. In quick brush strokes he painted God's actions:

He now wills to remove

He gives to both North and South, this terrible war

Yet, if God wills that it continue

Historians have continued to use Lincoln's engagement with fatalism as a young man as the main rubric to understand his thought as a mature president. Fatalism, a kissing cousin of Deism, is an attitude that all events are predetermined and therefore inevitable. But to say Lincoln remained a fatalist fails to do justice to the growth in his thinking, especially speeded up during the Civil War. If Lincoln was drawn to fatalism—what he often called a doctrine of necessity—in the 1840s, the ideas in his Second Inaugural give evidence to a quite different perspective on the nature of God's involvement in history.

The modern suggestion that fatalism and providence are part of a continuum would have surprised Protestant theologians and ministers in the middle of the nineteenth century. In 1859, Francis Wharton, a professor at Kenyon College, described fatalism as "a distinct scheme of unbelief." The author of *A Treatise on Theism and the Modern Skeptical Theories*, Wharton singled out fatalism as an opponent of Christianity because it did not acknowledge a God who acted in history. Wharton, who later became a professor at the new Episcopal Theological Seminary in Cambridge, Massachusetts, contrasted fatalism with the Christian faith where God is known to his followers by "his watchful care and love."[8]

Though affirming the inscrutable intentions of God, Lincoln did not retreat to agnosticism about the specific content of those purposes. Rather, he focused those purposes by invoking a fiery biblical quotation from Matthew 18:7:

> *"Woe unto the world because of offences! For it must needs be that offences come; but woe to that man by whom the offence cometh!"*

The purposes of God can also bring judgment. Lincoln had long believed that slavery was evil because one person held another in bondage. Whereas he had been willing to contain slavery politically and geographically, he had come to the conclusion in the midst of the Civil War that its moral implications could not be contained. He continued:

> *If we shall suppose that American Slavery is one of those offences*

What was there and then in the Bible had become here and now in American history. In quoting this second passage from the Gospel of Matthew, Lincoln employed the sanction of scripture to initiate his indictment of slavery and his formal charge against the American people.

Lincoln did not say *Southern* slavery. By saying *American* slavery, he again used inclusive language to declare that North and South must together own the offense. He was not simply trying to set the historical record straight. He was thinking of the future. Lincoln understood, as many in his own party did not, that the Southern people would never be able to take their full places in the Union if they felt that they alone were burdened with the guilt for what Lincoln believed to be the national offense of slavery.

Lincoln offered a biblical and theological sanctification for declaring that slavery must *now* come to an end. Starting in 1854, he had begun to use Thomas Jefferson's words in the Declaration of Independence, "all men are created equal," as a call for advocating some kind of political rights for African Americans. Now, in 1865, Lincoln appealed to Jesus's words in the Bible as part of his warrant for his conviction that the time for slavery had *now* come and gone.

Who was this God who *gives to both North and South, this terrible war*? Lincoln answered that question by observing that God's activity was no

> *departure from those divine attributes which the believers in a Living God always ascribe to him*

It is easy to skip over the word *attributes*. The theological affirmation that Lincoln made was that *divine attributes* presume and define *a Living God*. In the Christian idea of providence, God is a personal, living God who is the source of all life. Fatalism, on the other hand, was oriented around the concept of an impersonal God as a first cause.

Lincoln had heard Phineas Densmore Gurley, minister of the New York Avenue Presbyterian Church in Washington, a congregation Lincoln attended with more and more frequency as president, speak of *divine attributes*. Gurley, as a student of Professor Charles Hodge at Princeton Theological Seminary, would have learned from his professor the language of attributes. In Hodge's lectures, published in his three-volume *Systematic Theology*, he titled chapter 5 "The Nature and Attributes of God." He spent eighty pages making the case that these attributes are "essential to the nature of a divine Being."[9]

Hodge and Gurley were really building on the language of attributes from the Westminster Confession of Faith, written in England in 1646. English-speaking Presbyterians brought the Westminster Confession of Faith with them across the Atlantic at the beginning of the seventeenth century. Chapter 2 of the Westminster Confession, familiar to Lincoln as a participant in Presbyterian congregations in both Springfield and Washington, began with a discussion of the attributes of God. God was defined at the outset as the "only living and true God," whose attributes included that he was "gracious, merciful, long-suffering, abundant in goodness and love."[10] Lincoln turned to Presbyterian language when he affirmed that *believers* would *always ascribe* certain *attributes* to God.

As the address built towards its final paragraph, Lincoln made an unexpected move. Speaking on the eve of military victory, when many expected him to celebrate the successes of the Union, he called on his audience to recognize a perilous evil in their midst. Instead of self-congratulation, he asked his fellow citizens for self-analysis.

Inaugural addresses, if we are honest, have always been exercises of self-congratulation. Second inaugural addresses, especially, offer self-congratulation that the electorate has reelected the candidate. Inaugural addresses are also self-congratulation to the nation. Presidents seem to bend over backward telling the audience how great the nation, and by implication the audience, is.

Not so with Lincoln. He broke this pattern of self-congratulation when he carried to his speech the scales of justice. He did so knowing that Americans have always been uncomfortable facing up to their own malevolence. We might think that the Civil War forced such an encounter, but evil in any war always seems to be consigned to the other side. Many in the North felt quite righteous in criticizing the South for both rebellion and slavery. Many in the South believed they were acting in the spirit of 1776 in severing ties with a tyrannical and hypocritical federal government.

In his Second Inaugural, Lincoln sounded like a New England Puritan preaching a jeremiad that combined both criticism and reaffirmation to a nation that had lost its moral way. Because of the evil of the offense of slavery, the nation was deserving of God's indignation. The task of the preacher was to point out to the congregation the reason for God's anger: slavery. As in a jeremiad, Lincoln prosecuted his case not in generalities but with concrete, visual representations. In a complex sentence of seventy-eight words, he worked with imagery that brought the long, dark night of slavery under an intense light that allowed his audience to see both the breadth and depth of this American offense.

As Lincoln examined the consequences of evil, he placed his judgments within two large historical contexts. First, Lincoln reached back before the nation's birth in 1776 as he reminded his audience that the stain of slavery was enmeshed in the fabric of American history from its beginnings, with

two hundred and fifty years of unrequited toil

Lincoln's imagery reached its zenith when he implied that the sword of military battle was the judgment of God:

until every drop of blood drawn with the lash, shall be paid by another drawn with the sword

Second, speaking to an audience of people who knew their Bible, Lincoln reached much farther back in history when he quoted a fourth biblical passage, this one from Psalm 19:9:

As was said three thousand years ago, so still it must be said, "the judgments of the Lord are true and righteous altogether."

Certainly Lincoln believed that God had blessed America. Where Lincoln distinguished himself from most of his contemporaries was in his willingness to confront the ambiguities in America. Brooding over the honor and dishonor in his nation's actions, he was not willing to reduce political rhetoric to national self-congratulation.

Lincoln now moved quickly from the past to the future, from judgment to hope. In an address filled with surprises, he turned rapidly to his unexpected conclusion:

With malice toward none, with charity for all

Lincoln concluded by asking his audience to enter a new era, armed not with antagonism but with forgiveness. He summoned American citizens to overcome the boundary of sectionalism and come together in a new Union of reconciliation.

In the final paragraph, Lincoln offered an ethical imperative. This imperative was a response to the political and theological indicative of the first three paragraphs. The symmetry of the Second Inaugural rises from the close connections between indicative and imperative.

In the Presbyterian sermons Lincoln heard, the preacher would spend the major part of the sermon reciting a grand indicative. The indicative was what God had done. For Puritans, the indicative helped them understand themselves as God's new Israel. For African Americans, the indicative was the story of the redemption of Israel, which offered them consolation in suffering and a model for liberation. The indicative pattern of Christ's life, teaching, and death became the pattern for selfless love and reconciliation, a frequent motif in the sermons Lincoln heard from Gurley.[11]

Lincoln's majestic but mysterious indicative was that God had been present in the midst of the Civil War. His underscoring of Providence became the prism through which he refracted the meaning of the war.

Convinced of God's activity, Lincoln would not speak about God in the language of triumphalism or jingoism. He was distrustful of visiting delegations of ministers who knew exactly when, where, and how God was on Union's side. He could not have been comfortable with those voices in the rising evangelicalism of his day that seemed all too familiar with the Almighty. Lincoln, who did not wear his faith on his sleeve, never spoke glibly about God.

If the imperative in a sermon is a response to the indicative, we need to insert an unvoiced *Therefore* at the beginning of the fourth and final paragraph. *Therefore* is the connective tissue between what God has done and what men and women are to do.

If Lincoln's final imperative is ethical in content, it is pastoral in tone. Lincoln concluded his Second Inaugural Address with a coda of healing:

to bind up

to care for

to do all which may achieve and cherish a just and a lasting peace, among ourselves, and with all nations.

He was quite precise about who should be the objects of this new ethical duty:

him who shall have borne the battle, and for his widow, and his orphan

Portraits of widows and orphans now balanced the images of blood and swords.

The Second Inaugural received many comments in both the American and English press. Frederick Douglass confided to his diary that evening, "The address sounded more like a sermon than a state paper."[12]

The most important commentator was the president himself. When Thurlow Weed, the New York Republican boss, wrote to thank him for the address on the day of the inauguration, Lincoln replied, "I expect the latter to wear as well as—perhaps better than—any thing I have produced."[13]

Because we often view Lincoln's life through the lens of his assassination, we are tempted to see the Second Inaugural Address as an ending. Lincoln, and those who heard him that day, understood his Second Inaugural not as an ending but as a new beginning. Four years before, the nation had begun a dark night of the soul. Now, in the spring of 1865, it was nearly daylight. At this new dawning, Lincoln was the reelected leader who would lead the nation into a new era. The president was thinking and speaking about the future.

Lincoln defined the signpost toward winning the peace as the task of achieving reconciliation. He spoke for an inclusive God who was comprehensive in both judgment and reconciliation. In his final paragraph, he declared that the true test of the aims of war would be how they now treated those who had been defeated. If enmity continued after hostilities ceased, the war would have been in vain. These are no maudlin words crafted for emotional effect. Lincoln's words were directed to the tough, practical living actions that must replace retribution with *charity*.

In the spring of 1865, what did Lincoln hope would become America's pathway from war to peace? In his final paragraph, he offered the ultimate surprise. Instead of rallying his supporters, in the name of God, to extol a blameless North and denigrate a soon-to-be-defeated South, he asked his listeners to imitate the ways of God.

ABRAHAM LINCOLN
SECOND INAUGURAL ADDRESS
MARCH 4, 1865

At this second appearing to take the oath of the presidential office, there is less occasion for an extended address
than there was at the first. Then a statement, somewhat
in detail, of a course to be pursued, seemed fitting and
proper. Now, at the expiration of four years, during which
public declarations have been constantly called forth on
every point and phase of the great contest which still
absorbs the attention, and engrosses the enerergies [*sic*]
of the nation, little that is new could be presented. The
progress of our arms, upon which all else chiefly depends,
is as well known to the public as to myself; and it is,
I trust, reasonably satisfactory and encouraging to all.
With high hope for the future, no prediction in regard
to it is ventured.

On the occasion corresponding to this four years ago,
all thoughts were anxiously directed to an impending
civil-war. All dreaded it—all sought to avert it. While
the inaugural address was being delivered from this
place, devoted altogether to *saving* the Union without
war, insurgent agents were in the city seeking to *destroy* it
without war—seeking to dissol[v]e the Union, and divide
effects, by negotiation. Both parties deprecated war; but
one of them would *make* war rather than let the nation
survive; and the other would *accept* war rather than let it
perish. And the war came.

One eighth of the whole population were colored
slaves, not distributed generally over the Union, but lo-
calized in the Southern part of it. These slaves constituted
a peculiar and powerful interest. All knew that this interest was, somehow, the cause of the war. To strengthen,
perpetuate, and extend this interest was the object for
which the insurgents would rend the Union, even by war;
while the government claimed no right to do more than
to restrict the territorial enlargement of it. Neither party

expected for the war, the magnitude, or the duration, which it has already attained. Neither anticipated that the *cause* of the conflict might cease with, or even before, the conflict itself should cease. Each looked for an easier triumph, and a result less fundamental and astounding. Both read the same Bible, and pray to the same God; and each invokes His aid against the other. It may seem strange that any men should dare to ask a just God's assistance in wringing their bread from the sweat of other men's faces; but let us judge not that we be not judged. The prayers of both could not be answered; that of neither has been answered fully. The Almighty has His own purposes. "Woe unto the world because of offences! for it must needs be that offences come; but woe to that man by whom the offence cometh!" If we shall suppose that American Slavery is one of those offences, which, in the providence of God, must needs come, but which, having continued through His appointed time, He now wills to remove, and that He gives to both North and South, this terrible war, as the woe due to those by whom the offence came, shall we discern therein any departure from those divine attributes which the believers in a Living God always ascribe to Him? Fondly do we hope—fervently do we pray—that this mighty scourge of war may speedily pass away. Yet, if God wills that it continue, until all the wealth piled by the bond-man's two hundred and fifty years of unrequited toil shall be sunk, and until every drop of blood drawn with the lash, shall be paid by another drawn with the sword, as was said three thousand years ago, so still it must be said "the judgments of the Lord, are true and righteous altogether."

With malice toward none; with charity for all; with firmness in the right, as God gives us to see the right, let us strive on to finish the work we are in; to bind up the nation's wounds; to care for him who shall have borne the battle, and for his widow, and his orphan—to do all which may achieve and cherish a just, and a lasting peace, among ourselves, and with all nations.[14]

Notes

1. *Washington Daily Morning Chronicle*, March 4, 1865.

2. March 7 report "From Our Correspondent," *London Times*, March 20, 1865; *New York Herald*, March 6, 1865.

3. Michael Shiner, *Diary, 1813–1865* (Washington, DC: Library of Congress), 182; Noah Brooks, *Washington in Lincoln's Time* (New York: Century, 1896), 213.

4. "Civil War at 150: Still Relevant, Still Divisive," Pew Research Center for the People and the Press, April 2011, http://www.people-press.org/files/legacy-pdf /04-08-11%20Civil%20War%20Release.pdf.

5. David Herbert Donald, *Lincoln* (New York: Simon and Schuster, 1995), 566–67.

6. Mark Noll, "The Bible and Slavery," in *Religion and the American Civil War*, ed. Randall M. Miller, Harry S. Stout, and Charles Reagan Wilson (New York: Oxford University Press, 1998), 48–49.

7. "Story Written for Noah Brooks," [December 6, 1864], in *The Collected Works of Abraham Lincoln*, ed. Roy P. Basler, 8 vols. (New Brunswick, NJ: Rutgers University Press, 1953–55), 8:154–55.

8. Francis Wharton, *A Treatise on Theism and Modern Skeptical Theories* (Philadelphia: J. B. Lippincott, 1859), 147, 152.

9. Charles Hodge, *Systematic Theology*, vol. 1 (New York: Charles Scribner and Company, 1871), 368. Gurley would have heard Hodge's thinking on *divine attributes* in lectures. Hodge made the decision not to publish his lectures in book form until the end of his career.

10. "The Westminster Confession of Faith," in *The Constitution of the Presbyterian Church (U.S.A.)*, part 1, *Book of Confessions* (Louisville, KY: Office of the General Assembly, 1996), 128.

11. In a collection of Phineas Gurley sermons at the Presbyterian Historical Society, one hears a consistent indicative-imperative refrain. Gurley first speaks about the indicative of the love of Christ, manifest in Christ's death on the cross. He then calls for a selfless love as the response to Christ's love. Because these eighteen sermons are undated, I could not connect them definitively with Lincoln in the 1860s, but this was a consistent theme in Gurley's sermons.

12. Frederick Douglass, *Autobiographies* (New York: Library of America, 1994), 802.

13. Abraham Lincoln to Thurlow Weed, March 15, 1865, *Collected Works*, 8:356.

14. Lincoln, "Second Inaugural Address," *Collected Works*, 8:332–33.

5

Lincoln's Greatest Escapade:
Walking through Richmond on April 4, 1865

Richard Wightman Fox

I

The remembering of Abraham Lincoln has its own history. As time passes, some features of his career gain greater traction in Americans' minds, while others fade from memory. Nothing is fixed once and for all. Aspects of his character or career that grow dimmer for a stretch of decades may later revive and vice versa. Even a small event in Lincoln's life can rise or fall in recognition. A fascinating book could be written titled *Lincoln in American Forgetting*, to offer the other side of the story well told in Merrill Peterson's *Lincoln in American Memory* (1994).

One chapter of *Lincoln in American Forgetting* might dwell on his sneaking through Baltimore under cover of night in February 1861 to foil an assassination plot. His advisers believed the danger was real—it had been confirmed by two independent sources—and he willingly embraced their ruse, hiding out, lightly disguised in a soft cap and long overcoat, on the night train to Washington. When the newspapers, Republican and Democratic alike, discovered the subterfuge, Lincoln was lambasted for cowering in the face of a threat, and for doing so at a symbolically delicate juncture: the moment when citizens received the president-elect into the national capital and confirmed their choice of him. In a republic, the new chief magistrate was supposed to show that sort of deference to the people. Lincoln had chosen the course of a timid potentate, concerned for his own safety, not the path of a stalwart, republican representative.

His supposed flight from danger was well remembered in both North and South for the next four years. In April 1865, after his assassination, newspapers and orators referred often to the Baltimore episode and did not bother to spell it out; they took for granted that everyone knew the story. With Lincoln gone, the press retroactively absolved him of cowardice as president-elect, for now it seemed obvious that true peril must have been lurking in Baltimore too. The tale of Lincoln's weak-kneed debut in Washington was erased as new stories emerged to recall his steely personal and political courage.[1]

One such narrative grew to major significance in 1865 for the very reason that it so perfectly refuted the impression left by the Baltimore debacle. The apprehensive Lincoln of 1861 was replaced by the audacious Lincoln of April 4, 1865, who had marched through the crowded streets of Richmond, Virginia, leading a mass procession. That was the day after the city fell to Union troops, and ten days before Lincoln fell to John Wilkes Booth's derringer ball. In 1861, the national press had judged him harshly for failing to enter his own capital with confidence; in 1865, countless Northern speeches and newspaper editorials let him make up for it by shepherding a throng of citizens through the former rebel capital. In 1861, he had followed his advisers' orders; in 1865, he made his own orders, casting caution aside and revealing his inner core.

For many Northerners of Lincoln's time, the Richmond walk qualified as his greatest single escapade, the culmination of his career, a day to remember because it took the true measure of his life and political vision. He had made mixing with the people the centerpiece of his political practice since the 1830s. In mid-nineteenth-century America, nearly all Democrats and Republicans (most of whom, like Lincoln, were Whigs until the mid to late 1850s) considered themselves "republicans," with a lowercase *r*, antimonarchists who believed in government by the people's freely elected representatives. Understanding Lincoln's presidential career from 1861 to 1865 depends on keeping in mind that more than many of his political peers, he took republicanism seriously as a daily commitment—one that entailed constant contact between the people and their leaders. He enjoyed this contact immensely; his political ideology meshed nicely with his inborn sociability. By temperament and experience, he was well suited to the impersonal, yet personable, life of citizenship: individuals interacting locally and nationally as members of the body politic, not just as friends, coworkers, club or church members, or familial intimates.[2]

Until the Lincoln centennial celebration of 1909, the year when those who turned sixty-five years old had been twenty-one at the time of the assassination, the march through Richmond seems to have remained common knowledge in the North. As they referred to it, newspapers still assumed that readers knew the story.

In 2015, the sesquicentennial of his death, Lincoln's walk through the rebel capital appears to be almost completely forgotten. Five generations after his passing, most Americans measure Lincoln's greatness by his incomparable words and his sterling traits of character and leadership. His own coalition of Northerners and African Americans loved his words, character, and leadership too, but they took special pride in his deeds. In 1865, and for decades thereafter, Richmond was the site of one of his most memorable actions. For there he put his body on the line, and he did so wordlessly.

On April 4, 1865, in a spontaneous physical act, he showed many of his contemporaries—as they never tired of saying after his assassination—the essence of who he was. Sometime after 3 P.M., holding his twelve-year-old son, Tad's, right hand with his left, Lincoln strode slowly through the streets of Richmond at the head of a column of citizens that apparently grew into the thousands. (*Head* is the perfect word for it: Lincoln led from the front, and his head bobbed above everyone else's in the river of humanity.)

Twelve sailors had just rowed Tad, his father, and four military men —Admiral David Porter, Captain A. H. Adams of the navy, Captain Charles Penrose of the army, and Lieutenant W. W. Clemens of the Signal Corps—ashore at the downtown dock near the spot where today's Seventeenth Street meets Dock Street. To a twenty-first-century reader, it may seem inconceivable that no army vehicle was on hand to conduct Lincoln to his destination: the Confederate White House evacuated by Jefferson Davis on April 2 and occupied on April 3 by twenty-nine-year-old Union general Godfrey Weitzel and his staff. The president of the United States was simply left standing on a wharf wondering what to do next. Should he wait for the "ambulance" that Weitzel was supposed to provide, or should he strike out on his own?

Moreover, no one in Lincoln's entourage had any idea how to find the Confederate White House, another incredible fact. As they were supposed to be met at the river by a carriage of some sort, they had not bothered to consult a map before departing that morning from General Ulysses Grant's downstream headquarters at City Point, Virginia. As John Nicolay and John Hay, Lincoln's secretaries-turned-biographers, noted in 1889, "One cannot help wondering at the manifest imprudence of both Mr. Lincoln and Admiral Porter in the whole proceeding."[3]

The president apparently was not bothered by the momentary confusion at the dock. Before he could think twice, a large group of black laborers digging nearby, under the eye of the Union officer who had put them to work, threw down their shovels and greeted their hero. One of the African Americans volunteered to guide the president and his party to General Weitzel's location, and Lincoln saw no reason to decline. He launched out on foot, with the crowd behind him expanding rapidly as word spread that the president—rumored for days to be bound soon for Richmond—was indeed parading through town.

No one who joined Lincoln on the walk—not even a well-known Northern journalist fortuitously standing on the dock when he arrived—ever thought to record the exact route the president took to "Jeff Davis's house." And no one stopped to wonder whether this jaunt carried unacceptable security risks for Lincoln or his son. Everyone seems to have been caught up in the euphoric bedlam of the moment. The vast majority of those following him on what turned out to be a tiring, partially uphill, three-quarter-mile hike were ecstatic black Virginians celebrating the first day of their de facto freedom. They could scarcely believe the arrival in their midst, on this first day of their liberty, of the larger-than-life Lincoln, their hoped-for emancipator ever since 1861.[4]

Their exuberance was uncontainable, according to the reporter on the dock and other journalists who arrived on the scene in time to witness some of the walk. These writers were all astounded by the continuous "whoops," "contortions," and "prayerful ejaculations" of the African American marchers, including men, women, and children. They mostly stayed behind the president, but some ran up to his side or ran ahead to cry out in joy that Lincoln had come. A festival of freedom streamed through the city. For Lincoln, the lifelong opponent of slavery who had bided his time in order to make emancipation happen, being present at the actual moment of slave liberation carried immense satisfaction.[5]

Along with Tad and his other son, Robert, an officer serving on General Grant's staff, the president had witnessed a similar scene in Petersburg, Virginia, the day before, when the slaves in that city were celebrating their first day of freedom. As he and Tad traveled up the James River to Richmond on the morning of April 4, they knew exactly what kind of joyous outpouring they could expect: it would look like Petersburg, but on a far grander scale. Lincoln would be heralded as the slaves' emancipator, and Tad as the flesh-and-blood son of the nation's Father. One wonders if in Petersburg the president had watched and heard the slaves' revelry from such a "safe" distance—he was invited there to visit the security-conscious General Grant—that once in Richmond he eagerly dove into the middle of it.

For many of Lincoln's contemporaries, the walk through Richmond revealed a personal courage bordering on heedlessness. It disclosed an un-heard-of posture of forgiveness toward a defeated enemy. And it summed up a distinctive approach to leadership: the resolve to make himself acces-sible to his fellow citizens. All of these meanings of the march were plainly articulated in the nation's press before the news of his assassination broke over Northern telegraph lines in the wee hours of April 15.

With Lincoln's death, the memory of the Richmond event was desta-bilized, morphing into a religious as well as a political and ethical deed. Its republican core was blown open by a dazzling providential intrusion. Lincoln's courage as the people's champion and representative now counted as only one component of the walk's meaning. Now it was apparent that the president had entered Richmond just as Jesus had entered Jerusalem, in preparation for the sacrificial act carried out by both men on Good Friday.

Unbelievably, John Wilkes Booth had executed Lincoln on the very day of Christ's crucifixion. Millions of Northerners took immense com-fort from God's obvious message: the president had been called to higher service as a unique sentinel of charity and forgiveness. The rough work of Reconstruction—punishing the rebels and reshaping Southern society—had been left to men less saintly and more judgmental than Lincoln. Now the walk through Richmond disclosed a Christian paragon superimposed upon a republican hero.

II

Lincoln's first biographer, Josiah Holland, in his hugely successful *Life of Abraham Lincoln*, emphasized his subject's religious virtues but without minimizing his political ones. He gave an excellent one-page summary of the president's day in Richmond—excellent because unlike many later writers down to the present, he relied on the firsthand testimony of Charles C. Coffin, the journalist who actually walked with Lincoln on April 4, standing directly behind him.[6]

A war correspondent for the entire duration of the conflict, Coffin dis-played a knack for being in the right place at the right time. He "has always managed to be at the point of interest," said Charles Page, a fellow war reporter, "whether it were Vicksburg, Chattanooga, the Wilderness, Savan-nah, Charleston, Wilmington, or Richmond." Once in Richmond, Coffin alone among the journalists in town sniffed out Lincoln's actual point of arrival—not Rockett's Landing, two miles south of the city, where he was supposed to disembark and be met by General Weitzel's wagon, but the downtown dock much closer to his destination. Admiral Porter must have told the sailors rowing Lincoln's party upriver at the end of his voyage—

with the afternoon slipping away after a series of delays on the James River—that the fifty-six-year-old president and his twelve-year-old son did not have the time or energy to trek two miles to town from Rockett's Landing.[7]

The most reliable information about what happened between the time Lincoln set foot on the dock and the time he arrived at General Weitzel's headquarters comes from Coffin's dispatch written that evening, April 4, and published in the *Boston Journal* on April 10. That remains the most dependable report because it was never influenced at any point, from composition to publication, by news of Lincoln's assassination, and because its presentation of the facts was subject to immediate scrutiny—and correction—by the others in the party who took the same walk.

Josiah Holland's twenty-six lines devoted to the Richmond episode captured the two central points of Coffin's dispatch. Lincoln entered Richmond humbly—"in no triumphal car" and with "no brilliant cavalcade"—and without delay a gathering of "happy and humble people surrounded him." They were "the grateful blacks, who pressed upon him with their thankful ejaculations and tearful blessings on every side." The men threw their hats and the women their handkerchiefs into the air, calling out "Glory to God! Glory! Glory!" and "thank you, dear Jesus." Lincoln was engulfed in the celebrations of "the black multitude of liberated slaves."[8]

Coffin's dispatch contained one significant detail that Holland did not pick up. Only two-thirds of the "thousands" of people that marched along with the president, Coffin wrote, were African Americans. By deduction, readers learned that hundreds of marchers were white people. Coffin was so impressed by Lincoln's treating the jubilant black marchers as "citizens"—"the great deliverer, meeting the delivered"—that he did not think to note whether the whites in question were all Union soldiers or a mixture of soldiers and white Virginians. Maybe in the commotion, he did not register who they were. He indicated only that Northern soldiers "swelled the crowd, cheering in wild enthusiasm."

The whites specifically identified as Southern in Coffin's account were not walkers, but watchers: "a few white women looking out from the houses waved their handkerchief." He noticed only one woman who *might* have disapproved of the president: "One lady in a large and elegant building looked awhile, and then turned away her head as if it was a disgusting sight." In Coffin's firsthand report, only that single white person expressed even possible animosity toward Lincoln. What struck Coffin was the concord the president had created in letting himself be ogled and jostled at close range by "citizens, *black and white!*" According to him, "President Lincoln walked in silence" and simply acknowledged "the salutes" of one and all. Lincoln was satisfied to symbolize with his presence in the streets that a new birth of freedom had arrived for slaves, making them legally equal to all whites, including him, the president.[9]

To mid-nineteenth-century African Americans and white Northerners, Lincoln's silence during the march spoke volumes. They did not notice the absence of presidential speech. The walk carried the abundant meaning of a solemn, ritualized deed. Lincoln was acting out his "office," embracing his official duty and exhibiting his preferred self-conception. He was reconsecrating Richmond as national territory with every step he took, and with every salute to a black person he was acknowledging the former slaves' new civic status.

In an article written for the *Atlantic Monthly* right after the assassination, Coffin recorded the single most memorable encounter of all, one that combined silence and salute: "The walk was long, and the President halted a moment to rest. 'May de good Lord bless you, President Linkum!' said an old negro, removing his hat, and bowing with tears of joy rolling down his cheeks. The President removed his own hat, and bowed in silence; but it was a bow which upset the forms, laws, customs, and ceremonies of centuries. It was a death-shock to chivalry, and a mortal wound to caste."[10] Lincoln's silence magnified his physical performance as the head of the body politic.

Everything written about the Richmond walk after April 14, including this essay by Coffin, was shaped by general shock and sorrow over the loss of Lincoln. With the president dead, Coffin suddenly recalled that during the march, he saw white "men in the crowd who had daggers in their eyes."[11] From that point on, it was impossible for anyone to look back on April 4 and not see it as a rehearsal for Ford's Theatre. One writer after another asserted that Lincoln had risked his life—not just physical injury—by setting off on foot in the midst of a swelling crowd. And one writer after another sought to shape the nation's memory of Lincoln's last days by adding new facts to the story—details that would place the writer in the history books and provide the president with speech.

Decades after Lincoln's death, several authors supplied exact words that had supposedly come out of Lincoln's mouth in Richmond. The wordless trek through Richmond recorded by Coffin turned into a talkfest. History writing turned into historical fiction as the invented quotations piled up—quotations that twentieth-century writers accepted as Lincoln's true language because the words appeared in articles and books authored by people who claimed, often decades after the event, to have heard the president utter them.

Before April 14, not a single report from Richmond mentioned any exact words spoken by Lincoln in Richmond or any threat of assassination made or implied by anyone while he was there. After April 14, nearly everyone who wrote about the walk stated or implied that Lincoln had run a mortal risk by exposing himself to the tender mercies of the white Southerners—often including concealed military sharpshooters—who had remained in Richmond after the withdrawal of Confederate troops. It took decades for the most cherished words supposedly spoken by Lincoln on April 4 to enter the historical record.

The most beloved phrases of all were written by Admiral Porter and published in his 1885 memoir. He composed a dramatic scene on the Richmond dock, in which Lincoln—fresh from his grueling trip upriver and unsure what to do about not being picked up by Weitzel's carriage—allegedly conducted a long and eloquent conversation with the black laborers originally observed by Charles Coffin. Had this extravagant exchange really occurred, Coffin surely would have noticed it and made some mention of it in his dispatch that evening.

In Porter's rendering, a sixty-year-old "patriarch" spoke for the group. Lifting his arms and pointing to his eyes, he said of Lincoln, "he's been in my heart fo' long yeahs, an' he's cum at las' to free his chillum from deir bondage! Glory Hallelujah." At that point, the patriarch dropped to his knees to kiss the president's feet, and the other laborers joined in by trying "to kiss the hem of his garments!"

But according to Porter, Lincoln bristled at the fawning treatment. He ordered the African Americans to desist. He did not want them to exalt him the way first-century Jews had exalted Jesus on his arrival in Jerusalem for the Passover. He taught them a republican as well as a theological lesson. Porter's Lincoln preaches solemnly to "the poor creatures at his feet," telling them, "Don't kneel to me. That is not right. You must kneel to God only, and thank him for the liberty you will hereafter enjoy. I am but God's humble instrument; but you may rest assured that as long as I live no one shall put a shackle on your limbs, and you shall have all the rights which God has given to every other free citizen of the Republic."[12]

Later writers on Lincoln have often quoted some or all of these words, without identifying them in their texts as reconstructions twenty years after the fact, thus endorsing Porter's claim that Lincoln actually spoke them on the afternoon of April 4, 1865. And their doing so, ironically, may have helped preserve the memory of Lincoln's walk through Richmond for a readership no longer content to make sense of a silent but heavily symbolic Lincoln trek. Porter's Lincoln goes out of his way to command the African Americans to desist from greeting him with the physical symbolism they had learned from the Bible—kneeling and reaching for his garments—and gives them formidable words to help them remember not to do it again. No citizen bows down to his chief magistrate, and no Christian bows down to anyone but Jesus or his Father.

Porter's Lincoln, at the very start of his procession through Richmond, chooses verbal pronouncement over physical gesture and thus inadvertently makes his walk comprehensible to future generations, not just to the black laborers by river's edge. "His face was lit up with a divine look as he uttered those words," wrote Porter in 1885, and they ensured that Lincoln would "be honored thousands of years from now" for this "simple and humble affair" on the Richmond dock.[13]

III

Soon after the assassination, the religious interpretation of the Richmond walk took deep hold—not all at once replacing the republican story told by Charles Coffin but blending with it. This 1865 sacred-secular hybrid differed from David Porter's later joining of republicanism and religion. Porter's Lincoln resisted the idea that he had some religious mission to fulfill for the black men surrounding him on the dock. He thought the former slaves were worshipping him the same way that some first-century Jews had worshipped Jesus, and Lincoln told them to stop. He wanted to protect republican citizenship from contamination by religious habits of mind. He recoiled at the notion that one person might be judged essentially superior to another or, worse, that a morally gifted person might be elevated to quasidivine status.

But that's exactly what happened to Lincoln right after his death. The sermon preached by the Reverend Henry C. Badger in Cambridgeport, Massachusetts, on April 23 shows how this interweaving was accomplished. He told his flock to recollect "the fearful labors demanded" of Lincoln during the war, "remembering his course, how he watched and toiled and prayed; how he overcame evil with good . . . suffered, but threatened not." Without initially mentioning Jesus, Badger slid the president into the same template the gospel writers had created to describe the Son of God as he prepared for his sacrificial death. Lincoln had followed a time-honored path toward his martyrdom.

Then Badger mentioned Jesus explicitly. The single most telling feature of Lincoln's presidential career, said Badger, was his "humility as a victor," a trait he displayed as he entered Richmond without "self-exaltation or self-complacency." He grew "more humble as he was more exalted" by others. In the entire sweep of human history, only the "humble entry of Jesus into Jerusalem" could be compared to Lincoln's passage amid "that praying, weeping multitude of freedmen, showering prayers and blessings on his head where he walked, the humblest of them all, yet emancipator and conqueror, already with the martyr's halo round his brow."[14]

A moderate antislavery advocate of the Lincoln stripe, the Congregationalist Henry Badger dwelt on the spiritual dimension of the Richmond walk because it would help expose the president's republican commitment to black freedom. Radical abolitionist and Methodist preacher Gilbert Haven agreed: highlighting the religious meaning of the march would give a boost to the republican cause of equality for all. That cause would need a boost as it turned from ending slavery to the still tougher task of gaining citizen's rights for African Americans.

After the assassination, Haven called Lincoln's "advent into Richmond" his "jubilate," an archaic noun denoting a deed that combines glory, triumph, and joy. It was obvious to Haven that this jubilate would never be forgotten: "No picture of the war will be so frequently and so fittingly painted. It was in extraordinary agreement with his whole life and character."

> [Lincoln] walks up the central street of the capital of the rebellion, attended by twelve marines, half-a-dozen officers and friends, without music, or banners, or military, or civic pomp. Thousands of unshackled slaves dance around him in uncontrollable ecstasy of delight. They look upon the face of their liberator. To them it shines like that of Moses as he descended from the mount. Like the lame man unchained of his life-long fetters of infirmity, they precede and follow this, to them, chief of Christ's apostles, "walking and leaping and praising God." They too have been unchained of life-long fetters, that have made them sit at the beautiful gate of the temple of knowledge and liberty, powerless to move, hopeless of salvation.

To help spur them on through that gate of true equality, the Richmond story "will be wrought in song and on canvas. It will go over the world and down the ages—the most beautiful and most rare example of a Christian triumph."[15]

IV

Gilbert Haven turned out to be wrong about the lasting impact of Lincoln's republican and religious performance in Richmond. By the early twentieth century, at least among white people, it was still remembered but was fading in significance. Keyed to the cause of emancipation, Lincoln's interracial procession lost salience among white Americans as their fervor for extending African Americans' civil rights waned. Whites North and South had begun restitching their fraternal ties in the late nineteenth century, putting sectional reconciliation ahead of citizenship for blacks.

As Jim Crow segregation settled over the South and informal segregation deepened across the North, Lincoln's symbolic identity as emancipator weakened. Meanwhile, his cultural status as the champion of self-making, the epitome of eloquence, the master of morally based and politically deft leadership, and the iconic face of the nation became all the more firmly cemented.[16]

In the late twentieth century, the emancipator image made a substantial comeback, but Lincoln's Richmond walk was only fitfully retrieved. If he had delivered a major public speech while in Richmond, twentieth- and twenty-first-century Americans—attuned to his language more than his deeds—might well have taken notice. But even then, retrospective attention to a Richmond speech might not have extended to his spontaneous, silent procession. Had even a single photograph been taken during the march—showing the president mixing with the people and signaling his support, as Coffin put it, for "citizens, *black and white!*"—public memory of Lincoln's momentous day in Richmond might easily have persisted.

If documentary filmmaker Ken Burns had had access to such a photograph, his presentation of the president's April 4 Richmond visit in *The Civil War*, his ten-hour 1990 PBS television documentary, might have registered much more deeply in the minds of his 15 million viewers. The actual forty-second segment on the visit—four sentences read by narrator David McCullough while the screen showed a painting of the *carriage ride* through Richmond taken by Lincoln an hour or so after the march had concluded—reduced the walk to a minor and eminently forgettable incident in an error-filled script:

> On April 3 [read McCullough's script, off by a day], Abraham Lincoln and his son Tad arrived at Rockett's Wharf [they actually did not land here as planned, but at a dock closer to their destination] aboard a small barge and were escorted through the smoking city by a unit of black cavalry [the black cavalry escorted Lincoln on the carriage ride, not the walk]. Freed slaves mobbed the president, laughing, singing, weeping for joy, kneeling before him, straining to touch his clothes. "I know I am free," said one man, "for I have seen Father Abraham, and felt him." The president walked about a mile through the crowd [actually, the crowd was walking too], and loped up the steps of the Confederate White House, now Union headquarters.[17]

In this late twentieth-century rendition of the event, the republican daring and saintly egalitarianism that Lincoln's African American and

Northern white contemporaries beheld in it have been completely ex-
punged. The carriage ride painting, Dennis Malone Carter's 1866 *Lincoln's
Drive through Richmond*, depicts a racially mixed, but mostly white, crowd
of civilians saluting Lincoln as he sits peering out at them from his protected position inside the vehicle. This image gets the racial composition
of the crowd wrong and obscures the actual historical fact that during the
walk, Lincoln had chosen to consign his body to the protection of a mass
of friendly African Americans.

A far better choice to illustrate this segment of *The Civil War* would have
been Thomas Nast's 1866 drawing *President Lincoln Entering Richmond*,
which portrays Lincoln, hand in hand with Tad, striding through town.
Nast had corresponded with Charles Coffin to ensure the factual accuracy of his image, printed in *Harper's Weekly* on February 24. It depicted
a crowd of gleeful African Americans pressing forward to touch him as
they all marched together toward General Weitzel's headquarters. Ken
Burns's selection of Carter's artwork over Nast's contributed in a small
way to the forgetting of the Richmond walk, but it was the prior fading
of the march from American memory that made the choice of Carter's
image possible in the first place.

Twenty-two years after Ken Burns's *Civil War*, Steven Spielberg's 2012
film *Lincoln* came close to reviving the president's visit to Richmond but
ultimately left it aside. Screenwriter Tony Kushner's five-hundred-page
first draft of the script included the last several months of Lincoln's life,
and he explained in an interview with Charlie Rose that the president's
day in Richmond had piqued his interest. He was fascinated by Lincoln's
decision to court danger on April 4, 1865, and to allow young Tad to court
it with him. Kushner has not released his first draft of *Lincoln*, which
Spielberg now owns, but based on his comments to Rose, it seems likely
that it included a Richmond scene. And as he said to Rachel Maddow
of MSNBC, he has not ruled out the possibility of one day asking for
permission to let it see the light of day.[18]

Spielberg's decision to base his film on the first 150 pages of Kushner's
screenplay and to highlight Lincoln's political maneuvering in January to
obtain passage of the House resolution supporting the Thirteenth Amendment, abolishing slavery once and for all, did not stop him from including a
few April scenes. He showed Lincoln and Grant conversing in Petersburg,
Virginia, on April 3 and Grant and Lee silently doffing their hats to one
another after the April 9 Appomattox surrender.

Having opened up those early April scenes, the film missed a sol-
id-gold opportunity to dramatize its overall theme—Lincoln's devotion
to emancipation—by putting him on the Richmond streets on April 4.

A brief treatment of his walk, something short of a Cecil B. DeMille style crowd scene that would have broken Spielberg's $50 million budget, could have captured Lincoln's feelings about the slaves' freedom and the slaves' feelings about Lincoln's role in making it happen.

The film portrays such a vehement *indoor* emancipator—mulling over the politics of the amendment and mediating on the meaning of equality—that one wishes Spielberg had let Lincoln out of the White House to celebrate the new era with the masses of African Americans who gave him and God the credit for freeing them. Even a small glimpse of the Richmond walk in a film of this pedigree—a film actually shot in Richmond—could have jump-started the memory of what Gilbert Haven canonized as Lincoln's "final deed": the emancipator striding into the postwar world in the just-fallen capital of the Confederacy, shoulder to shoulder with the nation's newly liberated men and women.

Spielberg's inspired shot of Grant and Lee doffing their hats to one another in silence on April 9 could have been foreshadowed by the moment of the Richmond march that Charles Coffin loved the most: Lincoln stopping to greet the aged black man. That is the moment Coffin called "a death-shock to chivalry, and a mortal wound to caste." That's the moment when the old man removed his hat and bowed, with tears of joy streaming down his face. Lincoln took off his hat, too, and "bowed in silence."[19]

Three months after the release of Spielberg's *Lincoln*, the National Geographic Channel aired its two-hour television docudrama *Killing Lincoln*, which drew a sizable cable audience of more than three million viewers. Near the start, a two-minute segment showed the Richmond walk. But with only a couple dozen black and white participants, all of them marching in a subdued, almost funereal manner, the depiction missed the unabashed gaiety of the moment. It also transformed Lincoln's well-documented reserve into a string of amiable comments about what he was thinking and how he was feeling.

When a hatless and tattered old black man approaches to offer him God's blessing and then drops to his knees, Lincoln is moved to bend down himself. He whispers into the man's ear a version of David Porter's lines: "You are a free citizen of this Republic. Kneel to God only and thank him for the liberty that is yours." In this rendition of Coffin's scene, the equivalence of the two men doffing their hats, one after another, is lost. Lincoln's charity for all is nicely dramatized, but not his official deference to the citizenry.

Still, the National Geographic version succeeded in signaling the historical importance of the Richmond march—perhaps a first step in the cultural remembering of it. In his summation, narrator Tom Hanks skips the republican meaning of the walk but powerfully voices its unlikelihood: "It's one of the most unforgettable scenes in American history. An American president walking the streets of a fallen rebel capital, in the midst of a civil war. Scarcely 36 hours after Jefferson Davis has fled his capital, Abraham Lincoln arrives at the surrendered home of the Confederate President."[20]

Notes

1. In the twenty-first century, the Baltimore assassination plot has nearly disappeared from public memory. In 2009, when Barack Obama re-created Lincoln's inaugural train trip from Philadelphia to Washington, DC, the press did not contrast Obama's warm welcome in Baltimore—where he stopped to give a barnstorming outdoor address—to Lincoln's surreptitious passage through the city.

2. Lincoln's physical and political engagement in the body politic is a major theme of my book *Lincoln's Body: A Cultural History* (New York: W. W. Norton, 2015).

3. John G. Nicolay and John Hay, "A History of Abraham Lincoln," *Century* 39 (December 1889): 310. Many historians have asserted that Washington, DC, policeman William Crook—one of the president's appointed bodyguards—also came ashore with Lincoln and took part in the walk, for the very good reason that Crook claimed, in his 1910 recollections, to have done both. But none of the multiple 1865 sources that identified who landed and marched with Lincoln mentions Crook. In addition, general doubt has been cast on his trustworthiness since other misstatements of fact have been found in his text, and since he appears so eager to create scenes that show a special intimacy between him and the president. Margarita Spalding Gerry, ed., *Through Five Administrations: Reminiscences of Colonel William H. Crook* (New York: Harper and Bros., 1910). Nicolay and Hay had read Crook's memoir in manuscript, and thought they had adequately disposed of it, and of other Lincoln accounts "written from memory, after the lapse of years, . . . so evidently colored by fancy that they do not invite credence," in their 1889 *Century* article.

But Carl Sandburg freely exploited Crook's account of the Richmond visit in his mega-best-selling *Abraham Lincoln: The War Years* (1939), and many later biographers, equally eager for graphic details unavailable in nineteenth-century accounts, endorsed Crook's text and other treatments brightly "colored by fancy." Although twentieth-century academic historians generally scoffed at Sandburg's own credibility—scorning him the way Nicolay and Hay had scorned Crook—David Herbert Donald's now standard *Lincoln: A Biography* (New York: Simon and Schuster, 1995) followed Sandburg in valuing Crook as a source. In *Abraham Lincoln: A Life* (Baltimore: Johns Hopkins University Press, 2008), Michael Burlingame decertified Crook by omitting him and his recollections from the story of Lincoln in Richmond. But Donald's imprimatur has likely guaranteed Crook safe passage into future Lincoln historiography.

4. On April 5, the *Richmond Whig* identified the final stretch of the president's walk: "dressed in a long black overcoat, high silk hat, and black pants, giving to his form a very commanding appearance," Lincoln "moved up Governor to Twelfth St., out Twelfth to Marshall St. and the mansion of Jeff. Davis" (cited in the *Washington Evening Star*, April 8, 1865).

5. *New York Tribune*, April 8, 1865.

6. More than one hundred thousand copies of Holland's book sold after publication. Allen C. Guelzo, in his excellent introduction to J. G. Holland, *Life of Abraham Lincoln* (1866; Lincoln: University of Nebraska Press, 1998), x, explains why Holland's *Life*, and not other books on Lincoln published in 1865, qualifies as the first "biography": it covered his whole life, not just his political career.

7. C. A. P. [Charles Page], *New York Tribune*, April 10, 1865, 1. One of the many compelling reasons to doubt that William Crook was present with Lincoln in Richmond is his mistaken claim that he disembarked with the president at Rockett's—the place where the party was supposed to land but did not. See Gerry, *Through Five Administrations*, 52.

8. Holland, *Life of Abraham Lincoln*, 510.

9. [Charles] Carleton [Coffin], "The President's Entry into Richmond," *Boston Journal*, April 10, 1865, reprinted in *Littell's Living Age* 85, no. 1090 (April 22, 1865): 137, available at Cornell University's Making of America website.

10. C. C. Coffin, "Late Scenes in Richmond," *Atlantic Monthly* 15, no. 92 (June 1865): 755.

11. Ibid.

12. David D. Porter, *Incidents and Anecdotes of the Civil War* (New York: D. Appleton, 1885), 295. In their 1889 *Century* article, Nicolay and Hay criticized Porter as well as Crook for writings "colored by fancy." They were referring to Porter's work on naval history, but their judgment applies to his Richmond account too—which includes the fanciful claim that John Wilkes Booth was in Richmond on April 4 and that Porter saw him trying to get aboard the ship on which Lincoln was spending the night. Porter's *Incidents* contains so much concocted dialogue and scene-setting that it qualifies as historical fiction. That doesn't mean his writing is untrue, only that it's not strictly factual. Good historical fiction can deliver important truths in its dramatic recreations. Porter's scene at the Richmond dock contributes an eloquent statement of Lincoln's actual republican and theological beliefs.

13. Porter, *Incidents and Anecdotes*, 296.

14. Henry C. Badger, "The Humble Conqueror: A Discourse . . . Preached to the Cambridgeport Parish," April 23, 1865 (Boston: William V. Spencer, 1865), 6, 11, available at The Martyred President: Sermons Given on the Occasion of the Assassination of Abraham Lincoln, http://beck.library.emory.edu/lincoln/sermon.php?id=badger.001&keyword=Henry%20C.%20Badger,%20The%20Humble%20Conqueror.

15. Gilbert Haven, "The Last Word and Deed of Abraham Lincoln," *The Independent*, May 4, 1865, 1.

16. I trace these developments in my book *Lincoln's Body*.

17. Ken Burns, "War Is All Hell (1865)", *The Civil War*, episode 8, [1990], rebroadcast January 2001 (Arlington, VA: Public Broadcasting Service [PBS]), DVD.

18. Tony Kushner interview on *The Charlie Rose Show*, February 14, 2013; "Public Forum: Tony Kushner and Rachel Maddow," December 2, 2012 (http://www.youtube.com/watch?v=O3mtlnypqow).

19. Coffin, "Late Scenes in Richmond," 755.

20. *Killing Lincoln*, an adaptation of Bill O'Reilly and Martin Dugard, *Killing Lincoln: The Shocking Assassination That Changed America Forever* (New York: Henry Holt, 2011), aired February 17, 2013 (National Geographic Channel), DVD.

6

Why Was Lincoln Murdered?

Edward Steers, Jr.

"I suppose Lincoln is a man of courage . . . he would undoubtedly resist being captured and I could not stand the imputation to having consented to Mr. Lincoln being assassinated."[1] These words were not what the young officer sitting across from his president wanted to hear. But Jefferson Davis was no fool. The year was 1862, three full years before Lincoln's 1865 murder, and hopes of Confederate independence were then running high. Few Confederate officials were as yet prepared to accept the draconian policy shifts that would climax in the final year of the war.

Confederate major Joseph Walker Taylor, nephew of former U.S. president Zachary Taylor and first cousin of Sarah Knox Taylor, Davis's first wife, devised the 1862 plan to capture Lincoln and hold him for ransom. The major, known as Walker Taylor, had been stationed at Fort Donelson in western Tennessee under the command of Confederate general Simon Bolivar Buckner. Buckner was forced to surrender the besieged fort to General Ulysses Grant on February 16, 1862, but Taylor had made his escape along with several other officers the night before.

Wounded in the cheek and throat during the siege, Taylor made his way to Washington to the home of his uncle, Union brigadier general Joseph Pannell Taylor, where he spent time recuperating. His uncle was not pleased at the notion of hosting his Confederate nephew, but family trumped politics.

While moving about the city as a civilian, Walker Taylor paid particular attention to Lincoln's habit of often traveling alone on horseback to his summer residence at the Soldiers' Home, three miles north of the Capitol. Once fully recovered, Taylor made his way to Richmond, where he paid a visit to Jefferson Davis. Over breakfast, Taylor told Davis of his plan: he would take several of his best cavalrymen and raid the summer retreat, capturing Lincoln and heading across the river to Richmond. It was a good plan with reasonable expectation of success. Davis, however, wanted no part of putting his adversary's life at risk.

But 1862 was not 1864. While Davis's armies had rolled up a series of impressive battle victories early in the conflict, by 1864 they were losing the war. In the process, the war's character had changed dramatically from one of conventional practice to one of black flag warfare, a term introduced by the daily newspaper *Philadelphia Age* to describe a no-holds-barred style of warfare in which the laws of war were no longer followed. In 1863, the Confederacy's worst fears were realized when Lincoln issued his Emancipation Proclamation, a military order calling for the emancipation of slaves in Confederate territory along with the enlistment of black men into the Union army.

In the beginning, Lincoln had tried to mollify Southern fears about his policy toward slavery. Most Southerners remained unconvinced. In his inaugural address on March 4, 1861, Lincoln had spoken to the South directly: "I have no purpose, directly or indirectly, to interfere with the institution of slavery in the States where it exists. I believe I have no lawful right to do so, and I have no inclination to do so."[2] This attempt by Lincoln to assuage Southern fears fell on deaf ears. Most Southern slaveowners believed rightly that Lincoln's ultimate aim was the abolition of slavery, even at the cost of civil war. William L. Harris of Mississippi proclaimed to the Georgia state legislature that Mississippi "had rather see the last of her race, men, women, and children, immolated in one common funeral pile, than see them subjected to the degradation of civil, political, and social equality with the negro race."[3]

When Lincoln's efforts in 1862 to compensate slave owners in the border states of Missouri, Kentucky, Maryland, and Delaware were rebuffed, his position hardened. Lincoln believed that compensating owners for their slaves would save thousands of lives and millions of dollars. Aware of the great economic upheaval emancipation would cause the Southern economy, his plan called for the transfer of 6 percent interest-bearing bonds of the U.S. Treasury to each state equal to the aggregate value of the slaves within that state according to the 1860 census. Congress would set the price for each slave, and the funds would be transferred in coordination with emancipation. Lincoln pointed out to any who would listen that the cost of eighty-seven days of the war would purchase all of the slaves in the four border states plus the District of Columbia at $400 each. It was a generous offer, considering the alternative.

Having offered his compensation plan only to see it soundly rejected, Lincoln decided to take dramatic action. While the Constitution clearly prevented a president from interfering with slavery by executive action, legal experts advised Lincoln that it allowed the commander in chief far greater latitude under the vague war powers the Constitution granted the president.[4] Whatever action taken by a president that injured the enemy in time of war or rebellion was fair game under the war powers interpretation of the Constitution.

Exactly what prompted Lincoln to issue his proclamation when he did is open to debate, but its effect established several important objectives that dramatically changed the war and ultimately doomed both the Confederacy and Lincoln. First, declaring that all slaves held within areas in rebellion were "now and forever" free meant that any hope of reunion was irrevocably linked with emancipation. This objective was unacceptable to Confederate leaders. In his message to the Confederate Congress in response to Lincoln's proclamation, Jefferson Davis declared, "A restoration of the Union has now been rendered forever impossible." He went on to describe the proclamation as the "most execrable measure recorded in the history of guilty man."[5] Second, the most shocking aspect of Lincoln's proclamation to Southerners was the call for the enlistment of black men into the Union army. Placing guns in the hands of black men and sending them into the Confederacy struck terror into the hearts of most Southerners. And third, the proclamation blunted any thought of Great Britain recognizing the Confederacy as a sovereign country. This last point had enormous political consequences for the Confederacy.

Jefferson Davis understood exactly what the proclamation meant and what Lincoln's aims were. One must consider the significance of Davis's statement that restoration of the Union had been rendered impossible to fully understand the real effect of the proclamation. For Davis to have made this statement suggests that he thought there were circumstances under which restoration would be possible. A return to the Union as it once existed would have meant that slavery as an institution would continue as it had prior to the war. Lincoln's proclamation made clear that this was no longer an option. The fact that Davis felt restoration was no longer possible because of the proclamation shows us just how important the document was in changing the course of the war.

To Davis and his cohorts, the Emancipation Proclamation was a clear call to slaves throughout the South to rise up in revolt against their masters with the inevitable result, in Southern minds, of the massacre of women and children. The idea that black troops would now invade the South as part of the Union army abrogated any right to protection Lincoln may have warranted under the recognized rules of civilized warfare. To Davis and others in the South, Lincoln had shown himself to be nothing more than a barbarian, and a barbarian was entitled to no protection under the civilized laws of war or mankind.

The Southern reaction to Lincoln's call for black enlistment was virulent. Black soldiers who fell into Confederate hands would not be treated as prisoners of war. Black people were not entitled to equal treatment under the law of most Southern states and certainly not under the laws of war. Incidents of Confederate atrocities began to occur wherever black troops were involved in battle. Captured black soldiers were either executed summarily or taken south and sold into slavery.[6] Evidence of these atrocities appears in the correspondence of certain Confederate military leaders. Confederate general Kirby Smith's assistant adjutant general, S. S. Anderson, wrote to Confederate general Richard Taylor, commander of the District of West Louisiana, that "no quarter should be shown" to black soldiers. And Smith wrote to Taylor expressing his displeasure when Taylor's troops took black prisoners: "I hope this may not be so, and that your subordinates who have been in command of capturing parties may have recognized the propriety of giving no quarter to armed negroes and their officers."[7] On October 3, 1864, the day after a battle at Saltville, Virginia, Confederate forces under General John S. Williams systematically murdered black troops who had been captured or had surrendered, resulting in what historian Thomas D. Mays described as a "no-quarter racial massacre."[8]

In addition to the military's "no-quarter" policy, Davis announced to the Confederate Congress that he was ordering that upon capture, all Union officers in command of black troops be turned over to state authorities to be dealt with according to that state's laws governing incitement of slave rebellion. Captured officers were no longer to be treated as soldiers protected under the rules of war, but as inciters of slave rebellion. Since most Southern state laws called for the death penalty for such crimes, the policy was tantamount to murder. When Lincoln heard of the new policies, he issued his "Order of Retaliation," which stated in part that for every black soldier killed in violation of the laws of war, "a rebel soldier shall be executed; and for everyone enslaved by the enemy or sold into slavery, a rebel soldier shall be placed at hard labor on the public works."[9] Fortunately, both Davis and Lincoln backed off their positions, but although Davis never carried out his threat to turn captured officers over to state authorities, his military commanders continued to commit acts against black soldiers in violation of the laws of war.

As the war ground on with mounting casualties on both sides, desperation began to set in. The final act that convinced Confederate leaders of Lincoln's "execrable" nature occurred in February 1864. A daring plan was developed in Washington that aimed at the city of Richmond, the very heart of the Confederacy. The idea was first hatched in 1863 during the Chancellorsville campaign. Union major general George Stoneman was sent by the Army of the Potomac's commanding officer, Joseph Hooker, on a raid behind General Robert E. Lee's lines with orders to disrupt Lee's supply lines. Moving completely around Lee's army, contingents of Stoneman's cavalry broke through Richmond's defenses but fell short of entering the capital. Several Union officers held as prisoners in Richmond reported following their release that Stoneman's men could have easily entered Richmond without opposition and burned the city to the ground. Lincoln, on hearing from these officers, sent an angry message to General Hooker: "He says there was not a sound pair of legs in Richmond, and our men, could have safely gone in *and burnt everything & brought us Jeff Davis*."[10] This telegram, long ignored by Lincoln scholars, is quite remarkable. The words "burnt everything & brought us Jeff Davis" deserve close scrutiny. Clearly, Lincoln harbored thoughts of capturing Davis and bringing him to Washington. Lincoln was not one to write idle thoughts or use words loosely. The telegram has to be taken seriously.

On learning that Union prisoners were suffering terribly in Libby Prison in Richmond and Belle Isle Prison south of the city, Lincoln was concerned about how to free the prisoners and bring them home. Lee was hard-pressed to feed his own army, let alone enemy soldiers held captive. In February 1864, Brigadier General Judson Kilpatrick, commanding the Third Division of the Cavalry Corps of the Army of the Potomac, proposed a second raid on Richmond. Kilpatrick had been part of the earlier Stoneman raid and believed he could enter the city with little opposition. The objective of the new raid would be to free the Union prisoners, capture Davis, and torch the city just as Lincoln had written in his telegram to Hooker. The goal of liberating Union prisoners fell within the laws of war, but burning the city, with the obvious consequence of the death of numerous civilians, including women and children, was not part of the gentleman's concept of war. Yet Lincoln's telegram shows he approved the plan, at least in hindsight. And if Union troops could burn Richmond, the Confederates felt, turnabout was fair play. Within months, plans were afoot to burn several Northern cities, including New York, Boston, and Cincinnati.[11]

Accompanying Kilpatrick's forces was a young cavalry officer, Colonel Ulric Dahlgren, the son of Union admiral John A. Dahlgren. The younger Dahlgren was a favorite of Lincoln's and met with the president just before the raid. The topic of conversation was not recorded, but the two men must have talked about the upcoming raid and its chances for success.[12]

Kilpatrick's plan consisted of a two-pronged approach, with his men attacking from the northwest while Dahlgren, accompanied by five hundred troops, moved south of Richmond, crossed the James River, and freed the prisoners held at Belle Isle. Dahlgren, with the freed prisoners now armed and attached to his army, would then enter the city from the south and complete their mission. In the end, however, Kilpatrick ran into unexpectedly heavy resistance and aborted his attack, leaving Dahlgren to fend for himself. Dahlgren, unable to ford the swollen James River, decided to abort his end of the raid too and instead attempted to join General Benjamin Butler's forces on the peninsula east of Richmond. While heading east, Dahlgren ran into a Confederate ambush and, after a brief exchange of gunfire, was killed.

The raid would have been recorded as yet another failed attempt to take the Confederate capital except for an almost incredible occurrence. On searching Dahlgren's body, a young boy found several documents that created a sensation. Two of them contained written instructions from Dahlgren to his troops. One of the documents, with the heading "Headquarters, Third Cavalry Corps," ordered the men to free the prisoners from Belle Isle and lead them into Richmond to burn the city and take Davis and his cabinet prisoners. A second document was even more detailed and more damaging. It told the men "to keep together and well in hand, and once in the city it must be destroyed and *Jeff Davis and cabinet killed*."[13] The documents were in Dahlgren's handwriting.

The planned burning of Richmond was viewed by the Confederates as an act of terrorism, and the killing of Davis and members of his cabinet as a gross violation of the laws of war. The *Richmond Inquirer* wrote that in the future, Confederate armies must be relieved from the "restraints of chivalry." Henceforth, Confederate armies "will make war upon the rules selected by the enemy."[14] Most important, Confederate leaders believed that Lincoln had authorized the orders calling for Davis's murder, clearly making Lincoln a war criminal. It mattered little whether Lincoln knew of Dahlgren's plans; finding these orders was still a great propaganda coup for the Confederacy.

Delighted with the evidence, the Confederate authorities were quick to release the text of the orders to the press and made several photographic copies. Davis also instructed General Lee to give copies of the documents to the commanding general of the Army of the Potomac, George G. Meade, demanding an explanation.[15] Meade denied any knowledge of Dahlgren's instructions, writing to Lee, "In reply I have to state that neither the United States Government [President Lincoln], myself, nor General Kilpatrick authorized, sanctioned, or approved the burning of the city of Richmond and the killing of Mr. Davis and his cabinet."[16] According to Meade, Dahlgren had acted on his own initiative and without the approval of his superiors, including Lincoln. The young colonel was hung out to dry. Dahlgren was dead and unable to defend himself and tell what really happened. Nevertheless, the Confederates were not buying any of the Union denials. The *Richmond Examiner* published an editorial that pointed out that the conflict had now deteriorated into a "war under the Black Flag."[17] From now on, the gloves would come off.

Within days of Dahlgren's disastrous raid, Jefferson Davis authorized a bold initiative establishing a group of agents in Canada whose purpose was to disrupt the war effort throughout the North and bring about Lincoln's defeat in the upcoming election. Included in Davis's initiative was a plan to free Confederate prisoners held in Northern prison camps close to Canada. As had been the plan for Union prisoners held at Belle Isle, once freed, the Confederate captives would be armed and marched south to rejoin the Confederate army, destroying anything or anyone in their path.

Seven weeks later, Jefferson Davis sent three more emissaries to Toronto to oversee a series of actions designed to undermine Northern morale and support the large contingent of pro-Confederate supporters eager to overthrow Lincoln and his government. Davis chose Jacob Thompson and Clement C. Clay as his special commissioners to oversee the operation. Thompson and Clay proceeded to Canada, carrying a draft for $1 million in Confederate gold,[18] along with a letter from President Jefferson Davis that read in part, "I hereby direct you to proceed at once to Canada, there to carry out such instructions as you have received from me verbally, in such manner as shall seem most likely to be conducive to the furtherance of the interests of the Confederate States of America which have been entrusted to you."[19]

It was Thompson and Clay's charge to wreak as much havoc throughout the Northern states as they could, using a variety of resources and tactics. That havoc came, in part, in the form of attacks against civilian areas of major cities, the bombing of manufactories and ships, and attempts to introduce infectious disease into civilian populations. Such attacks can only be described as terrorist in nature. If Lincoln could sanction the burning of Richmond and the killing of Davis and his cabinet, then Davis could surely turn the tables on Lincoln. The war between gentlemen had ended. The *Richmond Inquirer* put it another way: "all rosewater chivalry" was over.[20]

With each passing month, Lincoln moved closer to the center of several Southern plots. The idea of capturing Lincoln and holding him for ransom grew in popularity. Although Davis had vetoed such a plan in 1862, he no longer felt constrained. During the spring of 1864, Brigadier General Bradley T. Johnson came up with a plan to take two hundred of his best cavalrymen and capture Lincoln during one of his visits to the Soldiers' Home in northeast Washington. The plot represented a resurrection of the plan Walker Taylor had presented to Jefferson Davis less than two years earlier. Johnson was under the command of General Wade Hampton at the time and sought his consent. Hampton approved Johnson's plan and forwarded it up the chain of command to General Jubal Early. About to mount a major campaign in the Shenandoah Valley, Early put Johnson's plan on hold until the campaign was completed. Unfortunately for Early, his army was destroyed by Union general Phil Sheridan in October 1864, and Johnson's plan died along with Early's army.[21]

At the same time that Early was maneuvering around Sheridan's army in the Shenandoah at Winchester, one Thomas Nelson Conrad, a lay preacher and scout who had worked for Confederate general J. E. B. Stuart, made his way into Washington on a secret mission. Reassigned to the Confederate Secret Service, Conrad slipped into the federal capital in September 1864 to reconnoiter the president by carefully observing his daily movements. As with Walker Taylor and Bradley Johnson's earlier plans, Conrad hoped to capture Lincoln during one of his trips to or from the Soldiers' Home. That Conrad had the approval of the Confederate hierarchy is evident from the fact that he received letters from both the Confederate secretary of state Judah P. Benjamin and secretary of war James A. Seddon in support of his operation.[22] Benjamin had reassigned Conrad to the Secret Service, providing him with sufficient funds to support his operation, while Seddon's letter ordered Colonel John Singleton Mosby "to aid and facilitate the movements of Captain Conrad where needed."[23] Mosby, known to his Union enemies as the "Gray Ghost," had moved between Virginia and Maryland with impunity. Helping Conrad penetrate Union territory was an easy matter for Mosby.

During his observations of the White House and Lincoln's movements around town, Conrad discovered that the president was occasionally accompanied by a troop of Union cavalry. Fearful that the sudden appearance of bodyguards meant he had been betrayed, Conrad decided to abandon his plan to capture Lincoln, concluding that there must have been "another set of Confederates seeking the same end, and some one of them had given it away by some indiscretion."[24] The risk had become too great for Conrad.

Conrad was correct in noting the recent assignment of cavalry to accompany Lincoln's movements, but there is no evidence that the Confederates had another plan in place at the time of Conrad's operation or that the federal government even suspected that such a plot existed. The assignment of a special unit of the Seventh Independent Company of Ohio Volunteer Cavalry, known as the Union Light Guard, was purely coincidental to Conrad's operation. Lincoln disliked the guard, finding it more of a nuisance than an aid. He frequently slipped out of the White House and traveled to the Soldiers' Home alone, leaving the guard behind. Had Conrad paid closer attention to Lincoln's movements, he would have noticed this risky behavior on Lincoln's part and may well have succeeded in capturing him. Like Walker Taylor and Bradley Johnson before him, Conrad lost a golden opportunity to capture the president.

Although the Confederates did not have another plan in place to capture Lincoln at the time Conrad was reconnoitering the president, there was indeed another similar plot afoot. John Wilkes Booth, perhaps aware of other schemes to capture Lincoln and wanting to upstage them, was beginning to put together a plan of his own. While Booth had no doubts about his own ability to capture Lincoln, he knew he could not do it alone. He would need help. Subduing the president, even under the best of conditions, would require muscle, and transporting him over a hundred miles through occupied enemy territory would require guidance through unfamiliar terrain and river crossings under treacherous conditions. Although Booth was known for his brashness and bravado, he was no fool.

To understand John Wilkes Booth's plan to rescue a failing Confederacy, it is essential to understand how he assembled his team of conspirators and arranged a path of escape to Richmond, where his prize could reap huge dividends. Booth did not set out at the time to kill Lincoln, although he had no moral objection to seeing Lincoln dead. The fact was that Lincoln was far more valuable alive than dead, and Booth, along with several others, knew it. Here was a way Booth could serve his beloved Confederacy and become a hero without having to face the threat of a soldier's death. The Confederate armies were dying by attrition, as soldiers taken prisoner could not be replaced. While Union forces were able to maintain their numbers and even increase them over time, Confederate forces were shrinking at an alarming rate. Grant had suspended prisoner exchange on assuming command of the Union armies, further exacerbating the Confederacy's dwindling manpower situation. In addition, Lee's habit of frontal assaults was costing him dearly in casualties. It is clear that capturing Lincoln and exchanging him for Confederate prisoners languishing in Northern prison camps was considered in several quarters of the Confederacy.

During the second week of August 1864, Booth registered at the Barnum Hotel in Baltimore, where he often stayed when visiting his hometown. Having decided to move ahead with his plan, he sent messages to two old childhood chums asking them to visit him at the Barnum for an afternoon of cigars and brandy.[25] The two men were delighted to hear from their old school friend and hastened to join him for an afternoon of reminiscing.

Samuel Arnold and Michael O'Laughlen were obvious recruits. Booth knew them from his Baltimore days, and both men fit his current needs quite nicely. They were safe recruits on whom Booth could rely. Both men had seen combat, were well versed in the use of firearms, and together might prove physically capable of overpowering the president and anyone accompanying him. Booth was lucky to have them as friends who shared his views on rescuing the Confederacy.

Once he had brought Arnold and O'Laughlen into the fold, Booth embarked on what seemed an unrelated move. On October 16, he headed north to Canada, where he landed at the St. Lawrence Hall hotel in Montreal. St. Lawrence Hall served as the headquarters for Confederate agents working out of Montreal under a man named Patrick Charles Martin.

Booth remained in Montreal for ten days, during which time he was seen on several occasions in company with Martin and George Nicholas Sanders.[26] Martin was in charge of Confederate operations in Montreal; Sanders, a Confederate agent and notorious revolutionary, was known for his advocacy of assassination as a means of achieving political goals. On October 27, Booth, accompanied by Martin, visited the Ontario Bank, where he purchased a bank draft for sixty-one pounds, twelve shillings, and six pence, paying for it with $300 in gold coin. At the same time, he opened a savings account, depositing $200 in Canadian money and a check for $255 signed by a "Mr. Davis," a Confederate money broker from Richmond whose office was across from the St. Lawrence hotel.[27] Booth left Montreal the following day and returned to Washington, where he opened a checking account, depositing $1,750. (Booth dispersed all of this money by March 16, 1865, one month before he assassinated Lincoln.) Altogether, Booth's money transactions following his trip to Montreal equaled $2,865 in U.S. greenbacks, the equivalent of approximately $45,000 in today's dollars. It is not clear where Booth was able to get hold of such a substantial amount of money at a time when he was essentially broke, as his last paid performance as an actor had been on May 28, four and a half months before his trip to Montreal.[28] The circumstances of his visit and meetings with Patrick Martin strongly suggest the possibility that Martin provided Booth the money from the Confederate Secret Service fund to help finance his capture operation.[29]

Booth's stay in Montreal was extremely productive. Not only did he leave the city with a large amount of money, which he used to finance his effort to assemble an action team, but he also left with a letter of introduction provided by Patrick Martin addressed to two men in southern Maryland, Dr. William Queen and Dr. Samuel Alexander Mudd. Queen was an elder statesman among the Confederate underground in Charles County, while Mudd was one of several active Confederate agents servicing the "mail line" that ran from Richmond to Washington and points north. The line ran past the Mudd farm, and both Mudd and his wife, Frances, routinely passed mail back and forth between Richmond and the North.[30]

It was after Booth's return to Washington that his recruitment picked up steam and he filled out his remaining cast of kidnappers. With Martin's letter in hand, Booth boarded the stagecoach in Washington on Friday, November 11, 1864, and headed for Bryantown in Charles County. A small village five miles due south of the Mudd home, Bryantown served as the commercial center for the surrounding community. It featured an inn and tavern, post office, blacksmith, and dry goods store. Booth arrived Friday evening and stayed the night at the tavern. On Saturday morning, he was met by Joseph Queen, the son of Dr. William Queen. The fact that Queen's son met Booth at the tavern the morning after his arrival in Bryantown suggests that prior arrangements had been made in anticipation of Booth's visit. How else would Queen have known to meet Booth at the inn?

Booth then went to the home of Dr. Queen, where he was introduced to John Thompson, a member of the Confederate underground in Charles County. Booth presented his letter of introduction from Martin, which assured Dr. Queen and the others that Booth could be trusted and needed help.[31] On Sunday morning, the Queens and Booth attended services at St. Mary's Catholic Church, just south of Bryantown not far from the Queen home. Also attending services there that Sunday was Dr. Samuel Mudd. Mudd's presence at St. Mary's was unusual in that the Mudds lived in a separate parish and regularly attended St. Peter's Catholic Church, two miles northwest of the Mudd farm and a good seven miles from St. Mary's. The Mudds had been married at St. Peter's in 1857, and their four living children had all been baptized there.[32] That Mudd traveled to St. Mary's on this particular Sunday suggests that he went there specifically to meet with Booth. Using the church as a congregating point for agents through-out the county made sense, as church gatherings were generally above the suspicion of Union forces. Agents could meet and exchange information there with impunity. That Queen's son and Dr. Mudd knew beforehand of Booth's visit suggests that the Confederate network was alive and well. Following the service, John Thompson introduced Booth to Dr. Mudd.

Booth's meeting with Mudd was the first of four meetings between the two men. The next time they met was a month later, in December 1864. On Friday, December 16, Booth again took the stage to Bryantown and stayed overnight at the tavern. The following morning, Joseph Queen met Booth and took him to William Queen's home for a second visit, where he spent the night. The next morning being Sunday, Booth attended services at St. Mary's Church for the second time. As in November, Dr. Mudd was in attendance that particular morning. After church services, Booth was invited back to Mudd's home for the noonday dinner. Later that afternoon, Mudd took Booth back to the Bryantown Tavern, where he had arranged a meeting with one of the Confederacy's top agents, Thomas Harbin.

Harbin, a former postmaster and resident of Charles County, knew Mudd well. Harbin joined the Confederacy's Signal Service following the outbreak of hostilities and operated a special signal camp in King George County on the Virginia side of the Potomac River. Harbin was among the many undercover operatives who handled "mail" for the Confederacy. Whether Booth knew about Harbin or whether Mudd recommended him to Booth is unclear, but either way, it was Mudd who introduced the two men to one another at the Bryantown Tavern on Sunday, December 18. The noted journalist and author George Alfred Townsend interviewed Harbin about his exploits in 1885 and wrote of the meeting in an article later published in the *Cincinnati Enquirer*:

> After church that [December] day, Booth went into Bryantown a mile or two distant and in plain sight was introduced by Dr. Mudd at the village hotel to Mr. Thomas Harbin who was the principal signal officer or spy in the lower Md counties. Harbin gave me all the particulars concerning Booth. He told that at the tavern that Sunday it was Dr. Mudd who introduced him to Booth who wanted some private conversation. Booth then outlined a scheme for seizing Abraham Lincoln and delivering him up in Virginia. Harbin was a cool man who had seen many liars and rogues go to and fro in that illegal border and he set down Booth as a crazy fellow, but at the same time said that he would give his cooperation.[33]

Crazy or not, Booth had added a very important and capable member to his action team of conspirators. Once across the Potomac with a captured Lincoln, Harbin would be an invaluable aid in getting their prize the rest of the way through Virginia to Richmond. But Harbin was valuable in another way as well. He was the link to the next recruit to join Booth's network: George Atzerodt, an accomplished riverboatman whose skills would be needed to cross the Potomac River safely past Union gunboats.

Following the meeting with Harbin at the Bryantown Tavern, Mudd invited Booth back to his home Sunday evening, where Booth was Mudd's guest for dinner and later stayed the night. On Monday morning, December 19, Mudd took Booth to the neighboring farm of George Gardner, where Booth purchased a horse that was peculiar because of a missing eye. Booth would ride the one-eyed horse back into Washington, where his loyal accomplice Lewis Powell would use it the night of Powell's assassination attempt on William H. Seward.[34]

With Arnold, O'Laughlen, Mudd, Harbin, and Atzerodt on board, Booth turned to his next recruit, John Harrison Surratt, Jr. Here again, Mudd was the key to this recruitment. Surratt was the youngest of innkeeper Mary Surratt's three children. John, born in 1844, was attending St. Charles College in Ellicott Mills, a few miles southwest of Baltimore, when war broke out. He remained at school until his father, John Harrison Surratt, Sr., died in August 1862. John then returned home to help his mother run their tavern in Surrattsville and assume his father's duties as postmaster for the surrounding area.

Suspected of "disloyal" activity, John was removed as postmaster on February 17, 1863. The government was right. John was serving as a Confederate agent, using his position as postmaster to conduct clandestine activities. Recruited by the Confederate Secret Service, John reported directly to Confederate secretary of state Judah P. Benjamin. He spent most of his time carrying messages and documents for Benjamin and escorting female agents between Richmond and Montreal, dealing directly with Patrick Martin. Young Surratt was a respected agent who had the trust of Benjamin and those working in Montreal and Toronto, where he was known by his favorite alias, "Charley Armstrong."[35] The trust placed in Surratt by Benjamin and his Canadian allies would prove valuable in helping him escape following Lincoln's assassination.[36]

On December 23, just four days after Booth returned to Washington from his meeting with Harbin, he met with Dr. Mudd in Washington for the purpose of being introduced to John Surratt. Mudd and Booth were walking along Seventh Street in Washington on their way to the Surratt boardinghouse on H Street, where John Surratt stayed when in the capital. As they walked along the street, they ran into Surratt and his friend and fellow boarder, Louis Weichmann. Introductions took place and Booth invited the three men back to his hotel room for drinks. During the meeting, Booth outlined his plan to capture Lincoln and take him to Richmond, where the president would be turned over to the Confederate authorities. Surratt listened carefully and, when Booth finished, agreed to join him along with Arnold, O'Laughlen, Harbin, Atzerodt, and Mudd.[37] Surratt was well acquainted with Mudd, Harbin, and Atzerodt and apparently approved their roles as members of Booth's team.

Thanks to the help of Samuel Mudd, John Surratt was now in the fold. Booth had convinced a key member of the Confederate Secret Service to cast his lot with him. Booth's recruitment efforts were moving along well, thanks to the help of Patrick Martin and Samuel Mudd. Next to join the team was David Herold. John Surratt recruited Herold in January 1865, a few days after Atzerodt cast his lot with the conspirators. Herold, twenty-two years old, brought two very important aspects to Booth's plot: he was an avid hunter, and as such, he was thoroughly familiar with every aspect of southern Maryland, where he spent considerable time roaming the marshes and fields in search of prey. Additionally, his employment at the Navy Yard pharmacy gave him access to chloroform, which might be needed to subdue a resistant president.[38] Herold was just the knowledgeable guide that Booth needed to safely make his way through Union-occupied territory with his prize captive. Atzerodt and Herold have since been characterized as slow-witted deadbeats whose only attribute to the scheming Booth was unquestioned loyalty. This simplistic view shows a lack of understanding about these two men and the valuable services they brought to Booth's conspiracy. Atzerodt had plied the Potomac River for four years without being arrested once, which speaks to his ability to navigate the heavily patrolled river. It is true that Herold was exceedingly loyal to Booth, but it was his knowledge of southern Maryland that helped Booth get as far as he did before being cornered in Virginia. It was this knowledge that Booth was anxious to acquire.

The final recruit to Booth's inner circle of conspirators came to him between January 21 and 22. It was through John Surratt that Lewis Thornton Powell was brought into the fold. Powell has been described by nearly every author as the "muscle" of Booth's action team. At the time he joined Booth, he stood six feet, two inches in height and weighed 175 pounds. Twenty-one years old, he was a powerful young man well suited to the difficult task of capturing the athletic president, who, despite his age, was still in excellent physical shape. Subduing Lincoln would not be easy, but Powell was the perfect man for the job.

Powell had originally served with Lee's Army of Northern Virginia through its campaigns culminating in the Battle of Gettysburg in July 1863. On July 2, he was wounded in the right wrist and taken prisoner. Eventually escaping while working as a nurse in the Confederate ward, Powell made his way to Baltimore, where he successfully hid out with the help of Confederate sympathizers. Surratt's contacts told him about Powell, and he concluded that the ex-soldier would make an ideal recruit for Booth's team. Surratt traveled to Baltimore and, after meeting with Powell, made arrangements for him to come to Washington.

Powell soon arrived at Mrs. Surratt's boardinghouse a few blocks north of Ford's Theatre.

With Powell's arrival in Washington, Booth's action team was now complete. Samuel Arnold and Michael O'Laughlen, the two former Confederate soldiers, complemented Powell's muscle. In David Herold, Booth had his pathfinder who could guide the fleeing team through southern Maryland during the day or at night. In George Atzerodt, he had his boatman to navigate the team safely across the heavily patrolled Potomac River to Virginia. And in John Surratt and Thomas Harbin, he had two experienced and highly respected Confederate agents who were connected directly to the hierarchy of the Confederate government. If Booth could have done better, it did not matter. He had what he needed, and his prospects for success were as good as he could get.

With his team intact, Booth called a meeting on March 15, 1865, summoning all six of his new recruits. They met at one of his favorite restaurants in Washington, Gautier's, on Pennsylvania Avenue a short distance from Ford's. Booth had reserved an upper room where he could privately lay out his plan to capture Lincoln during one of his visits to the theater. Dissension erupted almost immediately. Arnold and O'Laughlen thought Booth's plan foolhardy and impossible to carry out in a crowded playhouse. After a heated exchange, Booth backed off his plan and proposed that the group meet again to consider alternatives. Fortuitously for Booth, he learned two days later that Lincoln planned on traveling to Campbell Hospital, one of the hospitals on the northern edge of the city, to attend a play being staged for the convalescing soldiers. Here was the perfect opportunity. As Lincoln was known to travel with little or no protection, the team would have an ideal opportunity to capture him and whisk him south to Richmond. Booth sent word to his team to gather at a small restaurant not far from the hospital and wait for him there.

Arriving at the hospital, Booth was devastated to learn that the president had unexpectedly canceled his trip. Lincoln had decided to stay in Washington and receive a captured Confederate battle flag from an Indiana regiment. His decision, in all probability, saved him from capture or worse. Booth hurried back to the restaurant and informed his team that the capture plan was off. Thoroughly disappointed, the six men scattered, returning to their homes, not sure they would ever meet again.

Two weeks later, word reached Washington that Lee and the Confederate government had abandoned Richmond to Union forces. On April 4, the day after forces evacuated the capital, Lincoln made a surprise trip to the city, including a visit to Jefferson Davis's White House, where Lincoln sat at Davis's desk. Booth's anger grew with each passing day as

Washington celebrated the surrender of Lee's army and the fall of the Confederate capital. Worst of all, Booth's grand plan to save the Confederacy by capturing Lincoln no longer had a purpose. With Richmond in Union hands and Davis in flight, there was no place to take a captured Lincoln.

Celebration of the war's end was premature, however, at least to such devoted Confederates as Jefferson Davis and Booth. Three major Confederate armies were still in the field facing Union armies. As many as 160,000 Confederate soldiers were still in active service, and while some of these were accounted for only on paper and missing from their units, three intact fighting forces remained ready and willing to continue the fight.[39] The largest contingent, numbering 40,000 men, was serving under General Joseph E. Johnston in North Carolina. Two other large forces were in the field under Kirby Smith and Richard Taylor, totaling close to 70,000 men. Another 50,000 men lay scattered throughout the South. To rational people, the end of the war was clearly in sight. But not everyone was rational. To those still committed to a dying Confederacy, these troops meant hope. Davis, now forced to live part of his life in a boxcar for greater mobility as he fled pursuing Union troops, summoned Joe Johnston to a war council, at which he told his general that he had approved enlisting African Americans, including slaves, into the armed forces. These new troops, along with stragglers, would refill the depleted ranks, thus swelling the army. If Kirby Smith and Johnston could link up, it would make a formidable force to face Grant. There was still plenty of fight left in the Confederacy, he urged. All Davis needed was time and a small miracle. Booth intended to give Davis both.

At what moment Booth decided to kill Lincoln is not clear—certainly not before March 17, when hope was still alive for the Confederacy. But by April 11, Booth's world had turned upside down. His brain was filled with a mixture of hate, revenge, and the obsession that he must do something dramatic to alter history. While hiding in a pine thicket in Virginia three days after killing Lincoln, Booth would write in his little diary, "But our cause, being almost lost, something decisive and great must be done." What did Booth mean by "our cause, being almost lost"? Did he believe there was still hope for his cause? If we take Booth at his word, he did.

Having failed to capture Lincoln on his planned return from Campbell Hospital on March 17, Booth despaired of any hope of another kidnapping opportunity. Having witnessed Lincoln's inauguration at the Capitol on March 4, two weeks before the failed kidnap scheme, Booth had boasted to his friend Samuel Knapp that he had been clearly within reach of killing Lincoln: "What a splendid chance I had to kill the President on the 4th of March."[40] No one took him seriously. Booth was not a violent man. He had been raised by his famous actor father to respect all forms of life. He had also been raised to despise tyrants. After all, his father's middle name was Brutus, the man who had killed Caesar.

But Booth's world was crumbling. On the night of April 11, he joined a crowd of well-wishers on the lawn of the White House to hear the president speak. Lincoln laid out a plan for accepting the rebellious states back into the Union. Now that the Thirteenth Amendment had passed both houses of Congress, what would be the fate of newly freed black people? Lincoln did not evade the question. He spoke boldly: "It is unsatisfactory to some that the elective franchise is not given to the colored man. I would myself prefer that it were now conferred on the very intelligent, and on those who served our cause as soldiers."[41] It was all Booth could do to contain his rage. He firmly believed that black people were meant to serve white people, certainly not to share in the rights of citizenship. Lincoln's abolitionist policies had destroyed Booth's beloved South. Now Lincoln was proposing to destroy the white North. Hearing Lincoln's blasphemous words, Booth hissed under his breath, "Now, by God, I will put him through. That will be the last speech he will ever make."[42]

From the moment of his election in November 1860, Abraham Lincoln was in a sense a marked man. Despite his efforts to mollify the South and calm fears that the new government had no designs on disturbing slavery where it already existed, no one who owned slaves doubted that the new president's aims were the ultimate extinction of the peculiar institution. Lincoln had stated his position time and again, warning his fellow citizens as early as 1858 that the country could not survive half slave and half free. Now the slave owners' worst fears had come true, first with the Emancipation Proclamation, then the Thirteenth Amendment, and now the unthinkable, black citizenship. Anyone with any common sense knew that the statement in the Declaration of Independence that "all men are created equal" referred only to white men, they felt. Booth had said so in a letter to the editor of the *Washington National Intelligencer*: "This country was formed for the white, not for the black man."[43]

Three days after hearing Lincoln speak from the White House, Booth held a meeting with three members of his original capture team in Lewis Powell's room at the Herndon House, around the corner from Ford's Theatre. Lincoln would be attending the evening performance at Ford's Theatre. The moment had arrived. With Booth and Powell were David Herold and George Atzerodt. The meeting was short and to the point. Powell was assigned the task of killing Secretary of State William Seward. Atzerodt was assigned to kill Vice President Andrew Johnson. Booth would reserve Lincoln for himself. The attacks were coordinated for some-time between 10 and 10:30 that night.

Had the plot been successfully carried out, Booth was certain that it would have decapitated the federal government, leaving it in complete disarray. But whether or not the assassination succeeded in disrupting the government and allowing the dying Confederacy its small miracle, and a chance at recovery, was secondary to Booth's overweening desire to punish Lincoln for destroying not only the South, but white culture in general.

In his letter addressed to the *National Intelligencer*, Booth likened Lincoln to Caesar and himself to Brutus. "When Caesar had conquered the enemies of Rome and the power that was his menaced the liberties of the people, Brutus arose and slew him." And like Brutus, Booth proclaimed, "Caesar must bleed."[44]

Booth was right about one thing: the force of Lincoln's will had forever changed the South and America. Although Booth's bullet killed the man, it could not kill the dream.

Notes

1. Henry T. Louthan, "A Proposed Abduction of Lincoln," *Confederate Veteran* (June 1908): 157.

2. *The Collected Works of Abraham Lincoln*, ed. Roy P. Basler, 8 vols. (New Brunswick, NJ: Rutgers University Press, 1953–55), 4:262–71.

3. Charles B. Drew, *Apostles of Disunion: Southern Secession Commissioners and the Causes of the Civil War* (Charlottesville: University Press of Virginia, 2001), 89.

4. For an in-depth discussion of the war powers granted a president under the Constitution, see William Whiting, *War Powers under the Constitution of the United States* (Boston: Little Brown and Company, 1864).

5. Speech of Jefferson Davis before the Confederate Congress, January 12, 1863, in Dunbar Rowland, ed., *Jefferson Davis, Constitutionalist: His Letters, Papers and Speeches*, 10 vols. (Jackson: University of Mississippi Press, 1923), 5:409–11.

6. For two examples, see Ted Alexander, "Retreat from Gettysburg: Ten Days in July," *North and South* 2 (June 1999): 13; and Thomas D. Mays, *The Saltville Massacre* (Abilene, TX: McWhiney Foundation Press, 1998).

7. U.S. Congress, "House Report on the Assassination of Abraham Lincoln," 39th Cong., 1st sess., July 1866 (Washington, DC: Government Printing Office, 1866), 2. This report is commonly referred to as the Boutwell Report.

8. For a detailed account of this incident, see Mays, *Saltville Massacre*.

9. *Collected Works*, 6:357.

10. Ibid., 6:203 (emphasis added).

11. Edward Steers, Jr., "Terror: 1860s Style," *North & South* 5, no. 4 (May 2002): 12–18.

12. C. Percy Powell, ed., *Lincoln Day by Day*, 3 vols. (Washington, DC: Lincoln Sesquicentennial Commission, 1960), 3:237.

13. James O. Hall, "The Dahlgren Papers: A Yankee Plot to Kill Jefferson Davis," *Civil War Times Illustrated* 22, no. 7 (November 22, 1983), 33 (emphasis added).

14. Duane Schultz, *The Dahlgren Affair* (New York: W. W. Norton and Co., 1998), 157.

15. Joseph George, Jr., "Black Flag Warfare," *Pennsylvania Magazine of History and Biography* 115, no. 3 (July 1991), 309–10.

16. U.S. War Department, *The War of the Rebellion: A Compilation of the Official Records of the Union and Confederate Armies*, 128 vols. (Washington, DC: Government Printing Office, 1880–1901), ser. 1, vol. 33, 180.

17. *Richmond Examiner*, March 7, 1864, 2, quoted in George, "Black Flag Warfare," 317.

18. The $1 million came from a special fund appropriated by the Confederate Congress (February 15, 1864) designated "Secret Service." A request dated April 25, 1864, issued to Secretary of War Judah P. Benjamin with the notation "Thompson," was signed by Jefferson Davis. One dollar in gold was equal to $2.2 in greenbacks, the equivalent of approximately $23 million in current dollars. See William A. Tidwell, *April '65: Confederate Covert Action in the American Civil War* (Kent, OH: Kent State University Press, 1995), 129.

19. Wilfrid Bovy, "Confederate Agents in Canada during the American Civil War," *Canadian Historical Review* 11 (March 1921): 47. See also Albert Hemingway, "Neutral Border Violated," *America's Civil War* 1, no. 1 (May 1988): 43.

20. Schultz, *Dahlgren Affair*, 157.

21. William A. Tidwell, James O. Hall, and David W. Gaddy, *Come Retribution: The Confederate Secret Service and the Assassination of Abraham Lincoln* (Jackson: University of Mississippi Press, 1989), 235–36, 281–86.

22. Thomas Nelson Conrad, *A Confederate Spy* (New York: J. S. Ogilvie, 1892), 94–95.

23. Ibid., 119.

24. Thomas Nelson Conrad, *The Rebel Scout* (Washington, DC: National Publishing Company, 1904), 128.

25. Samuel B. Arnold quoted in Michael W. Kauffman, ed., *Memoirs of a Lincoln Conspirator* (Bowie, MD: Heritage Books, 1995), 22.

26. Testimony of Hosea B. Carter in Edward Steers, Jr., ed., *The Trial: The Assassination of President Lincoln and the Trial of the Conspirators* (Lexington: University Press of Kentucky, 2003), 38.

27. Edward Steers, Jr., *The Lincoln Assassination Encyclopedia* (New York: Harper Perennial, 2010), 414–15. The bank draft was still on Booth's body when searched following his death at the Garrett farm on April 26, 1865. See also testimony of Robert Anson Campbell in Steers, *Trial*, 45–46.

28. See Edward Steers, Jr., *Blood on the Moon: The Assassination of Abraham Lincoln* (Lexington: University Press of Kentucky, 2005), 59.

29. Tidwell, *April '65*, 234n35.

30. "Union Provost Marshal's File of Papers Relating to Two or More Civilians," U.S. National Archives and Records Administration (NARA), RG 109, M-416, file 6083.

31. Testimony of John C. Thompson in Steers, *Trial*, 178.

32. Samuel Mudd married Sarah Frances Dyer on November 26, 1857. In all, nine Mudd children were baptized at St. Peter's Church, four prior to 1865 and five after 1865. Father Peter B. Lenaghan was the priest in residence at the time.

33. George Alfred Townsend, *Cincinnati Enquirer*, April 18, 1892.

34. Edward Steers, Jr., *His Name Is Still Mudd* (Gettysburg, PA: Thomas Publications, 1997), 42–43.

35. Joan L. Chaconas, "John H. Surratt, Jr.," in Edward Steers, Jr., *Trial*, xlii.

36. For an accurate account of Surratt's escape and eventual capture, see Alfred Isaacson, *The Travels, Arrest, and Trial of John H. Surratt* (Middletown, NY: Vestigium Press, 2003).

37. John H. Surratt, Jr., "The Rockville Lecture," in *A True History of the Assassination of Abraham Lincoln and of the Conspiracy of 1865 by Louis J. Weichmann*, ed. Floyd E. Risvold (New York: Alfred A. Knopf, 1975), 431.

38. Steers, *Blood on the Moon*, 81.

39. E. B. Long and Barbara Long, *The Civil War Day by Day: An Almanac, 1861–1865* (Garden City, NY: Doubleday, 1971), 706.

40. William C. Edwards and Edward Steers, Jr., *The Lincoln Assassination: The Evidence* (Urbana: University of Illinois Press, 2009), 345.

41. For Lincoln's last speech, see *Collected Works*, 8:404.

42. Testimony of Thomas T. Eckert, May 30, 1867, Judiciary Committee, House of Representatives, Impeachment Investigation, 39th Cong., 2nd sess., and 40th Cong., 1st sess. (Washington, DC: Government Printing Office, 1867), 674.

43. John Rodehamel and Louise Taper, *Right or Wrong, God Judge Me* (Urbana: University of Illinois Press, 1997), 147.

44. Ibid., 149–50.

7

Military Justice, Right or Wrong:
Judging the Lincoln Conspirators

Frank J. Williams

The spring of 1865 marked a trying time in America's history. The nation had just endured a brutal, punishing four-year war. Just as the tide had begun to turn, in the midst of widespread national rejoicing at the restoration of peace, President Abraham Lincoln's assassination provided a sharp reminder of the harrowing days of war. The murder of Abraham Lincoln on Good Friday, April 14, 1865, struck the American psyche like a hammer blow. Lincoln died at the successful conclusion of an Armageddon that finally reconciled the living nation's values with those enshrined in the Declaration of Independence, so mass shock and mourning were surely not surprising. To America, Lincoln's murder seemed so gratuitous, so irrational, and so utterly un-American that it defied logic.

In the months that followed, Americans sought justice. Those accused of conspiring to kill the president were brought before a military commission, where they were tried in closed proceedings that lacked the usual presumptions afforded in civilian trials, including the presumption of innocence until proven guilty by a unanimous jury. All defendants were convicted. Four were sentenced to hanging, three to imprisonment for life, and one to six years' imprisonment. The convictions gave Americans some solace but opened a debate on the propriety of military trials that would continue almost 150 years later.

Justice has long been a part of civilized society. As Daniel Webster recognized, justice is "the ligament which holds civilized beings and civilized nations together."[1] But what is justice for one society may not be justice for another. Justice is informed by societal norms and culture but judged against a legal landscape. As Frederick Hatch aptly observes in his forthcoming book on the trial of the Lincoln assassination conspirators, "Legal decisions considered acceptable and proper under certain circumstances, or in certain times and places, can be seen to be inadequate, or even in error, upon later examination. This is also true in history. Those who write history must try their best to present the truth of each case as they see it, always aware that others may disagree with them, and that the passage of time, along with changing ideas and attitudes, may bring about a change of opinion."[2]

Mindful of this admonition, we must not judge the decision to try the Lincoln conspirators based on today's societal norms, climate, and legal landscape, but rather on the societal norms, climate, and legal landscape as they existed in May 1865. When viewed against that backdrop, the decision to try the Lincoln conspirators by military commission was not only defensible but also appropriate.

Military commissions, born of military necessity, have long been a feature of war.[3] They are neither mentioned in the U.S. Constitution nor created by statute, but derive their authority from powers vested in both and are recognized by this nation as a vital aspect of war. Military commissions are special courts operated by the military, not the civilian judiciary, and are used to adjudicate extraordinary cases during wartime. If anything is certain, it is that Lincoln's assassination in 1865 presented extraordinary circumstances.

In the wake of President Lincoln's assassination and the attempted murder of Secretary of State William H. Seward, President Andrew Johnson on May 1, 1865, authorized the establishment of a military commission to try those accused of these crimes and of conspiring to assassinate other government officers.

President Johnson ordered nine military officers to serve on a commission to try those suspected of conspiring to assassinate President Lincoln. It became known as the Hunter Commission, after Major General David Hunter, its chief.[4] Pursuant to the president's order, eight days later the tribunal convened to try David Herold, G. A. Atzerodt, Lewis Payne, Mary Surratt, Michael O'Laughlen, Edward Spangler, Samuel Arnold, and Dr. Samuel A. Mudd. Each was charged with conspiring with the intent to kill President Lincoln (at Ford's Theatre), then vice president Johnson (at the hotel in which he was residing), Secretary of State Seward (at his home), and General Ulysses S. Grant (who was reported to be accompanying Lincoln to Ford's Theatre).

Only four years earlier, Attorney General Edward Bates had advised President Lincoln that in times of war and insurrection, the president possessed great powers, including the right to suspend the writ of habeas corpus: "I am clearly of opinion that, in a time like the present, when the very existence of the nation is assailed, by a great and dangerous insurrection, the President has the lawful discretionary power to arrest and hold in custody persons known to have criminal intercourse with the insurgents, or persons against whom there is probable cause for suspicion of such criminal complicity."[5]

The situation presented after the assassination of President Lincoln was not unlike the situation Lincoln had faced at the onset of the war. There certainly was cause to suspect criminal complicity in the assassination of the president, and the reach of such complicity was unknown. It was not just a trial for murder or attempted murder—it was a trial that was expected to unveil a widespread conspiracy. As the *New York Times* explained, "The trial now in progress is not a trial for simple murder. Its object is not merely to punish one or more individuals for a specific act of crime. The government seeks to unravel a conspiracy—to follow every clue that may be offered for the detection and arraignment of every person in any way connected, directly or indirectly, with the extended and formidable conspiracy, in which the assassination of the President was only one of the objects sought."[6] Against this backdrop and in an era when military commissions were a common feature of war,[7] President Johnson ordered the establishment of a military commission.

From the outset, Major General Cyrus B. Comstock, who had been appointed to serve as one of the commissioners, was critical of the proceedings. During the commissioners' first meeting on May 8, Joseph Holt, the judge advocate general of the army, who led the prosecution team, insisted that the trial be conducted as a secret military court proceeding. Comstock took exception to this and advanced arguments much like the arguments made by those opposed to today's military trials at Guantanamo. In Comstock's opinion, closed proceedings were improper and likely to lead to false testimony because witnesses could not be held publicly accountable. Comstock believed that the defendants should be tried in an open trial in a civilian court. During the next day's session, Comstock voiced his concerns, and another commissioner, General Horace Porter, echoed those sentiments. Holt advised the commissioners that the attorney general had decided they had jurisdiction and that the proceedings were being conducted in accordance with Secretary Stanton's directives. When Comstock and Porter appeared at the court the next morning, they both received orders relieving them from the assignment. Later that day,

Stanton sent word through General Grant that the action represented no reflection on the officers, but that there may have been a conflict, as both men were members of Grant's staff, and the general, too, had been an object of the assassination.[8]

The secret sessions lasted less than a week, and on May 13, President Johnson, responding to pressure in the press and apparently on the recommendation of General Grant, ordered the trial opened to the public.[9] The government's decision to make the trial testimony public was seen as "an assurance that secrecy is no longer essential to the ends of justice."[10]

All of the alleged conspirators were represented by counsel before the commission and were afforded the right to call witnesses in their defense. However, unlike the process afforded in the civilian courts, the trial displayed little evidence of the presumption of innocence of the accused and strict impartiality on the part of the judges.[11] From the beginning, members of the military commission presumed the accused to be guilty. In their first appearance in court, the men were chained, their faces almost entirely covered with black linen masks.[12]

The military officers making up the court displayed their prejudice on several occasions. When Confederate general Edward Johnson was called to testify, one officer on the commission moved that Johnson be "ejected from the court as an incompetent witness on account of his notorious infamy." Because Johnson had been educated at West Point and then resigned from the army and bore arms against the United States, he appeared before the court with hands "red with the blood of his loyal countrymen." The motion to oust him was seconded, but before Johnson could be removed, Judge Advocate Joseph Holt intervened. He advised the commission that the "rule of law" would not authorize the court to declare the ex-Confederate an incompetent witness, "however unworthy of credit he may be."[13] Holt was also obliged to intervene when a member of the court challenged the right of Maryland senator Reverdy Johnson to appear as counsel for defendant Surratt, questioning his belief in the binding effect of an oath.[14] After some debate, the commission allowed the senator to represent his client, although he would appear only several times over the course of the proceedings.

During the trial, Holt presented testimony that exceeded the bounds of relevancy in that it had nothing to do with the charges against the defendants but would serve to adversely influence the judges and the public at large against the Confederacy and the defendants.[15] The government introduced evidence concerning plots by the Confederate Secret Service to stage raids from Canada on U.S. cities, the attempt to burn New York City, and the effort to spread disease throughout the Union army by the use of contaminated clothing. It likewise introduced witnesses and evidence dealing with the starvation of Federal army prisoners at Libby, Belle Isle, and Andersonville Prisons, which had no connection to the conspirators.[16] Nevertheless, Holt endeavored to find some connection between those atrocities and the chained and hooded prisoners accused of complicity in the murder of President Lincoln.

Over the course of the fifty-three-day trial, the judge advocate or the special judge advocate, John A. Bingham, raised objections to evidence introduced by the defense on thirty-four occasions. In all instances, the objections were sustained. Defense attorneys raised objections fifteen times. They were overruled on thirteen of those occasions. Perhaps offsetting the procedural failings of the military commission, more than 350 witnesses testified in the trial, a more generous number than the parties would be permitted to introduce in civilian courts today.[17]

In his closing statements, Mary Surratt's lawyer, Senator Johnson, delivered a powerful challenge to the military commission's jurisdiction.[18] In Johnson's opinion, "Grave doubts, to say the least, exist[ed] in the minds of intelligent men as to the constitutional right of the recent military commissions at Washington to sit in judgment upon the persons now on trial for their lives before that tribunal. Thoughtful men feel agrieved [*sic*] that such a commission should be established in this free country when the war is over, and when the common-law courts are open and accessible to administer justice according to law, without fear or favor."[19]

Johnson's argument, however, was a year too early. It was not until 1866 that the U.S. Supreme Court issued its decision in *Ex parte Milligan*, a decision that validated Johnson's argument in holding that although the suspension of habeas corpus was permissible, it could not be used to try individuals in military courts captured away from the battlefield where civilian courts were still functioning.[20]

When the military officers deliberated the fate of the defendants behind closed doors at the conclusion of the trial, they worked with Holt and Bingham, the judge advocates who prosecuted the conspirators. The judge advocates were persevering and urged that all eight defendants should be hanged, one of the judges, General A. V. Kautz, later reported. The commission voted, however, to condemn four to the gallows and the remaining four to prison terms. The judge advocates were rather surprised when five of the officers sitting on the commission signed a paper recommending clemency for Mary Surratt, one of the defendants sentenced to be hanged.

The next step was for the judge advocate general to take the commission's findings either to the secretary of war or, in this instance, to the president, as capital offenses were involved. As customary, Judge Holt added a statement of his own to the court record for the benefit of his superiors. In this case, Holt made a slight but significant change in this procedure.

In two military trials before July 1865, Holt specifically included in his comments accompanying the records sent to the president information that the commissions had found the defendants guilty but had also recommended clemency. Holt's note to President Johnson dealing with the conviction of the Lincoln conspirators, however, urged the president to approve the findings of the court, saying nothing of the recommendation for clemency on behalf of defendant Surratt.[21] Holt wrote:

> Having been personally engaged in the conduct of the foregoing case, ... I deem it unnecessary to enter in this report into an elaborate discussion of the immense mass of evidence submitted to the consideration of the court. After a trial continuing for fifty-three days, in which between three and four hundred witnesses were examined for the prosecution and defense, and in which the rights of the accused were watched and zealously guarded by seven able counsel of their own selection, the commission have arrived at the conclusions presented above. . . .
>
> The opinion is entertained that the proceedings were regular, and that the findings of the commission were fully justified by the evidence. It is thought that the highest consideration of public justice, as well as the future security of the lives of the officers of the government, demand that the sentences based on these findings, should be carried into execution.[22]

Holt later insisted that he had included the petition for clemency with the record of the trial when he delivered the documents to the president. Johnson claimed that he never saw that petition. But whether or not Holt had included the request for clemency, he should have informed the president of the recommendation in his covering statement, as he had done on previous occasions. His failure to do so was a serious dereliction of duty.

Not surprisingly, the trial resulted in convictions: four of the defendants were sentenced to death by public hanging, and four others received prison sentences. At 3 in the morning before the scheduled executions, lawyers for defendant Surratt, one of the four who were sentenced to be executed, went to the home of Judge Andrew Wylie of the Supreme Court of the District of Columbia and petitioned him for a writ of habeas corpus. They argued to the judge, who answered the door in his pajamas, that in time of peace, civilians could not be tried before a military commission. Judge Wylie granted their request and issued the writ of habeas corpus, but that writ was almost immediately suspended by President Johnson. General Winfield Scott Hancock, accompanied by Attorney General James Speed, returned the writ and refused to surrender defendant Surratt, following instructions of the president. Speed urged, "This country is now in the midst [*sic*] of a great war and the commander-in-chief . . . was slain in the discharge of his duties, and if the armies of the United States cannot, under the laws of war, protect their commander-in-chief from assassination, and destruction, . . . what has the government come to?"[23] When Hancock refused to give up his prisoner, Wylie declared himself powerless to take any further action. Four of the conspirators—Herold, Atzerodt, Payne, and Surratt—were executed on July 7, 1865.

Two months after the commissions were convened and after the executions of the conspirators, Johnson asked Attorney General Speed for an ex post facto (after-the-fact) legal opinion on whether the persons charged could be tried before a military tribunal.[24] In response to Johnson's request, Speed delivered a lengthy opinion to the president, titled *Opinion on the Constitutional Power of the Military to Try and Execute the Assassins of the President*.[25] Setting the stage for his analysis, the attorney general laid out the relevant facts:

> The President was assassinated at a theater in the city of Washington. At the time of the assassination a civil war was flagrant, the city of Washington was defended by fortifications regularly and constantly manned, the principal police of the city was by Federal soldiers, the public offices and property in the city were all guarded by soldiers, and the President's House and person were, or should have been, under the guard of soldiers. Martial law had been declared in the District of Columbia, but the civil courts were open and held their regular sessions, and transacted business as in times of peace.

Against this backdrop, Speed began his analysis by recognizing the importance of the question about which Johnson had asked him to opine. He acknowledged the clash between citizens' constitutional guarantees and the security of the army and government during a time of war. Nevertheless, he offered his opinion "that the conspirators not only may but ought to be tried by a military tribunal." According to Speed:

> A military tribunal exists under and according to the Constitution in time of war. Congress may prescribe how all such tribunals are to be constituted, what shall be their jurisdiction, and mode of procedure. Should Congress fail to create such tribunals, then, under the Constitution, they must be constituted according to the laws and usages of civilized warfare. They may take cognizance of such offences as the laws of war permit; they must proceed according to the customary

usages of such tribunals in time of war, and inflict such punishments as are sanctioned by the practice of civilized nations in time of war. . . .

. . . The legitimate use of the great power of war, or rather the prohibitions against the use of that power, increase or diminish as the necessity of the case demands. When a city is besieged and hard pressed, the commander may exert an authority over the non-combatants which he may not when no enemy is near. . . .

. . . Military tribunals exist under and according to the laws and usages of war, in the interest of justice and mercy. They are established to save human life, and to prevent cruelty as far as possible. The commander of an army in time of war has the same power to organize military tribunals and execute their judgments that he has to set his squadrons in the field and fight battles. His authority in each case is from the law and usage of war. . . .

. . . That the laws of war authorized commanders to create and establish military commissions, courts or tribunals, for the trial of offenders against the laws of war, whether they be active or secret participants in the hostilities, can not be denied. That the judgments of such tribunals may have been sometimes harsh, and sometimes even tyrannical, does not prove that they ought not to exist, nor does it prove that they are not constituted in the interest of justice and mercy.

Speed also recognized what war would look like without the ability to convene a military commission:

War in its mildest form is horrible; but take away from the contending armies the ability and right to organize what is now known as a Bureau of Military Justice, they would soon become monster savages, unrestrained by any and all ideas of law and justice. Surely no lover of mankind, no one that respects law and order, no one that the instinct of justice, or that can be softened by mercy, would, in time of war, take away from the commanders the right to organize military tribunals of justice, and especially such tribunals for the protection of persons charged or suspected with being secret foes and participants in the hostilities. . . .

. . . The fact that the civil courts are open does not affect the right of the military tribunal to hold as a prisoner and to try. The civil courts have no more right to prevent the military, in time of war, from trying an offender against the laws of war than they have a right to interfere with and prevent a battle. A battle may be lawfully fought in the very view and presence of a court; so a spy, or bandit or other offender against the law of war, may be tried, and tried lawfully, when and where the civil courts are open and transacting the usual business.

Thus, Speed said:

> My conclusion, therefore is, that if the persons who are charged with the assassination of the President committed the deed as public enemies, as I believe they did, and whether they did or not is a question to be decided by the tribunal before which they are tried, they not only can, but ought to be tried before a military tribunal. If the persons charged have offended against the laws of war, it would be as palpably wrong of the military to hand them over to the civil courts, as it would be wrong in a civil court to convict a man of murder who had, in time of war, killed another in battle.

This was not a universally accepted opinion. Secretary of the Navy Gideon Welles believed that Secretary of War Stanton had pressured Speed into this opinion and wrote in his diary on May 9, 1865, "The rash, impulsive, and arbitrary measures of Stanton are exceedingly repugnant to my notions, and I am pained to witness the acquiescence they receive."[26]

Former attorney general Bates shared the view that Stanton was behind Speed's opinion. He wrote in his diary on May 25, 1865, "I am pained to be led to believe that my successor, Atty Genl. Speed, has been wheedled out of an opinion, to the effect that such a trial is lawful. If he be, in the lowest degree, qualified for his office, he must know better." Bates then summed up the problem with a remarkable prophesy: "If the offenders be done to death by that tribunal, however truly guilty, they will pass for martyrs with half the world."[27]

Dr. Samuel Mudd was among those sentenced to prison for his involvement with the conspiracy to assassinate the president. The pro-Confederate Maryland physician was convicted by the commission and sentenced to life in prison for providing shelter and medical assistance to conspirators John Wilkes Booth and David Herold at his home on the night of Lincoln's assassination. Mudd also was convicted of having supplied the conspirators with horses the following day so that they could continue in their escape.[28] During his trial, Dr. Mudd argued that the Hunter Commission lacked jurisdiction and that his trial before the commission violated his constitutional right to a trial by jury in a civilian court with all its protections.

After the commission and Attorney General James Speed rejected Mudd's argument, he petitioned the U.S. District Court for the Southern District of Florida for a writ of habeas corpus.[29] By then, the U.S. Supreme Court had decided *Ex parte Milligan*, which held that although the suspension of habeas corpus is permissible, it cannot be used to try individuals in military courts captured away from the battlefield where civilian courts are still functioning.[30]

In September 1868, Judge Thomas Jefferson Boynton denied Mudd's petition on the basis that Lincoln's murder was a military crime, notwithstanding that the Civil War had ended prior to the president's assassination.[31] He reasoned that the president's assassination was an attempt to impair the effectiveness of military operations.[32] After all, the president is the commander in chief of the army, and thus it was not just the president who was assassinated, but the commander in chief. While serving his prison sentence, Mudd appealed Judge Boynton's decision to the U.S. Supreme Court, but when the case finally reached the high court, President Johnson already had fully and unconditionally pardoned Dr. Mudd for his service in battling a yellow fever epidemic at the Florida prison, and therefore Chief Justice Chase dismissed the case as moot.[33]

More than a century later, his great-grandson, Dr. Richard D. Mudd, filed an application with the Army Board for Correction of Military Records (ABCMR), seeking a declaration that Mudd had been innocent and that the military commission had lacked jurisdiction to try a Maryland citizen when fully functioning civil courts existed in Maryland that were competent to have tried Dr. Mudd. His great-grandson's argument focused on the Supreme Court's precedent in *Milligan*.[34]

By then, however, the legal landscape had changed again. In 1942, the U.S. Supreme Court decided *Ex parte Quirin*, a decision that held that although *Milligan* foreclosed the possibility of using military commissions to try individuals captured away from the battlefield where civilian courts are still functioning, when those individuals are uniformed, unlawful enemy combatants, they are subject to trial and punishment by military tribunals.[35]

After a hearing, the ABCMR found that it was not authorized to consider the actual innocence or guilt of Dr. Mudd, but it unanimously concluded that the commission had not had jurisdiction to try him and recommended that his conviction therefore be set aside.[36] In 2001, the U.S. District Court for the District of Columbia dismissed Dr. Mudd's great-grandson's appeal, finding that under *Ex parte Quirin*, "if Dr. Samuel Mudd was charged with a law of war violation, it was permissible for him to be tried before a military commission even though he was a United States and Maryland citizen and the civilian courts were open at the time of the trial."[37]

Although notions of justice change over time, even in 2001, a U.S. federal court applying modern-day law concluded that the use of military commissions was proper. At the time the decision was made to try the conspirators before the military commission, the Civil War was largely over, but unquestionably, a state of war still existed in Washington, DC. The city remained fortified and a declaration of martial law continued in place until August 20, 1866, more than a year after the trial.[38] Those circumstances cannot be ignored when passing judgment on the propriety of trial of the conspirators by military commission.

It is less likely that a court today would conclude that the process employed by the military commission was fair. Procedural due process would militate against the processes employed in the trial of the conspirators. However, even with all its procedural shortcomings, the military commission that tried the conspirators delivered justice. As assassination scholar Thomas R. Turner has observed, there is nothing to suggest that a civil jury would have been any more lenient than the military commission: "The members of the military commission seem to have been driven by the same emotional currents as the general public and the verdict of the commission was probably very similar to the decision that would have been rendered by a civil jury."[39] In the end, the commissions, judged by the law and societal norms of 1865, delivered justice.

Notes

1. Edwin Percy Whipple, *The Great Speeches and Orations of Daniel Webster* (Boston: Little Brown and Co., 1879), 533.

2. Frederick Hatch, *The Lincoln Assassination Conspiracy Trial and Its Legacy* (Jefferson, NC: McFarland Books, forthcoming).

3. Portions of this chapter are adapted from Frank J. Williams and Nicole J. Benjamin, "Military Trials of Terrorists: From the Lincoln Conspirators to the Guantanamo Inmates," *Northern Kentucky Law Review* 39 (2012): 609.

4. Anthony S. Pitch, *They Have Killed Papa Dead! The Road to Ford's Theatre, Abraham Lincoln's Murder, and the Rage for Vengeance* (Hanover, NH: Steerforth 2008), 313–14.

5. *Official Opinions of the Attorney General of the United States, Advising the President and Heads of Departments in Relation to Their Official Duties* 10 (Washington, DC: W. H. and O. H. Morrison, 1868), 81.

6. "Trial of the Assassins," *New York Times*, May 15, 1865.

7. During the Civil War, the Union army conducted at least 4,271 trials of U.S. citizens by military commission and another 1,435 during the Reconstruction period that followed. *United States v. Hamdan*, CMCR 09–002, 2011 U.S. CMCR LEXIS 1 at *135–36 (U.S. Ct. Mil. Comm. Rev. June 24, 2011).

8. Pitch, *They Have Killed Papa Dead*, 315.

9. James H. Johnston, "Swift and Terrible: A Military Tribunal Rushed to Convict after Lincoln's Murder," *Washington Post*, December 9, 2001, F01; "Trial of the Assassins," *New York Times*, May 15, 1865.

10. "Trial of the Assassins."

11. Thomas R. Turner, "What Type of Trial? Civil versus a Military Trial for the Lincoln Assassination Conspirators," *Journal of the Abraham Lincoln Association* 4 (1982): 35, 37; Vaughan Shelton, *Mask for Treason: The Lincoln Murder Trial* (Mechanicsburg, PA: Stackpole Books, 1965), 60–61.

12. Pitch, *They Have Killed Papa Dead*, 314.

13. Benn Pitman, *The Assassination of President Lincoln and the Trial of the Conspirators* (Lexington: University Press of Kentucky, 2003), 64.

14. Elizabeth Steger Trindal, *Mary Surratt: An American Tragedy* (Gretna, LA: Pelican Publishing Co., 1996), 150.

15. *The Trial of the Assassins and Conspirators at Washington City, D.C., May and June 1865 for the Murder of President Abraham Lincoln* (Philadelphia: T. B. Peterson and Brothers, 1865), 21.

16. Pitman, *Assassination of President Lincoln*, 46–62.

17. Ibid.

18. *Trial of the Assassins and Conspirators*, 158.

19. "Trial of the Assassins."

20. *Ex parte Milligan*, 71 U.S. 2, 127, 131 (1866).

21. Trindal, *Mary Surratt*, 203.

22. Robert Watson Winston, *Andrew Johnson: Plebeian and Patriot* (New York: H. Holt and Co., 1928), 288.

23. Ibid., 210.

24. "Legality of the Conspiracy Trial: Opinion of Attorney-General Speed," *New York Times*, August 13, 1865, 3.

25. James Speed, *Opinion on the Constitutional Power of the Military to Try and Execute the Assassins of the President* (Washington, DC: Government Printing Office, 1865).

26. Gideon Welles, *Diary of Gideon Welles: Secretary of the Navy under Lincoln and Johnson*, with an introduction by John T. Morse, Jr., 3 vols. (Boston: Houghton Mifflin Co., 1911), 2:304.

27. Howard K. Beale, *The Diary of Edward Bates, 1859–1866* (Washington, DC: U.S. Government Printing Office, 1933), 483.

28. *Mudd v. Caldera*, 134 F. Supp. 2d 138 (D.D.C. 2001).

29. Jeffrey F. Addicott, *Terrorism Law: The Rule of Law and the War on Terror*, 2nd ed. (Tucson, AZ: Lawyers and Judges Publishing Company, 2004), 100.

30. *Ex parte Milligan*, 71 U.S. 2, 127, 131 (1866).

31. Addicott, *Terrorism Law*, 100.

32. Susan Low Bloch and Ruth Bader Ginsberg, "Celebrating the 200th Anniversary of the Federal Courts of the District of Columbia," *Georgetown Law Journal* 90 (2002): 549, 449n42.

33. *Mudd v. Caldera*, 134 F. Supp. 2d 138.

34. *Ex parte Milligan*, 71 U.S. 2, 127, 131 (1866).

35. *Ex parte Quirin*, 317 U.S. 1, 22 (1942).

36. *Mudd v. Caldera*, 26 F. Supp. 2d 117.

37. *Mudd v. Caldera*, 134 F. Supp. 2d 146.

38. E. B. Long and Barbara Long, *Civil War Day by Day* (Cambridge, MA: Da Capo Press, 1983), 696.

39. Turner, "What Type of Trial?," 30.

8

Allies or Adversaries? Lincoln, Douglass, and Black Suffrage

Edna Greene Medford

$\mathcal{F}$rederick Douglass never let custom or tradition restrict his thinking or limit his actions. Hence, when Abraham Lincoln was inaugurated for the second time in March 1865, the former fugitive from slavery invited himself to the inaugural reception. As Douglass recalled years later, his presence at the entrance caused a bit of a stir among the White House guards, who, unaccustomed to people of color seeking admission to such events, barred his entry. Luckily, a passerby recognized him, and Douglass was able to enlist the man's aid, requesting that he inform Lincoln of the situation. Shortly thereafter, Douglass and his companion were admitted to the East Room, where he had a brief but cordial conversation with the president. Lincoln purportedly asked Douglass what he thought of the inaugural address, declaring to the man who had criticized his policies for much of the war that he valued no one's opinion more. According to Douglass, he assured Lincoln that the address was "a sacred effort."[1]

Douglass's encounter with Lincoln at the inaugural reception was only the third time that the two men had met. The first had been in August 1863, when Douglass requested a meeting with the president to discuss the injustices suffered by black soldiers. He was concerned particularly with pay inequities: although white enlisted soldiers received $13 per month *and* a $3 clothing allowance, the Militia Act of 1862 had established a plan of compensation for black military laborers such that African American men were paid only $10 per month with $3 *withheld* for clothing. Douglass insisted that the equal burden that black men bore in military service demanded that they receive equal compensation. Lincoln reminded Douglass that many white Americans had not supported the employment of black soldiers and that the lower rate of pay was a concession to that resistance. Lincoln counseled him to be patient and suggested that the inequity would be corrected once white Americans had grown more receptive to black men in arms. That moment came in June 1864, when Congress passed legislation to compensate black men at the same rate as their white counterparts.[2]

The second meeting, initiated by Lincoln, took place on August 19, 1864. This time the president was seeking Douglass's aid in facilitating the flight of African American men and women out of the Confederacy. Fearing that he would be forced to negotiate a premature peace with the rebels or that he might lose the fall election to a Democrat likely to rescind the Emancipation Proclamation, he asked Douglass to devise a plan to inform the enslaved residents of the Confederacy of the proclamation and to help them make their way to Union lines. After a period of deliberation, Douglass spoke confidentially with a few black friends and drew up a plan of action. Efforts at rescue proved unnecessary, however, as Union military fortunes improved and concerns about negotiation and a Democratic victory diminished.[3]

Sometime after the second inauguration, the president invited the abolitionist to join him at the Soldiers' Home, Lincoln's summer retreat on the outskirts of the city, but Douglass declined because of a prior commitment.[4] Hence, the inaugural reception marked the final time that the two men would meet. The incident was extraordinary, not simply because a black man dared crash the president's party or because the president appeared perfectly pleased with the intrusion. That Lincoln would be elected for a second term at all had remained uncertain through much of 1864. Even he had not been confident that victory was likely. The poor performance of Union troops on the battlefield and political opposition from elements throughout the North had suggested that Lincoln was headed for defeat.

In a sense, Lincoln's reelection was a victory for Douglass as well. The abolitionist had spent the first two years of the war pressing for a black military presence, equal treatment of black men once they were allowed to enlist, and freedom for the enslaved. Lincoln had helped realize these goals. A new president, especially if that man were George McClellan, could compromise hard-won gains, perhaps even crush the cause of black freedom.

Despite their limited contact, much has been made of the relationship between the president and the former bondman. Little direct information exists of what Lincoln thought of Douglass. Hence, we must rely primarily on Douglass's reports of Lincoln's cordiality at their three meetings. Mary Lincoln's later gift to Douglass of the president's favorite cane and Douglass's gracious note to her in response strengthen the argument that the two men respected and even liked each other. In gratitude for the gift, Douglass had written:

Dear Madam:

Allow me to thank you, as I certainly do thank you most sincerely for your thoughtful kindness in making me the owner of a cane which was formerly the property and the favorite walking staff of your late lamented husband—the honored and venerated President of the United States. I assure you, that this inestimable memento of his Excellency will be retained in my possession while I live—an object of sacred interest—a token not merely of the kind consideration in which I have reason to know that the President was pleased to hold me personally, but as an indication of his humane interest [in the] welfare of my whole race. With every proper sentiment of Respect and Esteem, I am, Dear Madam your obedt Servt.

Frederick Douglass[5]

A mutual respect had developed despite Lincoln's tendency toward cautiousness and Douglass's penchant for bold action. That respect survived even as the war neared its end and both men turned their attention to contemplating the political role African Americans would play in the reconstructed South. Characteristically, Lincoln assumed a moderate position, carefully weighing public opinion, while Douglass, impatient for change after having spent a lifetime in struggle, pressed vigorously for full participation in the political process.

For much of the war, Douglass had been an unapologetic critic of the Lincoln administration's policies regarding African Americans in general and the enslaved in particular. The man who had secured his own freedom through flight from slavery would not, indeed could not, accept the Lincoln administration's initial determination to keep the war's aim narrowly focused on Union rather than expanding it more expeditiously to include the liberation of black people. Douglass castigated the administration at every turn, especially for the tendency of some military commanders to return fugitives seeking asylum within Union lines to those who claimed ownership of them. He was no less agitated by the Lincoln administration's early refusal to permit black men to serve as soldiers. He reminded the administration that the slaveholders "have neither pride, prejudice nor *pity* to restrain them from employing Negroes *against white men, where slavery is to be protected and made secure.* Oh! that this Government would only now be as true to liberty as the rebels, who are attempting to batter it down, are true to slavery. . . . Every consideration of justice, humanity and sound policy confirms the wisdom of calling upon black men just now to take up arms on behalf of their country."[6]

The Emancipation Proclamation, which promised freedom to those in Confederate-held territory and the acceptance of black soldiers into the Union ranks, had helped temper Douglass's criticism, but it had not quashed it entirely. For a brief time during the 1864 presidential campaign, Douglass had contemplated giving his support to a Lincoln challenger. This notion subsided when the Democrats nominated McClellan, someone wholly unacceptable to Douglass and the abolitionists. Yet Lincoln's victory did not completely erase old concerns that had divided the two in the past.

Central to this continued division was the issue of African American citizenship and equality. Douglass and other black leaders had long before defined true freedom as the right and opportunity to share equally in all that America had to offer. In fact, a key incentive for black enlistment in the Union military, he claimed, was that once African Americans had risked all for their country by shouldering arms in its defense, it would be difficult, if not impossible, to deny them the rights of all other Americans.[7]

Acquisition of the elective franchise—for Douglass and other African Americans, a crucial ingredient of citizenship—occupied a central position in the aspirations of men who heretofore had been denied its enjoyment. On the eve of the Civil War, in only five states—Maine, Vermont, New Hampshire, Massachusetts, and Rhode Island—did black men have equal access to voting. In New York, property qualifications hampered the franchise for African Americans but did not restrict white men in the state. In 1860, despite a valiant effort on the part of African American men and their supporters, white New York voters overwhelmingly failed to approve a constitutional amendment that would have ended such discrimination against the state's black residents.[8]

All across the country, from coast to coast and from Wisconsin to Louisiana, African Americans took advantage of the disruptions of war to press for the right to vote. They petitioned state legislatures, threatened to withhold support for the Union until they received the same rights as other men, and laid their case before Congress and the president. In the fall of 1864, African Americans met in a national convention in Syracuse—144 delegates representing eighteen states, including seven in the Confederacy—where they expressed their dissatisfaction with the disabilities imposed on them. The call to meet in convention noted some of the issues with which the conveners were concerned: sound moral values, education, temperance, frugality, industry and thrift—"everything that pertains to a well-ordered and dignified life." The subsequent document the convention generated devoted considerable attention to political rights. The delegates called for the elective franchise for African Americans in all those states currently in the Union and all that would hereafter join in national affiliation. They pointed out that the argument that black men were not entitled to political rights because they did not provide military service would no longer withstand scrutiny, since as many as two hundred thousand African Americans were now serving the federal cause. And finally, they declared that they wanted and were entitled to such rights because, simply, "We are men, and want to be as free in our native country as other men."[9]

Lincoln's position on racial equality and black citizenship is often considered in the context of either his infamous Charleston speech of 1858 or his final public address given just three days before his assassination. The Charleston speech proclaimed that the then-Republican senatorial candidate would have nothing to do with black equality. In his effort to rebut incumbent senator Stephen A. Douglas's allegation that Lincoln *championed* racial equality, Lincoln had declared, "I am not, nor ever have been in favor of bringing about in any way, the social and political equality of the white and black races,—that I am not nor ever have been in favor of making voters or jurors of negroes, nor of qualifying them to hold office, nor to intermarry with white people . . . there is a physical difference between the white and black races which I believe will forever forbid the two races living together on terms of social and political equality."[10] But four years of war tempered Lincoln's views. A letter purportedly written by the president to General James S. Wadsworth sometime between December 3, 1863, and May 1864 suggests that Lincoln was willing to pair universal amnesty for the secessionists with universal suffrage for African Americans, although he signaled a willingness to qualify the latter, declaring that suffrage should be extended "on the basis of intelligence and military service."[11]

The letter to Wadsworth reveals what Lincoln believed to be his obligation: to do what was in the best interest of the freed men and women. "How to better the condition of the colored race has long been a study which has attracted my serious and careful attention," he wrote. "Hence I think I am clear and decided as to what course I shall pursue in the premises, regarding it a religious duty, as the nation's guardian of these people." But Lincoln's attitude was also shaped by long-standing notions of slavery's degrading impact on the black masses, by the recognition that certain classes of black men already possessed credentials—as defined by

Lincoln and many other men of his day—that prepared them for citizenship, and by a genuine gratitude for the service rendered by black men in defense of the Union. Lincoln believed that the intellect of many African Americans had been "clouded by Slavery" and that they would need the example and guidance of "intelligent colored men" to reverse the effects.[12] In August 1862, he had proposed that those men—many of whom had been free before the war—should be willing to lead the masses in an exodus from the country. Under their leadership, he argued, freed people could find the equality through colonization that surely would be denied to them in America.[13] Now, less than two years later, he was suggesting that perhaps those elites, if given political rights, could serve as examples right here at home.

Lincoln had also changed his mind about the usefulness of black men in uniform. During the first two years of the war, he had consistently rejected the notion that they could or should be engaged to fight for the Union. He had once believed that men conditioned to fear those who asserted ownership of their bodies could not confront them on the battlefield. Within weeks, he thought, Union arms would be in the hands of the enemy. But the bravery of black men in battle had convinced him otherwise: "[They] have so heroically vindicated their manhood on the battle-field, where, in assisting to save the life of the Republic, they have demonstrated in blood their right to the ballot, which is but the humane protection of the flag they have so fearlessly defended. The restoration of the Rebel States to the Union must rest upon the principle of civil and political equality of both races; and it must be sealed by general amnesty."[14]

Lincoln introduced his Proclamation of Amnesty and Reconstruction on December 8, 1863. By its provisions, he pardoned those who consented to an oath of allegiance and restored their rights and property, with the exception of their enslaved laborers. Exempt from this amnesty were certain classes of secessionists, including civil or diplomatic officers of the Confederacy; military officers above the rank of colonel in the army or lieutenant in the navy; and those who had taken oaths of allegiance to the federal government and had left those positions to aid the Confederacy. The seceded states would be returned to the Union when one-tenth of the voters in the 1860 election had sworn allegiance and constructed new state governments. As concerned the disposition of the freed people, Lincoln offered his support for any measures that would "recognize and declare their permanent freedom, provide for their education, and may yet be consistent, as a temporary arrangement, with their present condition as a laboring, landless, and homeless class."[15] This statement signaled his support for a period of apprenticeship, although he did not make it a requirement. And sensing, perhaps, that the public was not quite ready for black political participation, he remained silent on the matter of enfranchisement.

By March 1864, however, Lincoln was ready to share his thoughts about black voting rights at least privately with Michael Hahn, the newly elected governor of Louisiana. After congratulating Hahn for being elected the first governor of a free Louisiana, Lincoln moved to the issue of the elective franchise. He wondered if the state would be willing to admit African Americans to the body politic, "the very intelligent and especially those who have fought gallantly in our ranks," those who in the future might help to "keep the jewel of liberty within the family of freedom." Lincoln was quick to add that this was "only a suggestion, not to the public, but to you alone."[16] Unfortunately, his modest attempt to influence Louisiana did not bear fruit. When the state adopted a new constitution in September, it failed to include a provision for black enfranchisement. Instead, it authorized the legislature to determine such matters, thus making it unlikely that African Americans would ever enjoy suffrage in the state.

Lincoln's March 13 letter to Governor Hahn had followed by one day a visit by a delegation of free black men from New Orleans, who had presented the president with a petition signed by one thousand fellow residents of the city. Jean Baptiste Roudanez and Arnold Bertonneau represented the "very intelligent" African Americans that Lincoln thought deserving of enfranchisement. They were well-educated men of property and standing in their community, *gens de couleur* who enjoyed certain rights unknown to other free blacks, except suffrage. The petition they delivered described the signatories as descendants of those men who had fought with Andrew Jackson in the 1815 Battle of New Orleans, twenty-seven of whom claimed to have actually served with Jackson themselves. They cited the service they had rendered to the nation as soldiers in the current war and reminded the president that they were obligated to pay taxes on their landholdings, just like other citizens. Yet they could not participate in the reorganization of their state. They asked that political rights be extended to all natives of Louisiana of African descent, especially to those who had "indicated their right to vote by bearing arms."[17]

Despite Louisiana's negative response to his clandestine inquiry about black suffrage, Lincoln decided to make his thoughts public just three days before his assassination. Robert E. Lee had just surrendered his Army of Northern Virginia to General Ulysses S. Grant, ensuring Union victory. On such a momentous occasion, Lincoln took the opportunity to elaborate on his vision for reunification and respond to criticism that he had not exerted sufficient influence over Louisiana to include black enfranchisement in its new state constitution. In a speech delivered from a window of the White House, he offered as positive an interpretation of events as was possible. He asserted that he favored voting rights for the educated and the soldiers, and he hinted at disappointment that the state had not seen fit to extend that right. But he was encouraged by what the constitutional convention had accomplished. In his estimation, it was better to accept Louisiana back into the Union, even if the state had not resolved all its issues, rather than to deny its admission. He was encouraged by the support for ratification of the recently circulated Thirteenth Amendment among the organizers of the new government, their intention to provide public schools to black and white students alike, and the decision to give the legislature the authority to extend voting rights to black men at some future date. Rejection of the new state constitution because it did not immediately offer the elective franchise would delay readmission of the state and postpone even longer the time when black men might be accepted as voters.[18]

Lincoln's acceptance of black political rights obviously had been in advance of the views of most white Americans. Despite the efforts of black soldiers and sailors, and the general support African American civilians rendered to the Union cause, white Americans, with notable exceptions, found it difficult at best to conceive of black men securing equal access to the polls. And for pro-slavery, pro-secessionist men such as John Wilkes Booth, who was in the audience listening to Lincoln's speech on April 11, the idea was absolutely abhorrent. Lincoln's public pronouncement of his views on political equality convinced Booth that the president stood in the way of protecting the rights of white men.

Lincoln's moderate stance on black political rights appeared conservative in comparison to Douglass's views. As the demise of slavery had become more apparent, the famed orator had spoken repeatedly of his vision for black people in a postslavery America. At a dinner in Boston honoring Roudanez and Bertonneau, Douglass had argued that such men would be the future friends of the national government. Once the traitors had been defeated in the South, these black men would help restore the region's political integrity. Douglass urged his audience to use their influence "not so much for the abolition of slavery," as it was already doomed, "but for the complete, absolute, unqualified enfranchisement of the colored people of the South." Such enfranchisement, he insisted, not only would enable black men to serve as voters, but would give them the right to stand for election and hold public office as well.[19]

In the fall of 1864, the former bondman had taken his campaign for political equality south of the Mason-Dixon Line. The occasion was his return to Baltimore, where African Americans could now enjoy the freedom implemented by state action. Douglass was there to offer his congratulations but to make an appeal as well. "Make your good work complete and perfect," he urged white Marylanders, by ensuring "absolute civil and political equality." Declaring that any attack on liberty was harmful in a free society, he warned them to "keep any part of slavery above ground, now that the monster is dead. Let the shadow and the substance go down together, and let them sleep forever, in a common grave."[20] A shared purpose and common destiny made it unnecessary to give any man advantage over another. Douglass argued that white men should abandon the prejudices that heretofore excluded black men from enjoyment of law and justice: "If the negro knows enough to pay taxes, he knows enough to vote; if the negro can form an opinion respecting the claims of rival candidates and parties, and knows good from evil . . . he knows enough to vote. If he knows an honest man from a thief, he knows enough to vote. If he knows enough to commit crime and to be hanged or imprisoned, he knows enough to vote. If he knows enough to fight for his country when assailed by invasion from abroad, or rebellion at home, he knows enough to vote."[21]

Douglass addressed some of his remarks to the newly freed population as well. He urged them to remain in the countryside where they could secure labor, to acquire land and farm independently, to build schools and educate themselves and their children. And he urged them to strive to become the equal of white men. The man who had accomplished so much in his own life told them that "all men are equal naturally, but not practically." White men currently excelled in the sciences and the arts, but black men had the capacity for greatness. Through continuous effort, he declared, black men and women would be able to achieve all that was now the domain of white men and women.[22]

As the new year began, Douglass had intensified his efforts for political equality. He identified as the "fundamental principle of the reorganization of the South" the "absolute and complete enfranchisement of the entire black population of the South." He conceded that slavery was dying but warned that the Union might still be lost. Believing that the Confederacy might offer freedom, land, and the elective franchise to enslaved men who took up arms in defense of Southern independence, Douglass urged fellow Northerners to eliminate discrimination against men on the basis of race and adopt the idea that all who fought for the Union should "be invested with perfect and unqualified citizenship."[23] And to those who sought to solve the problem of race by encouraging colonization, he warned that black men and women had no intention of embracing self-deportation. Hence, the nation would have to determine what status they would occupy—an elevated position or a degraded one. Granting the elective franchise to black men, Douglass continued, would ensure loyalty to the nation. Black men cloaked in citizenship would "not merely give you ramparts of sand and granite, but they will give you ramparts of noble breasts, and human hearts, and steel and iron arms to uphold your government."[24]

A few weeks later, on the eve of the House of Representatives' passage of the resolution to send the Thirteenth Amendment to the states for ratification, Douglass repeated his argument for black enfranchisement while addressing attendees at the annual meeting of the Massachusetts Anti-Slavery Society in Boston. Irate over General Nathaniel Banks's policy toward the freed people in Louisiana, in which he forced them to accept labor contracts for fixed wages, Douglass offered a compelling case for why black men needed voting rights. The freedmen in Louisiana, he charged, had no control over either the duration of their labor or the rate of compensation, and they had no means of correcting this injustice. Without political protection, he argued, "you might as well almost retain the old name of slavery for his condition; for I fear, if he is not the slave of the individual master, he is the slave of society, and holds his liberty as a privilege, not as a right. He is at the mercy of the mob, and has no means of protecting himself."[25]

Douglass believed that black suffrage advantaged the country as well. He warned that a defeated South did not guarantee a peaceful one. It would take time for men certain of their cause to accept defeat. Enmity would linger, and some would dare disrupt the federal government. During these dangerous times, the national government would need to rely on its friends, on those who had remained loyal throughout the war despite the government's sometimes less than honorable behavior toward them. "They are our only friends in the South," he argued, "and we should be true to them in this their trial hour, and see to it that they have the elective franchise." To those who would argue that the franchise was premature and that black men were inferior, Douglass considered this "an old dodge," employed to justify the oppression of one group by another. He hoped that the nation would not "reward [its] enemies and trample in the dust [its] friends." When the nation was in trouble, it called upon black men to aid in its survival. "In time of trouble we are citizens," he pointed out and asked, "Shall we be citizens in war, and aliens in peace?"[26]

A few short months later, the man who could join forces with Douglass to assist him in fulfilling his quest lay dead, the victim of an assassin who could not abide black citizenship. In an address at Cooper Union on June 1, 1865, Douglass paid homage to the martyred president. "No people or class of people in the country have a better reason for lamenting the death of Abraham Lincoln, and for desiring to honor and perpetuate his memory, than have the colored people," he declared. "When measured against the actions of those who came before him, many of whom were merely the facile and servile instruments of the slave power," Abraham Lincoln was "in a sense hitherto without example, emphatically the black man's president: the first to show any respect for their rights."[27] Reiterating this sentiment near the end of the year, Douglass argued that if Lincoln had lived, "the negro of the south would have more than a hope of enfranchisement, and no rebels could hold the reins of Government in any one of the rebellious states. Whosoever else has cause to mourn the loss of Abraham Lincoln, to the Colored people of the country—his death is an unspeakable calamity."[28]

After Lincoln's assassination, Douglass and fellow abolitionists continued to press for political equality. In February 1866, a group of black leaders visited President Andrew Johnson after having met in convention, where they had discussed the issue of enfranchisement. The meeting with Johnson proved wholly unsatisfactory to the delegation. To their request that he support their effort to secure voting rights, the president argued that pressing for the franchise would lead to racial warfare. If the black man was dissatisfied with his position in America, then he could emigrate to a more agreeable place. The delegation left the White House fully aware that they had found no friend in Johnson but determined nonetheless to pursue their rights to the fullest. Douglass, a member of the delegation, quickly penned a reply to the president that was published in one of the local newspapers. He charged that Johnson's remarks had been "entirely unsound and prejudicial to the highest interest of our race as well as our country at large." He countered the argument that the hostility between black men and poor white men, cultivated under slavery, would continue into freedom. Even if that were true, he argued, peace "is not to be secured by degrading one race and exalting another, by giving power to one race and withdrawing it from another."[29]

African Americans would not enjoy the right of suffrage until 1870, when Congress passed and the requisite number of states ratified the Fifteenth Amendment. Once in receipt of voting rights, black men offered overwhelming support to Lincoln's Republican Party and, with Unionist allies in the South, helped enact legislation that sought to promote programs beneficial to all the region's people. That victory was short-lived, however; within a few decades, illegal and extralegal restraints and finally legislative assaults would dismantle the franchise that black men had labored to secure.

In confronting the issue of black suffrage, both Lincoln and Douglass had remained true to their nature. The president had tested the will of white men to extend to black men what the former enjoyed as a consequence of birth. When Louisiana would not accept the idea of suffrage for even a limited number of African Americans, Lincoln had concluded that a bold defense of universal enfranchisement would not meet with public favor. Hence, he proposed a plan of action that he hoped would appeal to the nation's sense of fairness and gratitude. Contrarily, Douglass would be satisfied with nothing less than full and unimpeded equality, especially since black men had fulfilled their promise to the nation. Ceding any ground on the issue was unthinkable and a betrayal of the men who had given their lives to the cause of freedom.

Despite their seemingly irreconcilable positions on black suffrage, the two men were perhaps not that far apart. Certainly, the willingness to extend the franchise to black elites—men of education and property—while excluding the masses suggests a degree of classism that was unacceptable to someone of Douglass's origins and sensibilities. But Lincoln's plan to include black military men in the body politic virtually ensured the eventual inclusion of the common folk from whose ranks many of these men had come and for whose freedom they had fought.

Notes

1. Frederick Douglass, *Autobiographies* (New York: Library of America, 1984), 803–4.

2. Douglass, *Autobiographies*, 786–87.

3. Ibid., 795–96. See also Benjamin Quarles, *Lincoln and the Negro* (New York: Da Capo Press, 1991), 215–16.

4. James Oakes, *The Radical and the Republican: Frederick Douglass, Abraham Lincoln, and the Triumph of Antislavery Politics* (New York: W. W. Norton, 2007), 207.

5. Frederick Douglass to Mary Todd Lincoln, Rochester, New York, August 17, 1865, the Gilder Lehrman Institute of American History, http://www.gilderlehrman .org/history-by-era/african-americans-and-emancipation/essays/"your-late-lamented -husband"-letter-from-fr.

6. Frederick Douglass, "How to End the War," in *Frederick Douglass: Selected Speeches and Writings*, ed. Philip Foner, abridged and adapted by Yuval Taylor (Chicago: Lawrence Hill Books, 1999), 448–49.

7. Douglass, "Men of Color, to Arms!" March 21, 1863, *Frederick Douglass*, 526–27.

8. For a discussion of the New York debate over equal voting rights for African Americans, see Phyllis F. Field, *The Politics of Race in New York: The Struggle for Black Suffrage in the Civil War Era* (Ithaca, NY: Cornell University Press, 1982).

9. "The Syracuse National Negro Convention," in *A Documentary History of the Negro People in the United States: From Colonial Times through the Civil War*, ed. Herbert Aptheker, 2 vols. (New York: Citadel Press, 1965), 1:511, 523.

10. Abraham Lincoln, "Fourth Joint Debate, Charleston, Illinois," September 18, 1858, in *Abraham Lincoln: Speeches and Writings, 1832–1858*, ed. Don E. Fehrenbacher (New York: Library of America, 2012), 636.

11. Abraham Lincoln, "Letter to James S. Wadsworth," [January 1864], in *The Collected Works of Abraham Lincoln*, ed. Roy P. Basler, 8 vols. (New Brunswick, NJ: Rutgers University Press, 1953–55), 7:101.

12. Lincoln, "Address on Colonization to a Deputation of Negroes," August 14, 1862, *Collected Works*, 5:372.

13. Douglass's response to Lincoln's solution to the race problem in America had been swift and biting. "In this address, Mr. Lincoln assumes the language and arguments of an itinerant Colonization lecture, showing all his inconsistencies, his pride of race and blood, his contempt for Negroes and his canting hypocrisy," he wrote. "How an honest man could creep into such a character as that implied by this address, we are not required to show." See Douglass, "The President and His Speeches," September 1862, *Frederick Douglass*, 511.

14. Lincoln, "Letter to James S. Wadsworth," *Collected Works*, 7:101–2.

15. Lincoln, Proclamation of Amnesty and Reconstruction, December 8, 1863," *Collected Works*, 7:53–56.

16. Lincoln, "Letter to Michael Hahn," March 13, 1864, *Collected Works*, 7:244.

17. James M. McPherson, ed., *The Negro's Civil War: How American Blacks Felt and Acted during the War for the Union* (New York: Ballantine Books, 1991), 282–83.

18. Lincoln, "Last Public Address," April 11, 1865, *Collected Works*, 8:404.

19. Frederick Douglass, "Representatives of the Future South: An Address Delivered in Boston, Massachusetts, on 12 April, 1864," *Frederick Douglass Papers*, Series 1: *Speeches, Debates and Interviews*, ed. John W. Blassingame and John R. McKivigan, 5 vols. (New Haven, CT: Yale University Press, 1991), 4:27–28.

20. Douglass, "A Friendly Word to Maryland: An Address Delivered in Baltimore, Maryland, on 17 November, 1864," *Frederick Douglass Papers*, 4:46–47.

21. *Frederick Douglass Papers*, 4:50.

22. Ibid.

23. "Black Freedom Is the Prerequisite of Victory: An Address Delivered in New York, New York on 13 January 1865," *Frederick Douglass Papers*, 4:56.

24. *Frederick Douglass Papers*, 4:59.

25. "What the Black Man Wants: An Address Delivered in Boston, Massachusetts, on 26 January 1865," *Frederick Douglass Papers*, 4:60.

26. *Frederick Douglass Papers*, 4:61–62.

27. Frederick Douglass, "Speech at Cooper Union," June 1, 1865, quoted in Michael Burlingame, *Abraham Lincoln: A Life*, 2 vols. (Baltimore: Johns Hopkins University Press, 2008), 2:829–30.

28. Frederick Douglass, "Abraham Lincoln, a Speech," ca. December 1865, Frederick Douglass Papers, Library of Congress.

29. Douglass, "Reply of the Colored Delegation to the President," February 7, 1866," *Frederick Douglass*, 588–89.

9

From Living Hero to Martyred Icon:
The Evolution of the Lincoln Image in 1865
Harold Holzer

On January 24, 1865, a calamitous fire broke out in the picture gallery of Washington's Smithsonian Institution, a building Abraham Lincoln had visited a number of times during his presidency. The blaze proved impossible to extinguish and soon engulfed much of the famous red "castle" landmark. It was "one of the momentous and saddest events of [our] lives," lamented Mary Anna Henry, daughter of the Smithsonian's presiding secretary, Joseph Henry. But then she added an observation that must have occurred not only to the institution's forlorn staff and their families but also to other eyewitnesses to the catastrophe, particularly artists: "Truly it was a grand sight as well as a sad one."[1]

Such a thought surely animated Alexander Gardner, the Washington-based photographer already widely known in the capital and the rest of the North not only for his masterful portraits of national celebrities— Lincoln included—but also for his searing images of dead soldiers and shattered landscapes at Antietam and other Civil War killing grounds. In other words, Gardner was no stranger to disasters; he saw part of his job as recording them for the public. Though his business within the capital was by then devoted principally to portraiture, Gardner still knew a "grand sight" when he saw one, so he quickly dispatched his cameras to record the conflagration at the Smithsonian. Gardner's ambition, however, outdistanced his technology. Apparently, the wet-plate process he used could not accurately record fire or smoke, which flickered and plumed too rapidly to be fixed on glass negatives during the lengthy exposures photography then required. Determined to produce a newsworthy image of the blaze anyway, Gardner offered customers the next best thing: a highly retouched photograph called *Burning of the Smithsonian Institution*, whose enhanced visual effects—a looming black curtain of smoke and overly neat fingers of vivid flame—had obviously been added by an artist, and not a very able one at that. The montage of art and photography, however, proved the closest thing to a genuine pictorial record of the fire.[2]

It is fair to say that Alexander Gardner by this time was no stranger to the confluence of art and photography, nor was his most famous subject, the president. Back in 1861, Lincoln's first sitting with Gardner had been supervised by a painter, George Henry Story. Two years later, Gardner had taken a series of now-famous Lincoln photographs for the exclusive use of a sculptor named Sarah Fisher Ames.[3] Now, just a few days after the Smithsonian fire, Lincoln and Gardner engaged in a similar collaboration that once again combined the two media, photography and painting, in this case to create an unforgettable visual record of Lincoln in what turned out to be the final months of his life.

The effort commenced when Secretary of the Navy Gideon Welles decided to hire a painter he had met in his home city of Hartford, Connecticut, Matthew Henry Wilson, to produce a portrait of the president. Welles wanted a nice painting of his chief to adorn the Navy Department, but as it happened, the resulting portrait reflected Lincoln at a crucial moment in American history: the final House passage of the resolution approving a constitutional amendment to end slavery. In fact, artist Wilson arrived in Washington just in time to rush to the Capitol and witness the tumultuous House session at which the amendment resolution triumphed. A few days later, on February 4, Welles's wife took Wilson to the White House to meet the president and Mary Lincoln. There, the president agreed to pose for the new portrait but apparently told the painter what he had been warning artists for years: he was willing to be painted, as long as the wielders of the brush did not expect him to freeze in place and hold still for prolonged sittings. He simply lacked the time to do so. Wilson responded to the challenge by proposing a remedy that other artists before him—including Thomas Hicks, Thomas M. Johnston, John Henry Brown, and more recently, Edward D. Marchant, Francis B. Carpenter, and Sarah Ames—had adopted: ordering specially commissioned Lincoln photographs to use as models to supplement sittings in the flesh.

Accordingly, the very next day, on February 5, Wilson met Lincoln and, as it turned out, his son Tad at Gardner's gallery on Seventh and D Streets. The primary object of the session was to produce a pose that would function as something of a stand-in for Lincoln, even though Wilson planned to augment the photographic source by producing his finishing touches from life. The artist certainly got what he hoped for, but the public got even more. Gardner produced five known photographs of Lincoln that day, one (fig. 1) featuring the adorable Tad leaning on a table and eyeing his father. The Gardner series also included the legendary out-of-focus, but eerily haunting "cracked plate" image (fig. 2), long mistakenly thought to have been taken in April and assumed to be the final photograph of Lincoln, although it was not. Looking haggard and worn, but barely able to conceal the first smile he had ever revealed at a photographic sitting, the Lincoln in all these February 5 images appears to have been defeated physically by the

PRESIDENT LINCOLN AND HIS SON THADDEUS.

THE LAST PHOTOGRAPH THE PRESIDENT SAT FOR.

Fig. 1. Alexander Gardner, *President Lincoln and His Son Thaddeus* [*sic*]. Photograph, Washington, February 5, 1865. From the Lincoln Financial Foundation Collection, courtesy of the Indiana State Museum and Historic Sites, LN-1464.

Fig. 2. Photograph by Alexander Gardner, Washington, February 5, 1865. From the Lincoln Financial Foundation Collection, courtesy of the Indiana State Museum and Historic Sites, LN-1467.

Fig. 3. Photograph by Alexander Gardner, Washington, February 5, 1865. From the Lincoln Financial Foundation Collection, courtesy of the Indiana State Museum and Historic Sites, OC-0235.

war even as the Union is about to triumph on the battlefield. Never before had the president sat for such raw, poignant, and haunting portraits, and Wilson no doubt gratefully chose one particularly disarming pose among them (fig. 3) as the model for his planned portrait in oils.[4]

Wilson then set up not one but two easels in the president's White House office and commenced painting a pair of portraits simultaneously—one for Welles and one, presciently, to keep for himself and employ as a model from which to make further copies. The artist was not about to let his precious opportunity pass without creating a record of it for his own use. Wilson worked diligently on his paintings through February 20, though whether he did the bulk of his work in the White House or in an artist friend's nearby studio is not known for certain. Wilson's surviving diary does show that one of the few days he missed working on his picture during that productive fortnight was February 12, his subject's fifty-sixth birthday.[5] Did Lincoln perhaps ask for solitude that day in order to observe that special event with his family? No one knows, though records for February 12, 1865, indicate that no such celebration took place; the president spent most of the morning and afternoon focusing only on routine military matters.[6]

A few weeks later, when the first picture was completed, Wilson had it hung up to dry in the presidential office. On Washington's Birthday, February 22, Welles examined the painting during a visit and delightedly pronounced it "a successful likeness." In an especially "cheerful" mood that day, Lincoln agreed, but then he jocularly added that the painting reminded him of the story of a westerner whose wife had commissioned a portrait of her husband as a birthday gift. When she first saw the result on canvas, she commented that she thought it "horridly like" the subject, "and that," Lincoln joked, "seems to me a just criticism of *this*!"[7] As it happened, the picture (fig. 4) soon entered a realm that took it beyond criticism. Matthew Henry Wilson's oil on board proved to be the last painting of Abraham Lincoln from life.

Fig. 4. Portrait from life by Matthew Henry Wilson, Washington, oil on board. From the Lincoln Financial Foundation Collection, courtesy of the Indiana State Museum and Historic Sites, 71.2009.081.0001.

But another life portrait, created in an altogether different medium, vies with Wilson's oil for the title of Lincoln's final artistic likeness. In that same month of February 1865, the well-known sculptor Clark Mills asked for permission to make a life mask of Lincoln to serve as the model for a planned Civil War monument that was to boast an impressive thirty-six heroic figures.[8] As Lincoln no doubt knew, Mills had sculpted the awkward but famous Andrew Jackson equestrian bronze that graced—or, as some said, disgraced—Lafayette Park across from the White House. The Jackson sculpture had once inspired the visiting British novelist William Makepeace Thackeray to wickedly observe, "To see other statues might do Mr. Mills no harm."[9]

Lincoln hesitated to comply with Mills's request for other than artistic reasons. He no doubt recalled the pain he had endured when another sculptor had tugged out his hairs in removing a hardened plaster life mask from his face after a similar sitting five years earlier in Chicago. To his delight, however, Lincoln soon learned that Mills had perfected a new and far less arduous process. For one thing, Mills placed a protective stocking on Lincoln's head to protect his hair. Then, before the mask was completely dry, Mills instructed his famous sitter simply to twitch his face so the mask could come loose in pieces. Mills then caught the fragments in a towel and reassembled them later. The entire sitting took only about fifteen minutes of the president's precious time. But the sculptor never took advantage of his opportunity to produce the statue that he had intended to create from the mask. Perhaps his ambition exceeded his talent.[10]

In the end, only a few nineteenth-century Americans ever viewed the early castings of the haunting Mills life mask (fig. 5), but those who did found the plaster portrait disturbing. So marked was the contrast between the two masks made only five years apart—the first by Leonard Wells Volk in 1860, the second by Mills in 1865—that Lincoln's secretary John Hay could not help mournfully observing how clearly they recorded his beloved boss's unmistakable deterioration in the intervening years:

> The first is of a man, fifty-one, and young for his years. The face has a clean, firm outline; it is free from fat, but the muscles are hard and full; the large mouth is ready to speak, to shout, or laugh . . . it is a face full of energy, of vivid aspiration. The other is so sad and peaceful in its infinite repose that the famous sculptor Augustus Saint-Gaudens insisted, when he first saw it, that it was a death mask. The lines are set, as if the living face, like the copy, had been in bronze; the nose is thin, and lengthened by the emaciation of the cheeks; the mouth is fixed like that of an archaic statue; a look as of one on whom sorrow and

care had done their worst without victory . . . the whole expression is of unspeakable sadness and all-sufficing strength. Yet the peace is not the dreadful peace of death; it is the peace that passeth understanding.[11]

For all his visible weariness, however, Lincoln was recorded twice more by photographers before his death two months later. On March 4, 1865, Alexander Gardner took several extraordinary photographs of the president delivering his Second Inaugural Address on the portico of the U.S. Capitol. Although some of the resulting poses are unavoidably blurry— Lincoln was, after all, in the midst of delivering a speech to a throng of thousands, making it impossible for him to stand still even if he desired to do so—but one or two clearly depict him towering over the wooden rostrum set up for his use and clutching his manuscript as he reads the unforgettable words of national redemption (fig. 6). An additional, long-lost photo discovered only in the 1960s (fig. 7) shows him seated on the portico waiting his turn to speak, looking gigantic and almost majestic in the sunless March chill.

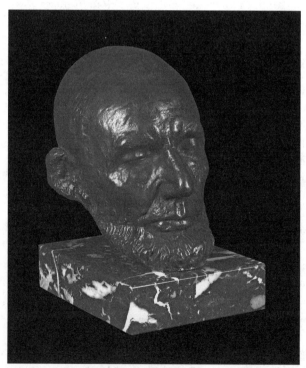

Fig. 5. Life mask by Clark Mills, Washington, February 1865. From the Lincoln Financial Foundation Collection, courtesy of the Indiana State Museum and Historic Sites, 71.2009.081.0838.

Fig. 6. Photograph by Alexander Gardner, the inauguration of Lincoln, Washington, March 4, 1865 (Lincoln delivering his inaugural address). From the Lincoln Financial Foundation Collection, courtesy of the Indiana State Museum and Historic Sites, LN-1588.

Fig. 7. Photograph by Alexander Gardner, the inauguration of Lincoln, Washington, March 4, 1865 (Lincoln seated). Library of Congress.

Just two days later, a visiting Massachusetts photographer named Henry F. Warren encountered the young Tad Lincoln riding his pony outside the White House gates and somehow persuaded him to take his father a message requesting a quick sitting. Lincoln not only obliged but went so far as to carry a chair onto the mansion's south balcony so he could pose in the daylight. But in the surviving prints, which may have taken too much time to arrange, Lincoln looks a bit annoyed that he is being subjected to the tedious process. His beard now reduced to a mere goatee, he squints against the sun and wind, looking even thinner than he had when he was captured by Gardner at the inaugural the previous month. Before very long, he impatiently inquired of Warren, "Is that all, sir?" Warren answered, "Yes, sir," and the brief sitting ended. The one publishable result (fig. 8), which the photographer believed offered a priceless record of the

H. F. Warren,   Waltham, Mass.

THE LATEST PHOTOGRAPH OF

PRESIDENT LINCOLN.

TAKEN ON THE BALCONY AT THE WHITE HOUSE, MARCH 6, 1865.

Fig. 8. Henry F. Warren, *The Latest Photograph of President Lincoln*, Washington, March 6, 1865. From the Lincoln Financial Foundation Collection, courtesy of the Indiana State Museum and Historic Sites, OC-1533.

president's "thought-chiseled and careworn aspect," proved to be the last photograph ever taken of the living Lincoln.[12]

On April 14, Matthew Henry Wilson made yet another entry in his diary: "About 10 was awakened by a commotion in the house and found it arose from the fact that the President had just been shot in the theater. Dressed and went about seeking news, the whole city in a ferment & universal horror & grief expressed." But within six days, Wilson, like many artists of his day, had cast off his depression and recovered sufficiently to turn his attention to the potentially lucrative market for Lincoln memorial portraiture. Within weeks, these enterprising picture makers transformed the hero into a national icon. By April 20, Wilson "began a copy of Mr. Lincoln's portrait for L. Prang & Co., print publishers, Boston." The Prang firm quickly issued a lithographic copy of the Welles-commissioned canvas (fig. 9), which reached the public by May.[13] Wilson earned only $85 from Welles for his original painting, discounted from his prevailing fee of $100 to $150, but selling copies to other patrons and offering the rights to printmaker Prang no doubt turned his project into a financial bonanza.[14]

Other artists similarly went to work reintroducing their existing Lincolns or producing new ones, some merely altering captions to update their recent Lincoln portraits in a manner that now fully acknowledged his martyrdom. Henry Warren, who had issued his photograph in late March as *The Latest Photograph of President Lincoln*, now republished it with a new title, *The Last Photograph of President Lincoln*. Others followed suit. Lincoln did not pass from understanding, to paraphrase John Hay; rather, the murdered president was born again as the nation's most preeminent— and profitable—subject of art, photography, and printmaking. It can be said with certainty that while he was widely portrayed in all artistic media during his presidential years, nothing Lincoln ever did for the picture industry in his life quite benefited it as much as his death. The moment he fell at Ford's Theatre, Lincoln was transformed in public memory from sectional political figure to national secular god. With preachers eulogizing him on the Easter Sunday after his death as a second Messiah, dying for the nation's sins, and as an American Moses, sacrificing his life just as he led people to the promised land, Northern artists not only illustrated but influenced the development of Lincoln's new image as a national saint. And part of that evolution came with embracing visualizations of Lincoln's final hours, however grisly or inaccurate.

"How shall the nation most completely show its sorrow at Mr. Lincoln's death?" the nation's most famous historian, George Bancroft, asked the two thousand people who crowded into Union Square in New York City for a memorial tribute to the fallen president on April 25, just ten days

Fig. 9. L[ouis]. Prang, after Matthew Henry Wilson,
*Abraham Lincoln. Copied by permission from the original
picture by Matthew Henry Wilson—now in possession
of Hon. Gideon Welles, Secy. of the Navy.* Lithograph,
Boston, 1865. From the Lincoln Financial Foundation
Collection, courtesy of the Indiana State Museum and Historic
Sites, 71.2009.081.0466.

after the assassination. "How shall it best honor his memory?"[15] The very
next day, New Yorkers had their answer, and it came from only a few
miles south in lower Manhattan, the crowded center of the city's robust
picture-publishing industry.

That morning, agents of the prominent local lithography firm headed
by Nathaniel Currier and James Merritt Ives arrived at the government
copyright office for the Southern District of New York to register a hastily
drawn but wrenching lithograph of the assassination of the president (fig.
10).[16] By the standards of the mid-nineteenth century, the artistic response
of Currier and Ives to the national tragedy was breathtakingly swift. And
the result provided American print-buying audiences with precisely the
kind of remembrance they could purchase to satisfy their hunger for news
and cherish to testify permanently to their sorrow.

THE ASSASSINATION OF PRESIDENT LINCOLN,
AT FORD'S THEATRE WASHINGTON.D.C.APRIL 14TH 1865.

Published by Currier & Ives, 152 Nassau St New York.

Fig. 10. Currier & Ives, *The Assassination of President Lincoln. At Ford's Theatre Washington, D.C. April 14th 1865*. Lithograph, New York, 1865. From the Lincoln Financial Foundation Collection, courtesy of the Indiana State Museum and Historic Sites, 71.2009.081.0060.

To be sure, this was not the kind of recollection Bancroft had in mind. In his Union Square speech, he had urged New Yorkers to celebrate Lincoln's life rather than dwell on his demise. But New Yorkers had their own ideas. Within days after the Currier and Ives print appeared, customers made it one of the great best-sellers in the history of graphic arts in America. No precise statistics exist to support that claim; the artists' own records did not survive. But judging from the sheer number of copies that remain extant, it was enormously popular.

As a work of graphic art, the lithograph had much to recommend it. Primarily, even though it did not appear for a full eleven days after the event it portrayed, the print still boasted genuine news value. According to the copyright registries for all the major publishing centers of America, the April 26 lithograph was the very first separate-sheet print to show the shooting at Ford's. Inevitably, its hasty production meant that the image was also somewhat flawed. There is certainly no proof, for example, that Lincoln had grasped an American flag at the moment John Wilkes Booth

crept up behind him. And it is difficult to believe that even as alert a theater guest as Major Henry Rathbone was already on his feet lunging for
the assassin just as the shot was fired, as the Currier and Ives print asked
audiences to believe. Yet in a sense, it was appropriate that this was the
assassination print America first saw: a president clutching the emblem of
his beloved Union as he becomes the final casualty of the war to preserve it.
Compared with the rival interpretations that were soon rolling off presses
in New York, Philadelphia, and other publishing centers, the lithograph
was virtually photographic in its accuracy.[17]

Errors also marred a heartfelt but poorly researched assassination scene
produced by an unidentified lithographer and titled *The Martyr of Liberty*
(fig. 11). Here, Lincoln was mistakenly placed in the center of the theater
box, looking as if he were about to plunge over the railing and into the
orchestra seats below. It was typical of the many fanciful assassination
scenes that began appearing for public sale in May and June 1865. Yet this
print was redeemed by the clever inclusion of four lines from Lincoln's
favorite play, Shakespeare's *Macbeth*.[18] "This Lincoln," the verse began,

> Hath borne his faculties so meek; has been
> So clear in his great office that his virtue
> Shall plead, trumpet-tongued, against
> The deep damnation of his taking off.[19]

The lines were entirely fitting and proper, neatly expressing national
sorrow. But Shakespeare originally had Macbeth pronounce the speech
to justify murdering King Duncan because of his "vaulting ambition."
Employed now as a caption for a Lincoln assassination print, it seemed
on the one hand to lament his passing, but on the other to invite justifi-
cation for Booth's murderous act—surely an unintended consequence of
the combination of "art" and literature.

Through such graphics, Americans were at least able to imagine the
great tragic event of their age. But where the Lincoln image was concerned, the prints represented only a beginning or, to be more accurate,
the second coming of a genre that had been dormant at the time: the
production and dissemination of the Lincoln image. The shot that killed
Lincoln may have snuffed out a great life, but it simultaneously breathed
unprecedented vitality into the picture-publishing industry, igniting
a major national demand for what passed at the time for "overnight"
pictures of the slain president. And it renewed demand for all Lincoln
photographs. Not only did American customers buy existing Lincoln
portraits by the thousands to fill their family albums, but engravers and
lithographers also turned to the photographs to serve as source models

THE MARTYR OF LIBERTY

Hath borne his faculties so meek; has been
So clear in his great office; that his virtues
Shall plead, trumpet-tongued, against
The deep damnation of his taking off."

Fig. 11. Printmaker unknown, *The Martyr of Liberty*.
Lithograph, city of publication unknown, 1865. From the Lincoln
Financial Foundation Collection, courtesy of the Indiana State Museum
and Historic Sites, 71.2009.081.0255.

for a new outburst of prints. In this way, the mutually beneficial inter-
dependence of the two media in the production of Lincoln art, with
paintings occasionally added to the mix as well, thrived unabated for
the remainder of the decade.

Though many post-assassination Lincoln prints suffered from poor research, limited imagination, constricting dependence on outmoded photographs as source models, and even occasional fakery, many achieved broad
popularity. And some achieved a timeless quality that makes it easy to
forget that they were part of the frenzied commercial response to Lincoln's
death. Prints inspired by the assassination were not limited to the murder
itself, and in calculating its true impact on Lincoln iconography, modern
audiences should be sensitive to the larger body of work.

The first category of assassination prints includes those that depict the shooting. The second might be called "cause-and-effect" prints. It is difficult to imagine that Americans would have wanted to purchase any pictures of the assassin, but enough curiosity about John Wilkes Booth existed to make the yearning for such pictorial anomalies understandable. Eventually, a carte-de-visite photograph of Booth was even acquired by a family that had more reason than any other to shun it: the Lincolns.[20]

Such photographs boasted unquestionable immediacy and, if unretouched, accuracy, but prints could do what straightforward camera portraits could not: attempt to explain visually, if sometimes unconvincingly, why a well-known stage actor had suddenly resorted to murder. One of the more preposterous of such 1865 prints, crafted by an anonymous artist, claimed that the "theory" behind the murder originated with the pro-slavery, anti-Union Catholic organization known as the Knights of the Golden Circle. Some Northerners seemed eager to believe that the mysterious group had inspired Booth into "practice," the "effect" being the elimination of the president. A similar print actually suggested that a kind of "magic bullet" had been involved in Lincoln's murder, proposing that the projectile, illuminated by a serpent's fiery breath, had enclosed the form and face of a miniature John Wilkes Booth presumably ready to plunge into Lincoln's brain. Did such art convince anyone? Surely not, but it apparently found an audience, so intense was public demand for visual analyses, however absurd, of the act that had deprived the nation of its leader. In the wise words framing the top of this particular print, "Death is not death; 'tis but the ennoblement of mortal man."

At least it seemed a more plausible explanation than that advanced by Philadelphia lithographer J. L. Magee, who suggested in another 1865 lithograph of note that it was Satan himself who tempted a pensive Booth to murder Lincoln (fig. 12). Here, the grotesque figure of the devil is contrasted sharply with that of the hypnotized matinee-idol assassin, as Lincoln is glimpsed in the background from behind, apparently enjoying the play whose conclusion the viewer knows he will never see. The implication is that only the darkest influences could have inflamed Booth to such villainy.

Public curiosity about the events of that Eastertime martyrdom was insatiable, and it also embraced a third type of print response to the assassination: the deathbed scene, as earnestly—and it sometimes seems, as frequently—created as Renaissance depictions of the crucifixion and resurrection. Americans had already learned that after Booth's attack, Lincoln had been carried gingerly across the street into the back bedroom of a boardinghouse, where he lingered for nearly nine hours before breathing

Fig. 12. J. L. Magee, *Satan Tempting Booth to the Murder of the President*. Lithograph, Philadelphia, 1865. From the Lincoln Financial Foundation Collection, courtesy of the Indiana State Museum and Historic Sites, 71.2009.081.0257.

his last on the morning of April 15. That is what Americans read. Beyond these raw and sketchy details, however, particulars could be imagined, and that is precisely what printmakers did.

Again, it was Currier and Ives who set the pace, with another lithograph copyrighted on April 26, 1865, the same day as their assassination print. Like most of the portrayals that soon followed it to the marketplace, this one showed the dying Lincoln without a trace of pain or discomfort. There was no sign of blood in these prints, either, and certainly no evidence of the black pallor that had discolored the president's eye by the morning of his death. His surgeons were usually depicted stoically surrounding his bedside, but not at work, as they periodically were, ill-advisedly probing their patient's wound with unsterilized instruments or plucking blood clots from his wound so bits of brain could ooze forth and stimulate his breathing. Nor was Lincoln's widow depicted in the hysterical frenzy that in reality overtook her that night; instead, she was presented as a calm, resolute woman moving almost gracefully through the event, gowned as if for an inaugural ball.

Like its companion print of the murder, however, the initial deathbed scene by Currier and Ives was not free of errors, such as the insertion of little Tad Lincoln crying on his mother's lap as she sat at the president's bedside. In reality, Tad was never brought to his father's deathbed that night, even though Mary Lincoln more than once cried out that she was sure her comatose husband would awaken if he could only hear the little boy's voice. What is perhaps more surprising, however, is how many details Currier and Ives did get right: the small size of the death chamber, the cluster of shocked witnesses, and even the print-within-the-print on the wall behind the deathbed. Many printmakers subsequently proved unaware, or unwilling to accept, the modest size of the chamber, but nearly all seemed to know that *The Village Blacksmith* had occupied a place in the Petersen House bedroom and took care to insert it into their Lincoln deathbed scenes.

The print by Currier and Ives was the first, and it was fairly accurate, yet the artists were unsatisfied. Within days, they had second thoughts about one major omission from their April 26 print: that of the new chief executive, Andrew Johnson. In a burst of artistic license, they removed General Henry W. Halleck from their group of bedside visitors and re-placed him with Lincoln's soon-to-be successor. In truth, the vice pres-ident's visits to the death chamber had been brief and perfunctory, and Mrs. Lincoln so despised him that it was beyond comprehension that the two could have occupied the same room at the same time, as this version of the print suggested. But with Johnson so included, a print of the last moments of President Lincoln could simultaneously become a print of the first moments of President Johnson and thus represent not only national tragedy but also national continuity in the face of unprecedented crisis. Perhaps that is why the third and final interpretation of Lincoln's death by Currier and Ives (fig. 13) proved the most politically correct, with Johnson advancing closer to the bedside and Mary banished to the doorway, now little more than a silhouette, weeping alone while her husband expired inside—much the way, ironically, events really transpired.

More expensive, lavish, and skillfully marketed deathbed scenes fol-lowed later. One of the most impressively produced and advertised, even if it was not the most historically precise, was a large engraving by Alex-ander Hay Ritchie, the same printmaker who had successfully undertaken the task of mass-producing the authorized adaptation of Francis B. Car-penter's acclaimed 1864 painting of the *First Reading of the Emancipation*

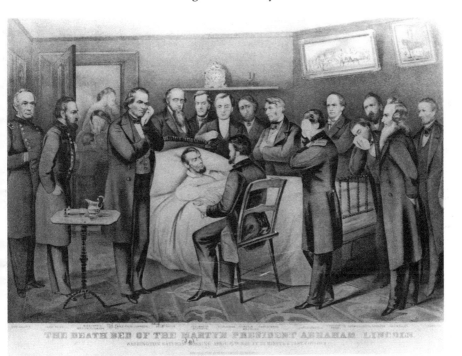

Fig. 13. Currier & Ives, *The Death Bed of the Martyr President Abraham Lincoln. Washington, Saturday Morning April 15th 1865, at 22 Minutes Past 7 O'Clock.* Lithograph, New York, 1865. (Library of Congress) From the Lincoln Financial Foundation Collection, courtesy of the Indiana State Museum and Historic Sites, 71.2009.081.0075.

Proclamation, a print destined to become what was probably the best-selling Lincoln image ever published.

Unfortunately, Ritchie consumed two years producing the painting *The Death of President Lincoln*, which he ultimately engraved himself. If one can believe his claim that he visited the house where Lincoln died to sketch the scene, then he surely came face-to-face there with the almost claustrophobic reality of the tiny chamber. Yet his work (fig. 14) depicted no fewer than twenty-six recognizable onlookers. In Ritchie's imagination, the boardinghouse bedroom took on the proportions of a royal chamber, and within it, Lincoln's final moments had the trappings of the death of a king. At the same time, Ritchie was scrupulous enough to exclude both Vice President Johnson and Mrs. Lincoln.[21]

"There is much variety of pose throughout the composition," a specially produced sales brochure boasted. "Every mind is absorbed by one idea, and we read it on every face." Here, the advertisement suggested, was a subject of irresistibly "deep national interest." Ritchie's print was not only ambitious in conception and large in size (nearly two by three feet) but

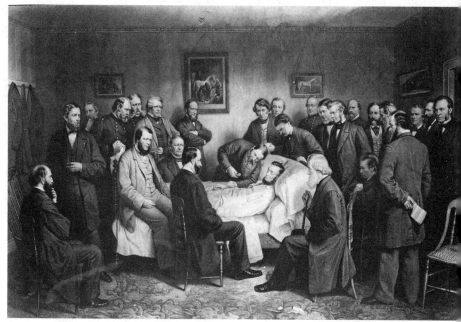

Fig. 14. A. H. Ritchie, *Death of Lincoln*. Engraving, New York, 1868. Library of Congress.

also expensive: $20 for plain proofs and $30 for signed proofs, hefty sums in post–Civil War America. But its promoters argued that it was a bargain for such a priceless "record of the passing history of the nation."[22]

Those portrayed in the scene agreed. The Reverend Phineas Gurley, who had spent three hours beside the deathbed, declared, "It renews to my eye and heart with surprising vividness, the scenes and impressions of that sadly memorable morning." Ritchie's picture was, he said, "a work of surpassing merit." Gideon Welles agreed, calling it "artistic and strikingly impressive of the scene on that memorable and sad occasion." And Quartermaster General Montgomery Meigs, another visitor to the death chamber that night, volunteered his hope "that the engraving may well have a place in thousands of American homes."[23]

But judging by its rarity today, Meigs's hope—and that of engraver Ritchie—went unfulfilled. Perhaps its large size and even larger cost hindered the print's chances for success. Perhaps it simply arrived on the market too late to win the kind of following that had greeted less accurate but more timely interpretations. In the end, however, Ritchie's ambitious project signaled the decline of the vogue for Lincoln deathbed scenes. The American marketplace for such prints had been oversaturated and now included an abundance of not only deathbed interpretations but also dazzling apotheosis scenes imagining Lincoln's subsequent ascent into heaven, including one that showed Lincoln rising from a tomb in a pleated nightshirt as the figures of Faith, Hope, and Charity ushered him into the afterworld (fig. 15). Few of the customers who purchased that particular hand-tinted print would have recognized that it was an adaptation of a George Washington apotheosis scene issued more than six decades earlier, with some of the original symbolic elements appropriate to the first president—including a weeping American Indian and a Masonic symbol—retained even though they had little or nothing to do with the sixteenth president.[24]

Fig. 15. D. T. Wiest, after Mathew Brady, based on a George Washington memorial engraving by John James Barralet after Gilbert Stuart, *In Memory of Abraham Lincoln—the Reward of the Just*. Lithograph, published by William Smith, Philadelphia, 1865. From the Lincoln Financial Foundation Collection, courtesy of the Indiana State Museum and Historic Sites, 71.2009.081.0168.

By then, the Lincoln assassination had inspired other highly popular pictorial genres as well: depictions of Lincoln's many funerals; images of the Lincoln family, none of which, significantly, had appeared before the assassination inspired demand for them; Great Emancipator prints that had been scarce before the assassination placed the late president's most famous act above controversy; portraits showing Lincoln together with his hitherto peerless hero and predecessor, Washington; and most ubiquitous of all, handsome memorial portraits that often framed his image with dedicatory captions identifying the depictions as "sacred to the memory" of the late chief executive—and presumably to the restored Union he had labored to save.

The very first such post-assassination tribute portrait may have appeared as early as a week after Lincoln's death. On that sad anniversary, Moore, Wilstach, and Baldwin advertised in the *Cincinnati Daily Gazette* a timely new Lincoln print priced at fifty cents. Their notice declared, "We will publish on Saturday Morning, April 22d, in tint, on Plate Paper 11 by 14 inches, the most recent, accurate and perfectly engraved Portrait of President Lincoln in the market. Himself, family and friends pronounced it the finest likeness that had been produced." But no copy of such a print has ever come to light. The same issue of that newspaper, however, also offered an advertisement from the printmaking firm of Middleton, Strobridge and Company, heralding their "just published . . . new and beautiful portrait of our late President, in fine Plate Paper, 19 by 24, in black and tint, with gold border," and priced at a dollar each. And this print most likely did appear that weekend. Elijah Middleton had been working on Lincoln lithographs since 1864 and had even elicited a comment on a preliminary proof from the president himself.[25]

But these tribute portraits did not have to boast tints and gold borders to make their point. Another notable martyr portrait of the day signaled its intentions by overtly naming Lincoln "the best beloved of the nation" and surrounding his profile portrait with such heroic symbols as a slain dragon of rebellion, a grateful liberated slave, and the representative figure of the entire nation, Columbia, overcome with emotion at Lincoln's gravesite.[26] Other memorial portraits, including works adapted from original paintings by Francis Carpenter, William Edgar Marshall, and John Littlefield, proved so popular they inspired rival advertising campaigns that featured battling juries of contemporaries who insisted that one or another of them was the best portrait ever made of the late president. For her part, Mary Lincoln favored the Frederick W. Halpin engraving (fig. 16) based on a life study by Carpenter, calling the original from which it was adapted "the most perfect likeness of my husband that I have ever seen." Her son

Robert agreed, stoking the Lincoln portrait wars further by adding, "Mr. Marshall has made a very good portrait, but there is something unsatisfactory about it which I cannot explain, and I would have no hesitation in choosing between the two."[27] Perhaps it was no accident that this family favorite was once again the product of a confluence of artistic media: an engraving by Frederick Halpin based on a painting by Francis Carpenter that had been modeled in part on a photograph by Mathew Brady.[28]

In the end, by canonizing Lincoln in the visual arts for fame and profit, artists forged an indelible legend and earned fame and commercial success in the bargain. They crafted indelible images of a victorious commander in chief struck down in his prime, dying for the nation's sins, and promptly rising into a pantheon of national secular gods. And the creators of these images left few elements of the tragic story uncovered.

Fig. 16. F[rederick]. W. Halpin, after Francis B. Carpenter and Mathew B. Brady, *Abraham Lincoln*. Line and stipple engraving, New York, 1866. From the Lincoln Financial Foundation Collection, courtesy of the Indiana State Museum and Historic Sites, 71.2009.081.0042.

On July 7, 1865, the War Department invited Alexander Gardner to photograph the execution of the Lincoln assassination conspirators. He was the only photographer allowed to record the hanging. Gardner was not alone in his fixation on the Lincoln theme. Throughout the spring and summer of 1865, artist Matthew Henry Wilson continued working away at copy after copy of the last painting of Abraham Lincoln from life, the great work of his career. At one point, he confided that he was laboring on what he complained were "the interminable, everlasting Lincolns."[29] That the popularity of such portraits would indeed be "everlasting," even the exhausted but enriched Wilson could not have predicted. Photographers, printmakers, and painters continued producing Lincoln images for the remainder of the decade, creating the building blocks that would inform and inspire Lincoln iconography for a century and a half to come, eventually in modern media that Lincoln's contemporaries could never even have imagined.

Henry Champion Deming, a Connecticut congressman who got to know Lincoln during the final two years of the president's life, fretted a few months after his death that Lincoln might still "descend the ages according to malicious caricature," so pervasive had been his original highly politicized image in the pictorial arts. But Deming need not have worried. The artists and photographers who so quickly and so inventively responded to Lincoln's death helped permanently transform him from a politician into a hero, and then from a hero into a saint. Through art, a transfigured Lincoln emerged, in the words of the Reverend Henry Bellows, as "the heir of Washington's place at the hearths and altars of the land"—hearths that quickly, and for generations thereafter, boasted revered icons of the national martyr who both triumphed and died in 1865.[30]

Notes

1. Excerpt from the manuscript diary of Mary Anna Henry, January 25, 1865, Collection of the Smithsonian Institution, Washington, DC.

2. D. Mark Katz, *Witness to an Era: The Life and Photographs of Alexander Gardner; The Civil War, Lincoln, and the West* (New York: Viking, 1991), 205, 235. On January 25, the *Washington Daily National Intelligencer* similarly observed, "The appearance of the fire at the Smithsonian yesterday was at once grand and saddening. We are glad to learn that Mr. Gardner was on the ground, and took photographs." Author Errol Morris ingeniously used the Smithsonian fire to introduce a four-part online discussion on 1865 Lincoln images, and I am indebted to him for including me in the discussion and for inspiring this entry point into the story of iconography in Lincoln's final year. See Errol Morris, "The Interminable, Everlasting Lincolns," *Opinionator* (blog), *New York Times*, December 1–4, 2013, http://opinionator.blogs.nytimes.com/2013/12/01/the-interminable-everlasting-lincolns-prologue/.

3. For more on the Gardner-Story sitting, see Harold Holzer, *Lincoln President-Elect* (New York: Simon and Schuster, 2008), 419. Lincoln's secretary John Hay noted in his diary for November 8, 1863, "Went with Mrs. Ames to Gardner's Gallery & were soon joined by [principal secretary John G.] Nico[lay] and the Pres[iden]t." Tyler Dennett, ed., *Lincoln and the Civil War in the Diaries and Letters of John Hay* (New York: Dodd, Mead and Co., 1939), 117.

4. Charles Hamilton and Lloyd Ostendorf, *Lincoln in Photographs: An Album of Every Known Pose* (Norman: University of Oklahoma Press, 1963), 401–2. For years, photographic historians, including Frederick Hill Meserve, Stefan Lorant, and at first Ostendorf himself, held that the pictures were made four days before Lincoln's assassination, on April 10.

5. William J. Sims, ed., "Matthew Henry Wilson, 1814–1892," *Connecticut Historical Society Bulletin* 37 (October 1972): 109–11. The Welles copy was later acquired by the Lincoln Museum in Fort Wayne, Indiana; Wilson used his own copy to paint another for Lincoln's old friend Joshua Fry Speed.

6. Earl Schenck Miers, ed., *Lincoln Day by Day: A Chronology, 1809–1865*, 3 vols. (Washington, DC: Lincoln Sesquicentennial Commission, 1960), 3:313.

7. Francis B. Carpenter, *Six Months at the White House: The Story of a Picture* (New York: Hurd and Houghton, 1866), 232–33. His cheerfulness was reported in Gideon Welles, *Diary of Gideon Welles: Secretary of the Navy under Lincoln and Johnson*, with an introduction by John T. Morse, Jr., 3 vols. (Boston: Houghton Mifflin Co., 1911), 2:245.

8. Rufus Rockwell Wilson, *Lincoln in Portraiture* (New York: Press of the Pioneers, 1935), 264.

9. F. Lauriston Bullard, *Lincoln in Marble and Bronze* (New Brunswick, NJ: Rutgers University Press, 1952), 7.

10. Hamilton and Ostendorf, *Lincoln in Photographs*, 232. Ostendorf owned the original, reassembled 1865 Mills life mask.

11. John Hay, "Life in the White House in the Time of Lincoln," *Century Illustrated Monthly Magazine* 41 (November 1890): 37.

12. Hamilton and Ostendorf, *Lincoln in Photographs*, 214–15; Wilson, *Lincoln in Portraiture*, 268.

13. Harold Holzer, Gabor S. Boritt, and Mark E. Neely, Jr., *The Lincoln Image: Abraham Lincoln and the Popular Print* (New York: Charles Scribner's Sons, 1984), 142–44. See also Sims, "Matthew Henry Wilson."

14. Mark E. Neely, Jr., "The Last Life Portrait of Lincoln," *Lincoln Lore* 1700 (October 1979): 1–3.

15. Waldo W. Braden, ed., *Building the Myth: Selected Speeches Memorializing Abraham Lincoln* (Urbana: University of Illinois Press, 1990), 66.

16. U.S. copyright records for the Southern District of New York for 1865, Library of Congress, Washington, DC.

17. Over the years, I have consulted print collections in the Lincoln Museum, Fort Wayne; the Library of Congress, Washington, DC; the Chicago Historical Society; the Museum of the City of New York; the Abraham Lincoln Museum at Lincoln Memorial University, Harrogate, Tennessee; and prints in the bins and catalogs of private dealers, such as the Abraham Lincoln Book Shop in Chicago, the Old Print Shop in New York, the Old Print Gallery in Washington, DC, and the Philadelphia Print Shop.

18. "Nothing equals Macbeth," Lincoln wrote to actor James Hackett on August 17, 1863. *The Collected Works of Abraham Lincoln*, ed. Roy P. Basler, 8 vols. (New Brunswick, NJ: Rutgers University Press, 1953–55), 6:392.

19. Shakespeare, *Macbeth*, act 1, scene 7.

20. Mark E. Neely, Jr., and Harold Holzer, *The Lincoln Family Album* (New York: Doubleday, 1990), 108–9.

21. Harold Holzer and Frank J. Williams, *Lincoln's Deathbed in Art and Memory: The "Rubber Room" Phenomenon* (Gettysburg, PA: Thomas Publications, 1998).

22. Sales brochure, Ritchie's Historical Picture, Death of President Lincoln (New York: A. H. Ritchie, 1868), 5.

23. Ibid., 7–8.

24. For information on the 1802 Washington original by John James Barralet, see Harold Holzer, *Washington and Lincoln Portrayed: National Icons in Popular Prints* (Jefferson, NC: McFarland and Co., 1993), 207.

25. *Cincinnati Daily Gazette*, April 22, 1865, copy in my collection. For the story of Middleton's print portrait of Lincoln, see Harold Holzer, Gabor S. Boritt, and Mark E. Neely, Jr., *The Lincoln Image: Abraham Lincoln and the Popular Print* (New York: Charles Scribner's Sons, 1984), 136–40; and Lincoln to Middleton, December 30, 1864, *Collected Works*, 8:191–92.

26. See C. Nahl, *To Abraham Lincoln the Best Beloved of the Nation. In Memoriam*, Lithograph, San Francisco, 1865, in Holzer, *Washington and Lincoln Portrayed*, 169.

27. Testimonials to "Abraham Lincoln. The Standard Portrait Now Ready. Painted from Life, at the White House, in 1864, by F. B. Carpenter," in Fred. B. Perkins, *The Picture and the Men. . . .* (New York: A. J. Johnson, 1867), 190. Mary's words of praise were actually directed at the Lincoln portrait in Carpenter's Emancipation Proclamation painting, on which the Halpin engraving was based. Mary Lincoln to Carpenter, December 25, 1866, in Justin G. Turner and Linda Levitt Turner, *Mary Todd Lincoln: Her Life and Letters* (New York: Alfred A. Knopf, 1972), 403.

28. Harold Holzer, Gabor S. Boritt, and Mark E. Neely, Jr., "Francis Bicknell Carpenter (1830–1900): Painter of Abraham Lincoln and His Circle," *American Art Journal* 16 (Spring 1984): 84–85.

29. Wilson diary entry in Sims, "Matthew Henry Wilson," 110.

30. Henry C. Deming, *Eulogy of Abraham Lincoln* (Hartford, CT: A. N. Clark and Co., 1865), 13; R. M. Whiting, ed., *Our Martyr President Abraham Lincoln: Lincoln Memorial Addresses* (New York: Abingdon Press, [1915]), 33.

Appendixes

Contributors

Index

Appendix A: Lincoln's Final Months
(January 1–April 15, 1865)

January 1   Lincoln writes a letter to endorse Robert H. Hender-
                shot for an appointment to the United States Military
                Academy:

> I know something of this boy, and believe he is very
> brave, manly and worthy.

January 2   President and Mrs. Lincoln hold the traditional New
                Year's Day reception at the White House. Guests from
                the diplomatic community, the military and the Supreme
                Court, and the public are assigned to specific time periods.

                Chief Justice Salmon P. Chase informs the president
                that he was unable to attend the holiday reception because
                of the death of his sister. Chase adds, "But let me assure
                you that no one more earnestly wishes every blessing of
                the New Year to you and yours." Lincoln responds to the
                chief justice:

> Without your note of to-day, I should have felt assured
> that some sufficient reason had detained you. Allow
> me to condole with you in the sad bereavement you
> mention.

Entries were compiled from the following sources: events—Earl Schenck Miers,
ed., *Lincoln Day by Day: A Chronology, 1809–1865* (1960; repr., Dayton, OH: Morn-
ingside, 1991); Lincoln's words—*The Collected Works of Abraham Lincoln*, 8 vols.,
ed. Roy P. Basler et al. (New Brunswick, NJ: Rutgers University Press, 1953–55).
Citations may be found in each source by the dates given.

January 4   The subject of availability of cotton supplies has been much discussed. In reference to that subject, Lincoln writes the following "Cotton Permit":

> Whereas satisfactory evidence, has been furnished to me by Fergus Peniston, that he is now and was prior to April 1864 the legitimate owner of large amounts of cotton and naval stores situated in Louisiana and Southern Mississippi and reposing special trust and confidence in said Peniston, I do by these presents, authorize him to proceed with steamboats barges and other conveyances, at his own risk, up and down the Mississippi River and land at any points on said river between Natchez and Port Hudson.

After naming other geographic sites, Lincoln continues:

> All officers of the army or navy of the United States & civil officers of the Government are hereby particularly required not only to not obstruct but to extend to said Peniston all facilities that may be required to carry out the design of this permit which is the introduction of cotton and naval stores within the Military lines of the United States.

January 5   The president is eager to push vigorously ahead with the war effort. Commenting on a message from General William T. Sherman to General Henry W. Halleck, in which Sherman reports from Savannah that he is preparing plans to make *"a good ready"* before advancing, Lincoln tells Secretary of War Edwin M. Stanton:

> Since parting with you, it has occurred to me to say that while Gen. Sherman's *"get a good ready"* is appreciated, and is not to be overlooked, *time*, now that the enemy is wavering, is more important than ever before. Being on the down-hill, & some what confused, keeping him going. Please say so much to Genl. S.

January 9   Busy as he is, the president continues to involve himself in the individual needs of soldiers. Today he writes:

> Let Solomon Young be examined to ascertain whether he possesses the physical qualifications for a soldier,

in which case he will be discharged from confinement in jail and enrolled as a substitute for William D McMahon drafted in the first Ward of this city.

January 10   After being relieved of command of the Department of Virginia and North Carolina two days earlier, the controversial General Benjamin Butler asks Lincoln for permission "to publish my report of the Wilmington [Delaware] affair."

Lincoln replies:

> No principal report of yours on the Wilmington expedition has ever reached the War Department, as I am informed there. A preliminary report did reach here, but was returned to Gen. Grant at his request. Of course, leave to publish, can not be given, without inspection of the paper, and not then, if it should be deemed to be detrimental to the public service.

General Ulysses S. Grant eventually gives his permission for publication.

January 12   Lincoln interviews a Mr. Duncan of Montreal regarding a discovery that was said to protect wood against fire.

Another instance of his willingness to deal with individual problems can be seen in a letter to General Grant:

> If Henry Stork of, 5th Pa. Cavalry has been convicted of desertion, and is not yet executed, please stay till further order & send record.

January 13   In another letter to General Benjamin Butler, the president writes:

> Yours asking leave to come to Washington is received. You have been summoned by the Committee on the Conduct of the War to attend here, which of course you will do.

January 14   Mrs. Lincoln holds her first reception of the season. In the receiving line, she is flanked by the president and their son Robert.

Lincoln responds to a message from vice president elect Andrew Johnson informing the president that delegates to a special convention had voted unanimously to abolish slavery in Johnson's home state, Tennessee:

> Yours announcing ordinance of emancipation received. Thanks to the Convention and to you. When do you expect to be here? Would be glad to have your suggestions as to supplying your place of Military Governor.

January 15　Orator Edward Everett, who was the principal speaker at Gettysburg in 1863, dies. Secretary of State William H. Seward sends notice to government offices to honor his memory.

Concerned about reports of violence in Missouri, Lincoln writes to Major General Grenville M. Dodge suggesting

> an appeal to the people there to go to their homes, and let one another alone, recognizing as a full right of protection for each, that he lets others alone.

January 18　Further evidence of the president's concern about the supply of cotton can be seen in his permission for Mrs. R. I. Ward to move these goods

> free from seizure or detention by any officer of the Government.

January 19　Overcoming resistance from his wife, Lincoln contacts General Grant regarding a staff position for his son, asking if Robert could,

> without embarrassment to you, or detriment to the service, go into your Military family with some nominal rank, I, and not the public, furnishing his necessary means?

January 21　Lincoln receives word from Grant that Robert may join his headquarters staff with the rank of captain.

January 22　Lincoln confers with New York governor Reuben E. Fenton regarding troop quotas for the Empire State. The president then writes to Secretary Stanton:

> The Governor has a pretty good case. I feel sure he is more than half right. We don't want him to feel cross and we in the wrong. Try and fix it with him.

January 23   Lincoln comments on a habeas corpus case involving former New York City detectives John Dugan and Christo-
pher V. Hogan. During Hogan's subsequent employment
with the Treasury Department, a paymaster's trunk was
stolen. Dugan and Hogan were arrested for the robbery.
Lincoln rules:

> The within named Hogan, or Dugan was arrested and
> imprisoned by my authority. This writ of habeas corpus
> is suspended, and the officer having Hogan or Dugan
> in custody is directed not to produce his body, but to
> hold him in custody until further orders giving this
> order in his return to the court.

January 24   After conferring with several cabinet members, Lincoln
writes to incoming vice president Andrew Johnson, who
had asked to be excused from attending the inauguration
on March 4:

> Several members of the Cabinet, with myself, consid-
> ered the question to-day as to the time of your coming
> on here. While we fully appreciate your wish to re-
> main in Tennessee until her State-Government shall
> be completely re-inaugerated [*sic*], it is our unanimous
> conclusion that it is unsafe for you to not be here on the
> fourth of March. Be sure to reach here by that time.

January 25   The president responds to a request for words marking the
birth of Robert Burns, one of his favorite poets:

> I can not frame a toast to Burns. I can say nothing
> worthy of his generous heart, and transcending genius.
> Thinking of what he has said, I can not say anything
> which seems worth saying.

Lincoln also writes a strange message to Stanton on
several matters involving Jewish supporters and soldiers:

> About Jews. I wish you would give Dr. [Isachar] Zacha-
> rie [his podiatrist and occasional emissary to the Jewish
> community] a pass to go to Savannah, remain a week
> and return, bringing with him, if he wishes, his father
> and sisters or any of them. This will spare me trouble
> and oblige me. I promised him long ago that he should

be allowed this whenever Savannah should fall into our hands. Blumenberg, at Baltimore. [Major Leopold Blumenberg had been dismissed from the military, one charge being cruelty to suspected deserters.] I think he should have a hearing. He has suffered for us and served us well—had the rope around his neck for being our friend—raised troops—fought, and been wounded [at Antietam]. He should not be dismissed in a way that disgraces and ruins him without a hearing.

January 26–27 Lincoln orders stays of execution for Franklin Smith, Barney Roorke, and Cornelius Preacher.

January 28 Lincoln speaks to Francis Preston Blair, Sr., about peace negotiations with Confederate president Jefferson Davis and notes:

To-day Mr. Blair tells me that on the 21st. Inst. he delivered to Mr. Davis the original of which the within is a copy, and left it with him; that at the time of delivering it, Mr. Davis read it over twice in Mr. Blair's presence, at the close of which he, Mr. B. remarked that the part about "our one common country" related to the part of Mr. D's letter about the "two countries" to which Mr. D. replied that he so understood it.

January 30 In regard to a proposed mission by peace representatives from the Confederacy, Lincoln writes to Major General Edward O. C. Ord:

Please procure for the bearer, Major Thomas T. Eckert an interview with Messrs. [Confederate vice president Alexander] Stevens [sic], [former senator Robert] Hunter and [former associate justice John] Campbell; and if on his return to you, he requests it, pass them through our lines to Fortress-Monroe, by such route, and under such other Military precautions as you may deem prudent, giving them protection and comfortable quarters while there. Let none of this have any effect upon your military movements or plans.

January 31 Lincoln directs Secretary of State Seward to go to Fortress Monroe in Hampton Roads, Virginia, to confer informally with Stephens, Hunter, and Campbell, giving him these instructions:

> You will make known to them that three things are indispensable, towit:
>
> 1. The restoration of the national authority throughout all the States.
> 2. No receding, by the Executive of the United States on the Slavery question, from the position assumed thereon, in the late Annual Message to Congress, and in preceding documents.
> 3. No cessation of hostilities short of an end of the war, and the disbanding of all forces hostile to the government.
>
> You will inform them that all propositions of theirs not inconsistent with the above, will be considered and passed upon in a spirit of sincere liberality. You will hear all they may choose to say, and report it to me.

Lincoln closes the letter with a reminder that he is in charge:

> You will not assume to definitely consummate anything.

The House of Representatives passes the Thirteenth Amendment to the Constitution.

February 1   Lincoln approves the resolution to submit the Thirteenth Amendment to the states for ratification. He adds his own signature, an unnecessary measure in the amendment process.

That same day, Illinois governor Richard J. Oglesby sends a telegram to the president informing him that the Illinois legislature has become the first to ratify. In response to a serenade that evening, Lincoln proudly acknowledges the swift action of Illinois.

February 2   The president leaves Washington, travels to Fortress Monroe, and meets with Secretary of State William H. Seward on board the presidential vessel, *River Queen*. Secretary of the Navy Gideon Welles reports in his diary this day: "The President and Mr. Seward have gone to Hampton

Roads to have an interview with the Rebel commissioners, Stephens, Hunter, and Campbell."

February 3   Lincoln hosts the Hampton Roads Peace Conference in the morning aboard his boat. Commissioners propose armistice without emancipation, and Lincoln refuses. Later that day, the peace initiative unsuccessful, he begins the trip back to Washington.

February 4   Lincoln authorizes Secretary of War Stanton to send the following telegram to General Grant:

> The President desires me to repeat that nothing transpired, or transpiring with the three gentlemen from Richmond, is to cause any change hinderance or delay, of your military plans or operations.

February 7   Though the president is generous in authorizing passes through military lines, he wants military commanders to maintain some control over the process. In a letter to General Grant, which also illustrates the ease with which ordinary citizens are able to meet with the president, he writes:

> Some time ago you telegraphed that you had stopped a Mr. Laws from passing our lines with a boat and cargo, and I directed you to be informed that you must be allowed to do as you please in such matters. To-night Mr. Laws calls on me, and I have told him, and now tell you that the matter, as to his passing the lines is under your control absolutely; and that he can have any relaxation you choose to give him & none other.

Regarding the potential for African American recruits, the president writes to Stanton:

> Complaint is made to me that our recruiting officers at, and in vicinity of Mayville, Ky are *forcing* negroes into the service. Please enquire into this & stop it if true.

February 8   Lincoln writes to General Grant asking if he may use one of Grant's comments regarding the meeting at Hampton Roads in a forthcoming report to Congress, in which among other things you say "I fear now their [referring to the representatives of the Confederacy] going back without any expression from any one in authority will have a bad influence." I think the despatch does you credit while I do not see that it can embarrass you. May I use it?

February 10   The president sends a message to Rear Admiral David Dixon Porter:

Sir: It is my agreeable duty to enclose herewith the joint resolution approved 24th January, 1865, tendering the thanks of Congress to yourself, the officers and men under your command, for their gallantry and good conduct in the capture of Fort Fisher, and through you to all who participated in that brilliant and decisive victory under your command.

The president keeps a personal promise he had made to Alexander H. Stephens at Hampton Roads—to have his old congressional colleague's nephew freed from a military prison in exchange for a Union prisoner held in the Confederacy:

According to our agreement, your nephew, Lieut. Stephens, goes to you, bearing this note. Please, in return, to select and send to me, that officer of the same rank, imprisoned at Richmond, whose physical condition most urgently requires his release.

February 13   After a request from General Benjamin Grierson on behalf of the people of the District of West Tennessee, Lincoln responds:

To the Military Officers Commanding in West Tennessee. While I can not order as within requested, allow me to say that it is my wish for you to relieve the people from all burthens, harrassments, and oppressions, so far as is possible, consistently with your Military necessities; that the object of the war being to restore and maintain the blessings of peace and good government, I desire you to help, and not hinder, every advance in that direction. Of your Military necessities you must judge and execute; but please do so in the spirit and with the purpose above indicated.

February 14   Lincoln meets with a Mrs. Hutter and a committee from Philadelphia to discuss plans for caring for orphans of soldiers and sailors.

February 17   The president officially orders the convening of an extra session of the Senate on March 4.

February 20   Lincoln writes to Missouri governor Thomas C. Fletcher expressing his concern that the state's citizens continue to be distrustful of each other:

> It seems that there is now no organized military force of the enemy in Missouri and yet that destruction of property and life is rampant every where. . . . It cannot but be that every man, not naturally a robber or cut-throat would gladly put an end to this state of things. . . . Each leaving all others alone solves the problem. . . . Please consider whether it may not be well to suggest this to the now afflicted people of Missouri.

February 26   Artist Francis B. Carpenter and party visit the president's office and get an advance peek at his manuscript in progress for the Second Inaugural Address.

March 1   The president receives a committee from Congress bearing official notification of his reelection. Lincoln responds:

> Having served four years in the depths of a great, and yet unended national peril, I can view this call to a second term, in nowise more flatteringly to myself, than as an expression of the public judgment, that I may better finish a difficult work, in which I have labored from the first, than could anyone less severely schooled to the task. In this view, and with assured reliance on that Almighty Ruler who has so graciously sustained us thus far; and with increased gratitude to the generous people for their continued confidence, I accept the renewed trust, with it's [sic] yet onerous and perplexing duties and responsibilities.

March 2   Worried about General Sherman's army as it marches east
           to the sea, Lincoln sends the following telegram to Gen-
           eral Grant:

> You have not sent contents of Richmond papers for
> Tuesday or Wednesday. Did you not receive them? If
> not, does it indicate anything?

> Grant responds: "There is every indication that Genl
> Sherman is perfectly safe."

March 3   Secretary of War Stanton confers with the president about
           a letter received from Confederate general Robert E. Lee
           proposing a meeting to end hostilities. Lincoln instructs
           Stanton to notify Grant that a conference may be granted
           only on the basis of Lee's surrender.

> Stanton writes to Grant: "The President directs me to
> say to you that he wishes you to have no conference with
> General Lee unless it be for the capitulation of Gen. Lee's
> army, or on some minor, and purely, military matter. He
> instructs me to say that you are not to decide, discuss, or
> confer upon any political question. Such questions the
> President holds in his own hands; and will submit them
> to no military conferences or conventions. Meantime, you
> are to press to the utmost, your military advantages."

March 4   Lincoln delivers his Second Inaugural Address and takes
           the oath of office from new chief justice Salmon P. Chase,
           who presents Mary Lincoln with the Bible used to admin-
           ister the oath. Chase, who had hoped to succeed Lincoln
           as president, notes that the sun broke through as Lincoln
           was sworn in, thus giving "an auspicious omen of the dis-
           persion of the clouds of war and the restoration of the clear
           sunlight of prosperous peace."

March 6   The presidential party attends the inaugural ball at the Pat-
           ent Office. Robert Lincoln escorts his future wife, Mary
           Harlan, the daughter of Iowa senator James Harlan.

March 7   Lincoln writes to General Grant:

> In accordance with a Joint Resolution of Congress,
> approved December 17, 1863, I now have the honor of

transmitting, and presenting to you, in the name of the People of the United States of America, a copy of said resolution, engrossed on parchment, together with the gold medal therein ordered and directed. Please accept, for yourself and all under your command, the renewed expression of my gratitude for your and their arduous and well-performed public service.

March 9 On the subject of Confederate prisoners of war, Lincoln discusses options in a letter to General Grant:

> I see your despatch to the Sec. of War, objecting to rebel prisoners being allowed to take the oath and go free. Supposing that I am responsible for what is done in this way, I think fit to say that there is no general rule, or action, allowing prisoners to be discharged merely on taking the oath. What has been done is that Members of Congress come to me from time to time with lists of names alleging that from personal knowledge, and evidence of reliable persons they are satisfied that it is safe to discharge the particular persons named on the lists, and I have ordered their discharge. These Members are chiefly from the border states; and those they get discharged are their neighbors and neighbors sons.

March 10 The president discusses with John A. Poor, a leading supporter of railroad development in Maine, the possibility of offering a cabinet position to former vice president Hannibal Hamlin.

March 11 Lincoln addresses the problem of Union deserters by issuing a proclamation that offers pardons to deserters who returned to service:

> Now, therefore, be it known that I, Abraham Lincoln, President of the United States, do issue this my Proclamation, as required by said act [of Congress] ordering and requiring all deserters to return to their proper posts, and I do hereby notify them that all deserters, who shall, within sixty days from the date of this proclamation, viz: on or before the tenth day of May 1865, return to service or report themselves to

a Provost Marshal, shall be pardoned, on condition that they return to their regiments and companies, or to such other organizations as they may be assigned to, and serve the remainder of their original terms of enlistment, and, in addition thereto, a period equal to the time lost by desertion.

March 15   Lincoln thanks Thurlow Weed, New York Republican boss, for a compliment on his inaugural address (which Weed actually had intended as a compliment on Lincoln's short pronouncement accepting formal notice of his re-election). In spite of this misunderstanding, the letter shows Lincoln's confidence in the future reputation of his address:

> I expect it to wear as well as—perhaps better than—any thing I have produced; but I believe it is not immediately popular. Men are not flattered by being shown that there has been a difference of purpose between the Almighty and them. To deny it, however, in this case, is to deny that there is a God governing the world. It is a truth which I thought needed to be told; and as whatever of humiliation there is in it, falls most directly on myself, I thought others might afford for me to tell it.

March 17   The president issues a proclamation to address problems regarding the supply of arms and ammunition to hostile Indians:

> Whereas, reliable information has been received that hostile Indians within the limits of the United States have been furnished with arms and munitions of war by persons dwelling in conterminous foreign territory, and are thereby enabled to prosecute their savage warfare upon the exposed and sparse settlements of the frontier. Now, therefore, be it known that I, Abraham Lincoln, President of the United States of America, do hereby proclaim and direct that all persons detected in that nefarious traffic, shall be arrested and tried by Court Martial at the nearest military post, and, if convicted, shall receive the punishment due to their deserts.

March 20   Lincoln responds to General Grant's invitation to visit City Point, Virginia:

> Your kind invitation received. Had already thought of going immediately after the next rain. Will go sooner if any reason for it. Mrs. L. and a few others will probably accompany me.

March 23   The Lincoln party, consisting of the president, Mary, Tad, Mary's maid, aide W. H. Crook, and Captain Charles B. Penrose, leaves Washington on the *River Queen*.

March 25   After arriving at City Point, Lincoln walks to Grant's headquarters and expresses a desire to visit the front. A special train is requisitioned to proceed to General Meade's headquarters. Lincoln then requests a horse so that he can ride over the battlefield at Petersburg. When the train returns to City Point, cars are attached to carry wounded soldiers. Lincoln sends a message to Stanton:

> I am here within five miles of the scene of this morning's action. I have nothing to add to what Gen. Meade reports, except that I have seen the prisoners myself and they look like there might be the number he states—1600.

> Stanton replies: "Your telegram and Genl Parkes report of the 'Scrimmage' this morning are received. The rebel rooster looks a little the worse as he could not hold the fence."

March 26   Lincoln reviews General Ord's division near Malvern Hill. Mary Lincoln, upset at the prominent position occupied by Mrs. Ord, has a temper tantrum of titanic proportions.

March 30   Secretary of State Seward arrives at City Point.
In a telegram to Stanton, Lincoln describes the current battle:

> I begin to feel that I ought to be at home, and yet I dislike to leave without seeing nearer to the end of General Grant's present movement. He has now been out since yesterday morning, and although he has not been diverted from his programme, no considerable effect has yet been produced, so far as we know here.

Last night at 10:15, when it was dark as a rainy night without a moon could be, a furious cannonade, soon joined in by a heavy musketry-fire, opened near Petersburg and lasted about two hours. The sound was very distinct here, as also were the flashes of the guns upon the clouds. It seemed to me a great battle, but the older hands here scarcely noticed it, and, sure enough, this morning it was found that very little had been done.

March 31   After several days of meetings with military leaders, both on the *River Queen* and on land, Lincoln receives a message from Stanton urging him to remain close to the front: "A pause by the army now would do harm; if you are on the ground there will be no pause."

April 1   Mrs. Lincoln and Seward leave for Washington. Tad remains with his father.

April 2   The president sends a telegram to Mary:

Last night Gen. Grant telegraphed that Sheridan with his Cavalry and the 5th. Corps had captured three brigades of Infantry, a train of wagons, and several batteries, prisoners amounting to several thousands. . . . Grant added, "All now looks highly favorable."

In the evening, Lincoln telegraphs Grant:

Allow me to tender to you, and all with you, the nations grateful thanks for this additional, and magnificent success. At your kind suggestion, I think I will visit you to-morrow.

The president also sends an additional message to Mary:

At 4:30 P.M. to-day General Grant telegraphs that he has Petersburg completely enveloped from river below to river above.

April 3   Lincoln meets with Grant and subsequently telegraphs Stanton from City Point:

Yours received. Thanks for your caution; but I have already been to Petersburg, staid with Gen. Grant an hour & a half and returned here. It is certain now that

Richmond is in our hands, and I think I will go there to-morrow. I will take care of myself.

April 4   The president travels on the *River Queen* to meet Rear Admiral Porter's fleet. He transfers to the flagship *Malvern* and then to the captain's gig for the trip to Richmond. With only twelve mariners as escorts, Lincoln, Tad, Admiral Porter, Captain Penrose, and W. H. Crook enter Richmond, where they are greeted with a tumultuous reception from the city's African Americans, and walk to General Godfrey Weitzel's headquarters, the house recently occupied by Jefferson Davis. Lincoln sits down in Davis's office and remarks:

This must have been President Davis's chair.

Weitzel later describes Lincoln's reception in Richmond as "enthusiastic in the extreme."

April 5   Lincoln replies to a message from Seward:

Yours of to-day received. I think there is no probability of my remaining here more than two days longer. If that is too long come down. I passed last night at Richmond and have just returned [to City Point].

At 6 P.M. Lincoln receives word that Secretary Seward has just been thrown from his carriage and is seriously injured.

Mrs. Lincoln and her party depart from Washington on the steamer *Monohasset* to return to City Point.

April 6   The president sends an authorization to General Weitzel:

It has been intimated to me that the gentlemen who have acted as the Legislature of Virginia, in support of the rebellion, may now desire to assemble at Richmond and take measures to withdraw the Virginia troops, and other support from resistance to the General government. If they attempt it, give them permission and protection, until if at all, they attempt some action hostile to the United States, in which case you will notify them and give them reasonable time to leave; & at the end of which time, arrest any who may remain.

Lincoln then informs Grant of this action:

> If the war be now further persisted in by the rebels, confiscated property shall, at the least, bear the additional cost; and that confiscations shall be remitted to the people of any State which will now promptly, and in good faith, withdraw its troops and other support, from resistance to the government. I do not think it very probable that anything will come of this [the possibility of an assembly in Richmond]; but I have thought best to notify you, so that if you should see signs, you may understand them. From your recent despatches it seems that you are pretty effectually withdrawing the Virginia troops from opposition to the government. Nothing I have done, or probably shall do, is to delay, hinder or interfere with you in your work.

April 7   Still at City Point, Lincoln interviews Assistant Secretary of War Charles Dana and remarks:

> Sheridan seemed to be getting Virginia soldiers out of the war faster than this legislature could think.

He then sends the following telegram to Grant:

> Gen. Sheridan says "If the thing is pressed I think that Lee will surrender." Let the thing be pressed.

April 8   The Marquis de Chambrun and U.S. senator Charles Sumner of Massachusetts board the *River Queen*. The presidential party then goes by train to Petersburg. Lincoln confers with generals and visits hospital camps. In the evening, a military band gives a farewell concert aboard the *River Queen*. Lincoln requests two songs, "The Marseillaise" and "Dixie." At 11 that evening the presidential party leaves City Point for the trip back to Washington.

April 9   Describing the trip up the Potomac, Chambrun writes, "That whole day the conversation turned on literary subjects. Mr. Lincoln read aloud to us for several hours. Most of the passages he selected were from Shakespeare."

Arriving at sundown in Washington, the party finds the city celebrating Lee's surrender at Appomattox. That evening, Lincoln visits the bedridden Seward.

April 10   Lincoln visits the Navy Yard and makes a few brief remarks.

At 5 P.M. a large crowd, including bands, congregates at the White House. The president promises to prepare a speech for the following day.

April 11   Lincoln meets with General Butler to discuss the "freed Negro problem." He delegates Ward Hill Lamon to travel to Richmond and report back on the Reconstruction Convention.

The cabinet meets to discuss the cotton business.

As promised, the president addresses a crowd at the White House in what would turn out to be his last public speech:

> We meet this evening, not in sorrow, but in gladness of heart. The evacuation of Petersburg and Richmond, and the surrender of the principal insurgent army, give hope of a righteous and speedy peace whose joyous expression can not be restrained. In the midst of this, however, He, from Whom all blessings flow, must not be forgotten.

The president then briefly discusses a general outline of "the re-inauguration of the national authority," using the term "reconstruction" to describe this process. He gives special emphasis to plans for Louisiana and suggests extending the right to vote to African Americans, especially the "very intelligent" and those who had served in the army.

Hearing this from the crowd gathered below, John Wilkes Booth vows that it will be the last speech that Lincoln will ever make.

April 12   Lincoln participates in numerous meetings. The Marquis de Chambrun reports that the president "spoke at length of the many struggles he foresaw in the future and declared his firm resolution to stand for clemency against all opposition."

Lincoln visits Secretary Stanton and decides to revoke the permission he gave on April 6 for a meeting of the Virginia Assembly. In this regard, he sends the following message to General Weitzel:

Is there any sign of the rebel Legislature coming together on the understanding of my letter to you? If
there is any such sign, inform me what it is; if there is
no such sign you may as [well] withdraw the offer.

Lincoln bases this decision on the belief that these are "the
gentlemen who have acted as the Legislature of Virginia
in support of the rebellion."

In response to Stanton's reprimanding Weitzel for not
ordering prayers for the president in churches, Lincoln
tells the general:

I do not remember hearing prayers spoken of while I
was in Richmond; but I have no doubt you have acted
in what appeared to you to be the spirit and temper
manifested by me while there.

April 13 Lincoln visits the War Department telegraph office in the
morning and later meets with several people, most notably
General Grant and Secretary Stanton, and later Secretary
Welles.

Lincoln rides to his country retreat, the Soldiers' Home,
and is described by Assistant Secretary of the Treasury
Maunsell B. Field as "weary and sad." Looking ahead,
the president writes his "Memorandum Respecting Re-
duction of the Regular Army." Looking at past statistics,
he proposes "one soldier to 1000 souls."

April 14 Robert Lincoln arrives at the White House after being
present at Appomattox. He and his father have breakfast
together, and Robert describes the event and shows the
president a souvenir photograph of General Lee.

Lincoln's meeting calendar is crowded with both formal
and informal meetings.

Lincoln writes to General James H. Van Alen:

I thank you for the assurance you give me that I shall
be supported by conservative men like yourself, in the
efforts I may make to restore the Union, so as to make
it, to use your language, a Union of hearts and hands
as well as of States.

The president visits the telegraph office and invites General Thomas Eckert to attend a play.

At a meeting of the cabinet at 11 A.M., Grant reports on the surrender at Appomattox, and Secretary Stanton presents the draft of a plan to reestablish authority in the Confederate states. There is an informal discussion regarding the status of President Davis and other leaders of the Confederacy.

At 2 P.M. the president meets Mrs. Lincoln for a private lunch. Meetings and visits continue throughout the afternoon until Lincoln and his wife leave the White House for a carriage ride. They stop at the Navy Yard to view three damaged ironclads. Lincoln talks of their future.

When they return to the White House, they find Governor Richard Oglesby and other friends from Illinois waiting for them. Lincoln reads four chapters of a humorous book, *The Nasby Papers*, to Oglesby and General Isham Haynie.

Meetings resume after supper, including one with former congressman from Massachusetts George Ashmun, who is given the following note: "Allow Mr. Ashmun and friend to come in at 9 A.M. tomorrow."

At approximately 8:30 P.M., the presidential party arrives late at Ford's Theatre to watch Laura Keene in *Our American Cousin*. At 10:20, John Wilkes Booth shoots the president from behind.

The mortally wounded Lincoln is carried across the street to a boardinghouse owned by William Petersen. Family members and friends visit the stricken president's room throughout the night.

April 15 — Dr. Charles Taft notes that Lincoln stops breathing "at 7:21 and 55 seconds in the morning of April 15th, and at 7:22 and 10 seconds his pulse ceased to beat." Secretary Stanton utters the now iconic observation on Lincoln, "Now he belongs to the ages."

Appendix B: Chronology for 1865

United States

Military and Political

January 11	Robert E. Lee calls for slaves to join the depleted Confederate army.
January 15	Edward Everett, "the other speaker at Gettysburg," dies.
January 16	Union general William T. Sherman issues Field Order 15, approved by Lincoln, which sets aside forty-acre plots of land along the coasts of South Carolina and Georgia to be distributed to black families. Families are also to be given mules that the army no longer needs. This is the genesis of the phrase "forty acres and a mule."
January 18	Charleston, South Carolina, surrenders.
January 31	House of Representatives passes the resolution sending the Thirteenth Amendment to the states for ratification.
February 3	Lincoln meets Confederate peace commissioners at Hampton Roads.
February 17	Senate cancels Confederate debts.
February 22	The last open Confederate port, Wilmington, North Carolina, is taken by General John Schofield.
March 2	Lincoln refuses Lee's request for peace talks and demands unconditional surrender.
March 3	The Freedmen's Bureau is established.
March 4	Abraham Lincoln is inaugurated for a second term. Andrew Johnson is sworn in as vice president.

March 11	Lincoln proclaims amnesty for all deserters who return within sixty days.
March 13	Jefferson Davis signs a bill that gives freedom to slaves who have fought in the army.
April 9	General Robert E. Lee signs a surrender document at Appomattox.
April 14	Abraham Lincoln is shot by John Wilkes Booth.
April 15	Lincoln dies at 7:22 A.M.
May 1	President Andrew Johnson orders that the assassination conspirators be tried by a military tribunal.
May 9	The Military Commission meets for the first time.
May 10	Jefferson Davis and his wife are captured in Irwinville, Georgia. The conspirators are arraigned before the Military Commission.
June 23	President Andrew Johnson ends naval blockade of Southern ports.
June 30	The Military Commission hands down the following sentences to the conspirators: Herold, Surratt, Powell, and Atzerodt are to hang. O'Laughlen, Arnold, and Mudd receive life terms. Spangler is to spend six years in jail.
July 7	Four assassination conspirators are hanged.
November 10	Captain Henry Wirz, commandant of Andersonville, is hanged.
December 1	Johnson restores the writ of habeas corpus.
December 13	The Joint Committee on Reconstruction is established, cochaired by Congressman Thaddeus Stevens and Senator William Pitt Fessenden.
December 24	Ku Klux Klan is founded by six Confederate veterans in Pulaski, Tennessee. The eventual leader of the group is Nathan Bedford Forrest.

Education

The following universities are founded in 1865: Cornell, Lehigh, University of Kentucky, University of Maine, Massachusetts Institute of Technology.

Yale establishes the nation's first Department of Fine Arts.

At Vassar College, Maria Mitchell becomes the first female astronomy professor.

Business, Industry, Science, and Discoveries

In Philadelphia, John B. Stetson manufactures the first Stetson hat.

John D. Rockefeller founds an oil refining company near Cleveland.

Thaddeus Lowe invents a compression ice machine.

William Sheppard is granted a patent for liquid soap.

The Freedmen's Savings and Trust Company is founded in Washington to focus on African Americans.

The world's first oil pipeline is opened between Oil Creek and Pithole in Pennsylvania.

Benjamin Altman opens a dry-goods store in New York City.

The Union Stock Yards are opened in Chicago.

Andrew Carnegie founds the Keystone Bridge Company.

Shipping firm W. R. Grace and Company opens.

Oliver Gibbs introduces electronic analysis for spectroscopy.

First railroad sleeping cars, designed by George Pullman, appear in the United States.

San Francisco Examiner and *San Francisco Chronicle* (initially called *Daily Dramatic Chronicle*) newspapers are founded.

The first train holdup in the United States occurs in North Bend, Ohio.

Art, Music, and Literature

Popular songs of 1865 include "Johnny Is My Darling," "Little Brown Church in the Vale," and "Marching through Georgia."

Mark Twain's first well-known story, "The Celebrated Jumping Frog of Calaveras County," is initially published in a New York newspaper under the title "Jim Smiley and His Jumping Frog."

Drum-Taps, a book of poetry by Walt Whitman that includes one of his most famous poems on Lincoln's death, "When Lilacs Last in the Dooryard Bloom'd," is published.

Mary Mapes Dodge publishes *Hans Brinker; or, the Silver Skates*.

The expression "Go West, young man, go West," appears in an editorial by Horace Greeley in the *New York Tribune*.

Appendix B

Births

Warren G. Harding, twenty-ninth president of the United States

Frederick Cook, explorer

International

July 2   In Great Britain, William and Catherine Booth launch the Christian Mission, which later becomes the Salvation Army.

October 4   Prussian chancellor Otto von Bismarck and French emperor Napoleon III meet in Biarritz, France, and Napoleon recognizes Prussian supremacy in Germany.

October 10   The United States demands that France withdraw the troops they sent to Mexico to support the French-appointed emperor Maximilian I.

October 29   Lord John Russell becomes prime minister of Great Britain, succeeding Lord Palmerston.

Science, Medicine, Exploration, and Discoveries

Edward Whymper of Great Britain leads the first successful climb of Switzerland's Matterhorn. Four members of the party fall to their death during the descent.

Starting in December, German explorer Gerhard Rohlfs is the first European to cross the Sahara Desert.

English surgeon Joseph Lister uses carbolic acid to kill germs during surgery.

Austrian monk and botanist Gregor Mendel publishes a paper on the laws of heredity.

French microbiologist Louis Pasteur develops the process that leads to pasteurization.

French chemist George Leclanché invents the zinc-carbon battery, the first dry cell battery.

Sweden's Alfred Nobel invents the blasting cap.

Art, Music, Literature

Claude Monet paints *Cart on the Snow-Covered Road at Honfleur*.

Edgar Degas paints *Woman with Chrysanthemums*.

Winslow Homer paints *Prisoners from the Front*.

English writer and mathematician Lewis Carroll publishes *Alice's Adventures in Wonderland* (originally titled *Alice's Adventures under Ground*).

Johannes Brahms completes Cello Sonata no. 1.

Hungarian Franz Liszt composes *Rákóczy March*.

Russian composer Nikolai Rimsky-Korsakov completes his Symphony no. 1.

First performance of Richard Wagner's *Tristan and Isolde* is presented in Munich.

German mathematician Julius Plücker invents line geometry.

Births

Future King George V of Great Britain

William Butler Yeats, Irish poet

Erich Ludendorff, German general

Appendix C: Lecture at the Inauguration of the Douglass Institute, by Frederick Douglass

THE DOUGLASS INSTITUTE, Lecture at Inauguration of Douglass Institute, Baltimore, September 29, 1865

I have, during my public career, had the honor to address many assemblies, both at home and abroad, and in furtherance of various objects; but I do not remember ever to have appeared anywhere under a deeper sense of the importance of the occasion than I feel tonight. I know it is common to call all occasions, upon which we assemble in large numbers, great and important, and in some sense the characterization is just and proper; for the movement of large bodies of men in this or that direction, for any purpose, good or ill, is always important, and worthy of note. But the present occasion is one of no ordinary character. We come here to dedicate an institution which, in my opinion, is destined to play an important part in promoting the freedom and elevation of the colored people of this city and State, and I may say of the whole Union.

Let me at the outset put myself at ease by expressing to the founders of this Institution my sincere and heartfelt thanks for assigning to me the high place I occupy on this occasion, and above all, for associating my name with the Institute here established. It is an honor. I look upon this proceeding on your part not merely as a compliment to me personally, but as an open avowal of the great principles of progress, liberty, justice and equality, which I have for years endeavored to advocate. When I left Maryland, twenty-seven years ago, I did so with the firm resolve never to forget my brothers and sisters in bondage, and to do whatever might be in

From Philip S. Foner, ed., *Frederick Douglass: Selected Speeches and Writings* (Chicago: Lawrence Hill Books, 1999), 580–85.

my power to accomplish their emancipation; and I have to say to-night, that in whatever else I may have failed, in this at least I have not failed. No man can truthfully say I ever deserted the post of duty.

The establishment of an Institute bearing my name by the colored people in the city of my boyhood, so soon after the act of emancipation in this State, looms before me as a *first* grand indication of progress. I say it is a *first*, and first indications, whether observed in the silent, mysterious phemomena [*sic*] of physical nature, or in the moral or intellectual developments of human society, are always interesting to thoughtful men. Every age has its prophet or its Messiah. We are ever waiting and watching like good old Simeon for our babe of Bethlehem. John Brown used to say he had looked over our people as over a dark sea, in the hope of seeing a head rise up with a mind to plan and a hand to deliver. Any movement of the water arrested his attention. In all directions, we desire to catch the first sign. The first sign of clear weather on the ocean after a season of darkness and storm; the first sign of returning health after long and weary months of wasting fever; the first sign of rain after a famine, threatening drouth; the first indication of spring, silently releasing the knotty and congealed earth from the frosty fetters of winter; the first sign of peace after the ten thousand calamities, horrors, desolations and alarms of war, evermore bring joy and gladness to the human heart.

The mind of man has a special attraction towards first objects. It delights in the dim and shadowy outlines of the coming fact. There is a calm and quiet satisfaction in the contemplation of present attainments; but the great future, and the yet unattained, awaken in the soul the deepest springs of poetry and enthusiasm.

The occasion that brings us here this evening may be properly viewed in the spirit of these brief reflections. It is an indication of the rise of a people long oppressed, enslaved and bound in the chains of ignorance, to a freer and higher plane of life, manhood, usefulness and civilization.

Peace, says the noble Sumner, has its trumphs [*sic*] no less than war. I avail myself of the aphorism, and claim the dedication of the Douglass Institute in this, the city of Baltimore, in the State of Maryland, dedicated as it will be to knowledge, virtue and liberty, as one such triumph. I think it quite difficult to over-estimate the importance and significance of the first effort of the kind in the city of Baltimore. I confess that the establishment of such an Institution here and now was a source of apprehension as well as joy; joy in the thought of its success, apprehension lest the effort should fail. It seemed too much to expect.

A people hitherto pronounced by American learning as incapable of any thing higher than the dull round of merely animal life—held to be originally and permanently inferior—fit only for the coarser and heavier labors of human society—shut out for ages from the arts, from science, and from all the more elevating forms of industry—deprived of the social incentives to excellence which everywhere act upon other men, dare here and now to establish an Institute, devoted to all the higher wants and aspirations of the human soul. It is a great fact.

Your very enemies, looking upon this event, will admit that it speaks well for the colored people of Baltimore. It is in itself a powerful appeal from the popular judgment under which the colored people of this city and of this State, and of the whole country, have staggered during more than two hundred years. I would bestow no extravagant and indiscriminate praise upon the founders of the Douglass Institute. You are sensible men, and would not thank me if I did. The colored people of this country have as much reason to deprecate flattery as they have disparagement. What they want is the simple truth, and this renders honor where honor is due. I say to you, gentlemen, what you all know, that this institution, viewed in comparison with those established by our white fellow-citizens for similar objects, stands but as a dwarf to a giant; but regarded in the light of our history, in view of our numbers and opportunities, the Douglass Institute is the equal of any in credit, and far more significant than most of them. It is a beginning, and though like all beginnings it is small, it is, nevertheless, a prophecy of larger and better things. It represents something, and important as it is for itself, it is ten-fold more important for what it represents in the character of its founders. It implies something. It implies that the colored people of Baltimore not only have the higher qualities attributed to the white race, but that they are awakening to a healthy consciousness of those qualities in themselves, and that they are beginning to see, as the dark cloud of slavery rolls away, the necessity of bringing those qualities into vigorous exercise. It implies an increased knowledge of the requirements of a high civilization, and a determination to comply with them. This Institute, in character and design, in some measure represents the abilities and possibilities of our race.

My friends, the present is a critical moment for the colored people of this country; our fate for weal or for woe, it may be yet for many generations, trembles now in the balance. No man can tell which way the scale will turn. There is not a breeze that sweeps to us from the South, but comes laden with the wail of our suffering people. Heaven only knows what will be in store for our people in the South. But dismal as is the hour, troubled and convulsed as are the times, we may congratulate ourselves upon the establishment of this institution. It comes as a timely argument on the right side of the momentous questions which now agitate the nation. It comes at a time when the American people are once more being urged to do from necessity what they should have done from a sense of right, and of sound statemanship [*sic*]. It is the same old posture of affairs, wherein our rulers do wrong from choice and right from necessity. They gave us the bullet to save themselves; they will yet give the ballot to save themselves. My hope of the future is founded just where it was during all the war. I always said that I had much faith in the virtue of the great North, but that I had incomparably more in the villainy of the South. The South is now on its good behavior, we are told. They have been invested with powers merely to see how they will use them. If they do certain things we are told, it will be well, but if they do certain other things—well, somebody will interfere. Very well. I expect to see the rebels consistent with their whole past. They are sworn now as at the beginning of the war, and with like results. They take the oath to support a Government they hate. They are sure to abuse the power given them, and I believe there will be virtue enough in the country, when it shall see that the loyal whites can only be saved by giving the ballot to the Negro, to do the thing now called impossible.

This Institute comes to our help. It comes at a time when hesitation to extend suffrage to the colored people finds its best apology in our alleged incapacity. I deem it fortunate that, at such a time as this, in such a city as this, so near the capital of the nation as this, there has arisen here an Institution in which we can confront ignorance and prejudice with the light and power of positive knowledge, and array against brazen falsehood the rightful influence of accomplished facts.

The very existence of this Institution, established and sustained by colored men in the city, so recently a slaveholding city—in this State, so recently a slaveholding State—in this community, among whom freedom of speech was scarcely known by even the white citizens only a few months ago—is a most striking, cheering and instructive fact. It attests the progressive spirit, the sagacity, the courage, the faith, the intelligence and manly ambition of the colored people of this city and State, and reflects credit upon the colored people of the country generally. Its effects upon those who disparage us will be good, but its effects upon ourselves will, I trust, be far better. While to them it will be a standing contradiction, to us it will be a happy concurrence with all our hopes, with all that is high, noble and desirable.

The colored boy and girl now, as they walk your streets, will hold themselves in higher estimation and assume a prouder and a more elastic step as they look up to the fine proportions of this ample and elegant building, and remember that from foundation to roof, from corner-stone to coping, in purpose and in value, in spirit and in aspiration, it is all the property of the colored citizens of Baltimore.

The establishment of this Institution may be thought by some a thing of doubtful expediency. There was a time when I should have thought it so myself. In my enthusiasm, perhaps it was my simplicity, it is not material which, I once flattered myself that the day had happily gone by when it could be necessary for colored people in this country to combine and act together as a separate class, and in any representative character whatever. I would have had them infuse themselves and their works into all the political, intellectual, artistical and mechanical activities and combinations of their white fellow countrymen. It seemed to me that colored conventions, colored exhibitions, colored associations and institutions of all kinds and descriptions had answered the ends of their existence, and might properly be abandoned; that, in short, they were hindrances rather than helps in achieving a higher and better estimation in the public mind for ourselves as a race.

I may say that I still hold this opinion in a modified degree. The latent contempt and prejudice towards our race, which recent political doctrines with reference to our future in this country have developed, the persistent determination of the present Executive of the nation, and also the apparent determination of a portion of the people to hold and treat us in a degraded relation, not only justify for the present such associate effort on our part, but make it eminently necessary.

It is the misfortune of our class that it fails to derive due advantages from the achievements of its individual members, but never fails to suffer from the ignorance or crimes of a single individual with whom the class is identified. A Benjamin Franklin could redeem, in the eyes of scientific Europe, the mental mediocrity of our young white Republic, but the genius and learning of a Benjamin Banneker of your own State of Maryland, the wisdom and heroism of Toussaint, are not permitted to do the same service for the colored race to which they belong. Wealth, learning and ability made an Irishman an Englishman. The same metamorphosing power converts a Negro into a white man in this country. When prejudice cannot deny the black man's ability, it denies his race, and claims him as a white man. It affirms that if he is not exactly white, he ought to be. If not what he ought to be in this particular, he owes whatever intelligence he possesses to the white race by contract or association. Great actions, as shown by Robert Small, the gallant captain of the Planter, and by William Tilghman, and other brave colored men, which by the war slavery has tossed to the surface, have not been sufficient to change the general estimate formed of the colored race. The eloquence and learning of Doctor Smith, Professors Vashon, Reason, Garnet Remond, Martin, Rock, Crummell, and many others, have done us service; but they leave us yet under a cloud.

The public, with the mass of ignorance—notwithstanding that ignorance has been enforced and compelled among our people, hitherto—has sternly denied the representative character of our distinguished men. They are treated as exceptions, individual cases, and the like. They contend that the race, as such, is destitute of the subjective original elemental condition of a high self-originating and self-sustaining civilization.

Such is the sweeping and damaging judgment pronounced in various high quarters against our race; and such is the current of opinion against which the colored people have to advance, if they advance at all. A few years ago, we met this unfavorable theory as best we could in three ways. We pointed our assailants and traducers to the ancient civilization of Northern Africa. We traced the entangled threads of history and of civilization back to their sources in Africa. We called attention to the somewhat disagreeable fact—agreeable to us, but not so to our Teutonic brethren—that the arts, appliances and blessings of civilization flourished in the very heart of Ethiopia, at a time when all Europe floundered in the depths of ignorance and barbarism. We dwelt on the grandeur, magnificence and stupendous dimensions of Egyptian architecture, and held up the fact, now generally admitted, that that race was master of mechanical forces of which the present generations of men are ignorant.

We pointed to the nautical skill, commercial enterprise and military prowess of Carthage, and justly claimed relationship with those great nations of antiquity. We are a dark people—so were they. They stood between us and the Europeans in point of complexion, as well as in point of geography. We have contended—and not illogically—that if the fact of color was no barrier to civilization in their case, it cannot be in ours.

Our second answer has been drawn from modern examples. These have not, I confess, been very numerous or striking, but enough to demonstrate the presence of highly progressive and civilizing elements in the colored race. We find them in Africa—we find them written down in the interesting travels of Barth, Livingston and Wilson. We find them in Hayti, and we find them in our own country. Our third answer has been the unfavorable influence under which our race has been placed by Christendom during the last three centuries. Where under the whole heavens was there ever a race so blasted and withered, so shorn and bereft of all opportunities for development as ourselves? It would seem that the whole Christian world had combined for the destruction of our race, and had summoned heaven and hell, philosophy and revelation, to assist in the work. Our history has been but a track of blood. Gaunt and hungry sharks have followed us on slave ships by sea, and the hungrier and greedier slave-drivers have followed us during all these years with the bloody slave-whip on land.

The question forced upon us at every moment of our generation has not been, as with other races of men, how shall we adorn, beautify, exalt and ennoble life, but how shall we retain life itself. The struggle with us was not to do, but to be. Mankind lost sight of our human nature in the idea of our being property, and the whole machinery of society was planned, directed and operated to the [sic] making us a stupid, spiritless, ignorant, besotted, brutified, and utterly degraded race of men.

Thus far we have derived little advantage from any apologies we have made or from any explanations we have patiently given. Our relationship to the ancient Egyptians has been denied; the progress made by the emancipated people of the West Indies is not believed, and men still insist that the fault of our ignorance is not in slavery, but in ourselves. So stood the question concerning us up to the second year of the fierce and sanguinary rebellion now subsiding. Since then, the colored man has come before the country in a new light. He has illustrated the highest qualities of a patriot and a soldier. He has ranged himself on the side of Government and country, and maintained both against rebels and traitors on the perilous edge of battle. They are now, many of them, sleeping side by side in bloody graves with the bravest and best of all our loyal white soldiers, and many of those who remain alive are scarred and battered veterans—mere stumps of men; armless, legless, maimed and mutilated ones are met with in the streets of every city. The veriest enemies of our race must now admit that we have at least one element of civilization. It is settled that we have manly courage, that we love our country, and that we will fight for an Idea. Both Governments—the Rebel as well as the Federal—admitted the energy that slumbered in the black man's arm, and both, at the last, endeavored to render that energy useful. But the charge still remains. Now, what are those elemental and original powers of civilization about which men speak and write so earnestly, and which white men claim for themselves and deny to the Negro? I answer that they are simply consciousness of wants and ability to gratify them. Here the whole machinery of civilization, whether moral, intellectual or physical, is set in motion.

Man is distinguished from all other animals, but in nothing is he distinguished more than in this, namely, resistance, active and constant resistance, to the forces of physical nature. All other animals submit to the same conditions and limitations from generation to generation. The bear today is as he was a thousand years ago. Nature provides him with food, clothing and shelter, and he is neither wiser not [sic] better because of the experience of his bearish ancestors. Not so with man. He learns from the past, improves upon the past, looks back upon the past, and hands down his knowledge of the past to after-coming generations of men, that they may carry their achievements to a still higher point. To lack this element of progress is to resemble the lower animals, and to possess it is to be men.

The mission of this Institution and that of the colored race are identical. It is to develop manhood, to build up manly character among the colored people of this city and State. It is to teach them the true idea of manly independence and self-respect. It is to be a dispenser of knowledge, a radiator of light. In a word, we dedicate this Institution to virtue, temperance, knowledge, truth, liberty and justice:

> In this fair hall, to Truth and Freedom given,
> Pledged to the right before all earth and heaven—
> A free arena for the strife of mind,
> No caste, or sect, or color are confined.

We who have been long debarred the privileges of culture may assemble and have our souls thrilled with heavenly music, lifted to the skies on the wings of poetry and song. Here we can assemble and have our minds enlightened upon the whole circle of social, moral, political and educational duties. Here we can come and learn true politeness and refinements. Here the loftiest and best eloquence which the country has produced, whether of Anglo-Saxon or of African descent, shall flow as a river, enriching, ennobling, strengthening and purifying all who will lave in its waters. Here may come all who have a new and unpopular truth to unfold and enforce, against which old and respectable bars and bolts are iron gates. Here, from this broad hall, shall go forth an influence which shall at last change the current of public contempt for the oppressed, and lift the race into the popular consideration which justly belongs to their manly character and achievements.

Appendix D: Letter to Francis Bicknell Carpenter from Mary Todd Lincoln, November 15, 1865

Mary Todd Lincoln to Francis Bicknell Carpenter

Chicago November 15, 1865

My Dear Sir:

Your last letter, has been received—It would be utterly impossible for me, in my present nervous state, to sit for a photograph—although, I should like to oblige you, very much. There is an excellent painted likeness of me, at Brady's in N.Y. taken in 1861—have you, ever seen it? I am sure you will like it & I believe, it was taken, in black velvet. I enclose you one of my precious, sainted Willie. You have doubtless heard, how *very* handsome a boy, he was considered—with a pure, gentle nature, always unearthly & in intellect *far, far* beyond his years— When I reflect, as I am always doing, upon the overwhelming loss, of that *most* idolized boy, and the crushing blow, that deprived me, of my *all in all* in this life, I wonder that I retain my reason & live. There are hours of each day, that my mind, cannot be brought to realize, that *He*, who is considered, so great and good, a God has *thus* seen fit to afflict us! How difficult it is to be reconciled to such a bereavement, how much sooner, each one, of our stricken family, if the choice had been left to us, would have preferred "passing away," ourselves.

It strikes me how strangely, how such a rumor, should be circulated—that Robert is in Europe. The thought of leaving home, I am sure, has never *once*, entered his mind. He is diligently applying himself, to his law studies—a most devoted Son & brother. Everything is *so fabulously* high *here*, that his third of the estate, an income of $1800 apiece—with taxes deducted—It required the most rigid economy, with Robert & the rest of us to clothe ourselves, plainly & weekly settle our board-bills. Is not this, a sad change for us! As a matter of course living, every where, *now* in the U.S. is high—Yet I cannot express to you, how painful to me, it is, to have *no* quiet home, where I can freely indulge my sorrows—*this, is* yet another of the crosses, appointed unto me. With my beloved husband, I should have had, a heart, for any fate, if "need be." Dear little Taddie! was named, for my husband's father, Thomas Lincoln—no *T*—for a middle name—was *nicknamed, Taddie,* by his loving Father. Taddie—is learning to be as diligent in his studies, as he used to be *at play* in the W. H. he appears to be rapidly making up, for the great amount of time, he lost in W— [Washington.] As you are aware, *he* was always a *marked character.* Two or three weeks since, a lady in an adjoining room, gave him, a copy of Mr Raymond's life of the President for me to read & return to her. After reading it, I remarked to Robert, in Taddie's presence, that it was *the most* correct history, of his Father, that has been written—Taddie immediately spoke up & said, "Mother, I am going to save, all the little money, you give me and get one of them." R. told him, he need not, as he would buy, a copy. I press the poor little fellow closer, *if possible*, to my heart, in memory of the sainted Father, who loved *him, so very dearly*, as well as the rest of us—How I wish you could have seen my dear husband, the last three weeks of his life! Having a realizing sense, that the unnatural rebellion, was near its close, & being most of the time, *away* from W, where he had endured such conflicts of mind, within the last four years, feeling *so encouraged*, he freely gave vent to his cheerfulness. Down the Potomac, he was almost boyish, in his mirth & reminded me, of his original nature, what I had always remembered of him, in our own home—free from care, surrounded by those he loved so well & *by whom*, he was so idolized. *The Friday*, I never saw him so supremely cheerful—his manner was even playful. At three o'clock, in the afternoon, he drove out with me in the open carriage, in starting, I asked him, if any one, should accompany us, he immediately replied— "No—I prefer to ride by ourselves to day." During the drive he was so gay, that I said to him, laughingly, "Dear Husband, you almost startle me by your great cheerfulness." He replied "and well I may feel so, Mary, I consider *this day*, the war, has come to a close—and then added, "We must *both*, be more cheerful in the future—between the war & the loss of our darling Willie—we have both, been very miserable." Every word, then uttered, is deeply engraven, on my poor broken heart. In the evening, his mind, was fixed upon having some relaxation & bent on the theater. Yet I firmly believe, that if he had remained, at the W. H. on that night of darkness, when the fiends prevailed, he would have been horribly *cut to pieces*—Those fiends, had too long contemplated, this inhuman murder, to have allowed, *him*, to escape. Robert informs me, that the best likeness of himself, is at Goldin's, in Washington, taken last spring. We have none, unframed. The attitude in the one, you sent me, of myself, is very good, my hands are always *made* in *them*, very large and I look too stern. The drapery of the dress, was *not* sufficiently flowing—and my hair, should not be so low down, on the forehead & so much dressed. I am sending you a long & most hastily written letter, which I pray you excuse. My sons desire to be remembered to you. Whilst I remain

Very Sincerely Mary Lincoln

Original in Lilly Library, Indiana University, Bloomington.

Contributors

Harold Holzer (coeditor) is the Roger Hertog Fellow at the New-York Historical Society and the chairman of the Abraham Lincoln Bicentennial Foundation. He is also the author, coauthor, or editor of forty-seven books on Lincoln and the Civil War, including *Lincoln at Cooper Union: The Speech That Made Abraham Lincoln President* and *Lincoln and the Power of the Press: The War for Public Opinion*, which won the 2015 Lincoln Prize.

Sara Vaughn Gabbard (coeditor) is the executive director of Friends of the Lincoln Collection of Indiana and a recipient of the 2015 Order of Lincoln Award from the state of Illinois. She is the editor of *Lincoln Lore* and a coeditor (with Harold Holzer) of *1863: Lincoln's Pivotal Year* and *Lincoln and Freedom: Slavery, Emancipation, and the Thirteenth Amendment* and (with Joseph Fornieri) of *Lincoln's America, 1809–1865*.

Michael B. Ballard, professor emeritus of libraries at Mississippi State University, is the author or editor of fourteen books, twelve of which are on the Civil War, including *Vicksburg: The Campaign That Opened the Mississippi* and *Grant at Vicksburg: The General and the Siege.*

Richard Wightman Fox is a professor of history at the University of Southern California. His books include *Lincoln's Body: A Cultural History* and *Trials of Intimacy: Love and Loss in the Beecher-Tilton Scandal.*

John F. Marszalek, the executive director of the U.S. Grant Presidential Library at Mississippi State University, is the editor of the *Papers of Ulysses S. Grant* and the author of many books, including *Sherman: A Soldier's Passion for Order* and *Lincoln and the Military.*

Edna Greene Medford is the chair of the history department at Howard University and a member of the Board of the Abraham Lincoln

Bicentennial Foundation. She cowrote *The Emancipation Proclamation: Three Views* and edited *The Price of Freedom* (two volumes).

Edward Steers, Jr., is the author, editor, coauthor, or coeditor of twelve books, including *Blood on the Moon: The Assassination of Abraham Lincoln*; *His Name Is Still Mudd*; and *Lincoln's Assassination.*

Richard Striner, a professor of history at Washington College, is the author of *Lincoln and Race*; *Lincoln's Way: How Six Great Presidents Created American Power*; and *Father Abraham: Lincoln's Relentless Struggle to End Slavery.*

Michael Vorenberg is an associate professor of history at Brown University and the author of *The Emancipation Proclamation: A Brief History with Documents* and *Final Freedom: The Civil War, the Abolition of Slavery, and the Thirteenth Amendment.*

Ronald C. White, Jr., is a fellow at the Huntington Library and a senior fellow at the Trinity Forum. He is the author of *A. Lincoln: A Biography*; *Lincoln's Greatest Speech: The Second Inaugural*; and *The Eloquent President: A Portrait of Lincoln through His Words.*

Frank J. Williams is a former chief justice of the Rhode Island Supreme Court and the founding chair of the Lincoln Forum. He is the author or editor of fourteen books, including *Judging Lincoln*; *The Mary Lincoln Enigma*; and *Lincoln as Hero.*

Index

Italicized page numbers indicate figures.

Index

Benjamin, Judah P., 88, 93
Bertonneau, Arnold, 119–20
Bible: Lincoln's dilemma of how
    to read, interpret, and apply, 56;
    quoted in inaugural addresses, 55
Bingham, John A., 105
black flag warfare, 82, 87
black people. *See* African Americans
Blair, Francis P., Sr.: Davis's message
    delivered to Lincoln by, 41–42; at
    Hampton Roads conference, 45;
    peace negotiations with Davis, 9,
    11–12, 33, 40–41
Blair, Montgomery, 10
Booth, John Wilkes: assassination of
    Lincoln, 70, 96–97; Gautier's meet-
    ing, 95; Herndon House meeting,
    97–98; images of, 140, *141*; letters
    to *Washington National Intelligencer*,
    97–98; at Lincoln's second inau-
    guration, 53; in Montreal, 90–91;
    plot against Lincoln, assembly
    of conspirators and funding for,
    89–95; response to Lincoln's policy
    address on enfranchisement of
    black people, 5, 97, 120
Boynton, Thomas Jefferson, 110
Bradford, Augustus, 14
Brady, Mathew B., 146–47, *147*
Bragg, Braxton, 24
Brooks, Noah, 49
Bryantown, Maryland, 91
Buckner, Simon Bolivar, 81
Burlingame, Michael, 79n3
Burning of the Smithsonian Institution
    (Gardner montage), 126–27
Burns, Ken, 76–77
Burnside, Ambrose, 23–24, 32
Butler, Benjamin, 18

Campbell, John A., 33, 42, 44–45, 47
Carlton, William Tolman, 1–2

Carpenter, Francis B., 1, 142–43,
    146–47, *147*, 150n27, 186–88
Carter, Dennis Malone, 77
casualties of North versus South, 29–32
Chancellorsville campaign, 85
Chandler, Zachariah, 42, 48
Chickamauga Creek, 24
chronologies for 1865: art, music, and
    literature, 175, 176–77; births, 176,
    177; business, industry, science, and
    discoveries, 175; education, 174–75;
    international, 176–77; Lincoln's
    activities and writings, 153–72;
    military and political, 173–74
churches, Lincoln's perception of, 57
Cincinnati Daily Gazette (newspaper),
    146
Cincinnati Enquirer (newspaper), 92
City Point (Hopewell, Virginia),
    31–32, 35–36
Civil Rights Act (1866), 19
Civil War: Atlanta Campaign, 27;
    black flag warfare, 82, 87; Chan-
    cellorsville campaign, 85; changed
    character of, 82; Cold Harbor
    battle, 30; North Anna River
    battle, 30; 120th Colored Infantry,
    3; Pew Research Center survey on
    attitudes toward, 55; Red River
    Campaign, 27; Spotsylvania Court
    House battle, 29; Union military
    victories in western theater, 22–24;
    Wilderness Campaign, 28–29. *See
    also* Confederate army; Union army
Civil War, The (Burns television docu-
    mentary), 76
Clay, Clement C., 87
Clemens, W. W., 68
Coffin, Charles C., 70–72, 77–78
Cold Harbor battle, 30
compensated emancipation, 14
Comstock, Cyrus B., 103